MACMILLAN

LANGUAGE ARTS TODAY

Great literature is an inspiration. Jan Andrews's *Very Last First Time* inspired artist Don Daily to create the illustration on the cover of your book. The story begins on page 32. We hope that you enjoy the story and the illustration!

SENIOR AUTHORS

ANN McCALLUM   WILLIAM STRONG   TINA THOBURN   PEGGY WILLIAMS

Literature Consultant for Macmillan Language Arts and Macmillan Reading   Joan Glazer

Macmillan Publishing Company   **New York**
Collier Macmillan Publishers   **London**

ACKNOWLEDGMENTS

The publisher gratefully acknowledges permission to reprint the following copyrighted material:

"Ben Franklin's Glass Armonica" from *Ben Franklin's Glass Armonica* by Bryna Stevens. Copyright © 1983 Carolrhoda Books. Reprinted and recorded by permission of the publisher, Carolrhoda Books, Inc., 241 First Avenue North, Minneapolis, MN 55401.

"Dear Aunt Helen" is excerpted from "Dear Aunt Helen" by Helen S. Munro. This originally appeared in *Cricket* Magazine, 1985. Copyright © 1985 Helen S. Munro. Reprinted and recorded by permission of the author.

"Fish Fry" from *Fish Fry* by Susan Saunders. Text copyright © 1982 by Susan Saunders. Reprinted and recorded by permission.

"The Great Mystery" from *Childcraft—The How and Why Library*, Vol. 5. Copyright © 1982 U.S.A. by World Book-Childcraft International.

"The Knee-High Man" from *The Knee-High Man and Other Tales* by Julius Lester. Text copyright © 1972 by Julius Lester. Reprinted by permission of the publisher, Dial Books for Young Readers. Reprinted also by permission of Penguin Books Ltd., publishers of the Kestrel Books edition of this title (1972). Recorded by permission of Claudia Menza Literary Agency.

"The Lady and the Spider" is the complete text with specified illustrations from *The Lady and the Spider* by Faith McNulty, illustrated by Bob Marstall. Text copyright © 1986 by Faith McNulty. Illustrations copyright © 1986 by Bob Marstall. Reprinted and recorded by permission of Harper & Row, Publishers, Inc.

"Very Last First Time" excerpted from *Very Last First Time* by Jan Andrews. Copyright © 1985 Jan Andrews. Reprinted with the permission of Margaret K. McElderry Books, an imprint of Macmillan Publishing Company. Reprinted also and recorded by permission of Douglas & McIntyre Ltd.

Poems, Brief Quotations, and Excerpts:

Excerpt from "I Don't Know Why" (and full poem) in *Whispers and Other Poems* by Myra Cohn Livingston, Copyright © 1958 by Myra Cohn Livingston. Reprinted by permission of Marian Reiner for the author.

Excerpt from "Reach for a Book" (and full poem) by Eve Merriam. Copyright © 1986 by Eve Merriam. Reprinted by permission of Marian Reiner for the author.

"Notice" from *One at a Time* by David McCord. Copyright © 1952 by David McCord. By permission of Little, Brown and Company.

Excerpt from "The Funny House" (and full poem) by Margaret Hillert. Used by permission of the author, who controls all rights.

"On Tuesday" is an excerpt from *A Week in the Life of Best Friends* by Beatrice Schenk de Regniers. Copyright © 1986 Beatrice Schenk de Regniers. Reprinted with the permission of Atheneum Publishers, an imprint of Macmillan Publishing Company. By permission also of the author.

"The Birthday Child" from *Round the Mulberry Bush* by Rose Fyleman. Copyright © 1928 by Dodd, Mead & Company, Inc. Copyright renewed 1955 by Rose Fyleman. Reprinted by permission of Dodd, Mead & Company, Inc.

Haiku from *More Cricket Songs*, Japanese haiku translated by Harry Behn. Copyright © 1971 by Harry Behn. All rights reserved. Reprinted by permission of Marian Reiner.

Excerpt from *Flying to the Moon and Other Strange Places* by Michael Collins. Copyright © 1976 by Michael Collins. Reprinted by permission of Farrar, Straus and Giroux, Inc.

(Acknowledgments continued on page 475.)

Cover Design: Barnett-Brandt Design
Cover Illustration: Don Daily

Macmillan Publishing Company
866 Third Avenue
New York, N.Y. 10022
Collier Macmillan Canada, Inc.

Printed in the United States of America

ISBN: 0-02-243505-0

9 8 7

MACMILLAN

LANGUAGE ARTS TODAY

CONTENTS
THEME: NEW TRAILS

AWARD WINNING
SELECTION

THEME: *FRIENDS*

AWARD WINNING
SELECTION

THEME: *INVENTIONS*

THEME: *PEN PALS*

THEME: *PET PARADE*

AWARD WINNING
SELECTION

THEME: *FAVORITES*

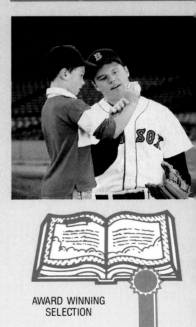
AWARD WINNING
SELECTION

THEME: *MYSTERIES*

WRITER'S REFERENCE

How can I get
ideas for writing?

This book can really help you there.
There's great literature between these
covers. I noticed that after reading
a good story, biography, or poem, I
wanted to respond. Sometimes I
wanted to write about the same topic
or in a similar style. Sometimes I
wanted to write a journal entry.

Writers
are readers,
and readers
are writers!

I know that sometimes, no matter how hard I try, the ideas won't come. Reading a story doesn't work. Talking with my friends doesn't help. Then, I take a look at the **PICTURES** SEEING LIKE A WRITER section in this book, and presto! Ideas start to flow. The pictures turn up the volume on my imagination.

What will I write about today?

IMAGINE

Writers observe, and observers can find lots of ideas for writing.

How will
I remember all
my ideas?

JOURNAL Personally, I don't know how I'd keep all my ideas straight without my journal. I write in it every day— facts, thoughts, feelings. I draw pictures, too. A journal is a great place to keep track of what you've learned.

A journal is a writer's best friend.

Writing doesn't have to be something that you do alone. I get lots of ideas when I work with my classmates. During group writing, we write and conference together. When it's time to write on my own, I'm all warmed up and ready to go.

How does working with a group help?

Writing together builds confidence; conferences get the ideas flowing.

How do thinking and writing go together?

I really give my brain a workout when I write. I can't help it. To write, you have to think about many things: sequence; main idea; beginning, middle, and end; likenesses and differences.

Writing is thinking on paper.

What is the writing process, and how will it help me?

Writing isn't something that just happens 1-2-3. It takes time to write. The writing process allows me the time I need.

Prewrite

At this stage I can get ideas and plan my writing. I need to think about my purpose and audience. Graphic organizers can really help here.

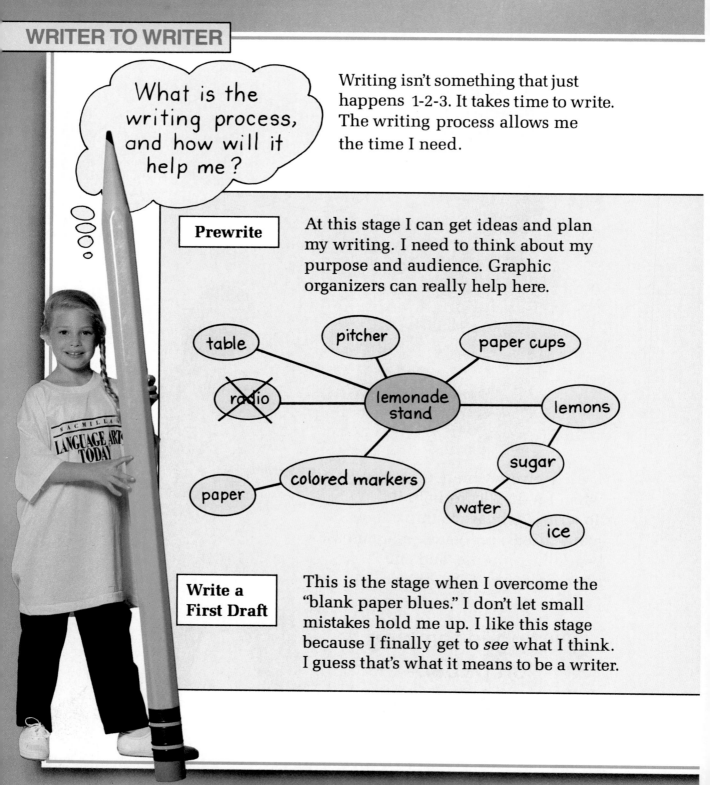

Write a First Draft

This is the stage when I overcome the "blank paper blues." I don't let small mistakes hold me up. I like this stage because I finally get to *see* what I think. I guess that's what it means to be a writer.

Don't tell anyone, but I feel most like a writer when I revise. It's such a thrill to be in control!

Revise	Before I revise, I take some ⏱ **TIME-OUT**. I need to let my writing settle a bit. Then I read my writing to myself and to a friend. I then take pencil in hand and go to it. I add, take out, move around, and combine some sentences. I even go back to prewriting for more ideas.
Proofread	During this stage, I fix all my grammar, spelling, capitalization, and punctuation mistakes. I proofread for one error at a time. (Take my advice. Learn the proofreading marks. You can use them to make changes simply and easily.)
Publish	I knew I was an author when I saw the word "publish." Publishing can mean reading your writing out loud or taking it home to show your family—anything that involves sharing your writing with your audience.

1

Sentences

In this unit you will learn about different kinds of sentences. You can use all of the different kinds of sentences when you speak and write.

Discuss Read the poem on the opposite page. When do you skip and run? Do you ever tiptoe?

Creative Expression The theme of this unit is *New Trails.* Which new trails have you traveled? Write two or three sentences to tell about a new trail that you know. Write your sentences in your journal.

THEME: *NEW TRAILS*

Yesterday I skipped all day,
The day before I ran,
Today I'm going to tiptoe
Everywhere I can.

—Karla Kuskin
from "Tiptoe"

1 WHAT IS A SENTENCE?

A sentence is a group of words that expresses a complete thought.

A sentence names the person or thing you are talking about. It also tells what happened.

SENTENCE: Carol strolled along the road.

NOT A SENTENCE: Climbed the hill.

Use a capital letter to begin a sentence.

Carol   crossed   a   stream.

Guided Practice

Tell which groups of words are sentences.

Example: Carol walked along the path. *sentence*

1. Rosa wandered into the woods.
2. Saw a moose.
3. Rosa stumbled over a big rock.
4. Scared an owl.
5. Mosquitoes buzzed all day.

?! THINK

- How can I decide if a group of words is a sentence?

REMEMBER

■ A **sentence** is a group of words that expresses a complete thought.

More Practice

Read each group of words. Write **yes** if the words make a sentence. Write **no** if they do not.

Example: Colorful leaves fall from the trees. *yes*

6. The happy girls hike up the trail.
7. The trail is very steep.
8. The trees are beautiful in autumn.
9. Many shades of red and yellow.
10. Frisky squirrels.
11. The girls build a fire near a pond.
12. Across the pond.
13. Gail and Nancy walk two more miles.
14. A big, old house.
15. Nancy looks through the window.
16. Three animals sleep in the corner.
17. A sandwich for lunch.
18. The girls eat lunch by the tree.
19. Many ants.
20. Ham and cheese sandwich.

Extra Practice, page 22

WRITING APPLICATION Sentences

Imagine that you explored a park. Write some sentences describing the things in nature that you saw. Check to see that each sentence expresses a complete thought.

2 STATEMENTS AND QUESTIONS

When you write or talk, you use different kinds of sentences.

A **statement** is a sentence that tells something. A statement ends with a period.

Mountain climbing is fun.

A **question** is a sentence that asks something. A question ends with a **question mark.**

Have you ever climbed a mountain?

It is right here.

Do you have your pack?

Guided Practice

Tell which sentences are **statements** and which sentences are **questions.**

Example: Did you climb the mountain? *question*

1. Why do people climb mountains?
2. Many people like adventure.
3. Is a mountain dangerous?
4. How many people climbed the mountain?
5. I would be too afraid.

?! THINK

■ How can I tell the difference between a statement and a question?

REMEMBER

■ A **statement** is a sentence that tells something.
■ A **question** is a sentence that asks something.

More Practice

Write the sentences. Add the correct end punctuation to each sentence.

Example: Should we climb with them*?*

6. Dale climbed a mountain in Alaska
7. Did she climb it easily
8. Did she follow a trail
9. Climbers faced strong winds
10. The temperature changed as they climbed
11. Would you climb these mountains
12. There is a great view from the top
13. Where is the mountain
14. This mountain is high
15. Do you think it is dangerous
16. Will you climb it with me
17. Will we need special shoes
18. Some people live near mountains
19. They like to climb them
20. They are not afraid

Extra Practice, page 23

WRITING APPLICATION A Post Card

Imagine that you went to the top of a tall building. Write a post card to a friend about the view. Exchange post cards with a classmate. Identify the statements and questions in each other's work.

3 COMMANDS AND EXCLAMATIONS

A **command** is a sentence that tells or asks someone to do something. A command ends with a **period**.

Pack your bags for the trip.
Make sure you bring boots.

An **exclamation** is a sentence that shows strong feeling. An exclamation ends with an **exclamation mark**.

I had a wonderful time in Hawaii!
The trip was great!

Follow me.
Be careful!

Guided Practice

Tell which sentences are **commands** and which sentences are **exclamations**.

Example: Put on your boots.   *command*

1. Wear your heavy jacket.
2. How funny you look!
3. Get the map, Neil.
4. Today is a great day for a hike!
5. Help me find my boots.

?! THINK

- How do I know if a sentence is an exclamation or a command?

REMEMBER

- A **command** tells or asks someone to do something.
- An **exclamation** shows strong feeling.

More Practice

Write the sentences. Add the correct end punctuation to each sentence.

Example: Let us sit under the tree

Let us sit under the tree.

6. Take water with you
7. Do not forget your gloves
8. Wow, I see a rock slide
9. Dana, pick up that rock
10. You are very brave
11. What a big tree that is
12. Come and rest under it
13. How tired you look
14. Take out our lunch
15. Do not make a fire
16. Wow, here comes a squirrel
17. Give it some nuts
18. How fast the squirrel runs
19. What a beautiful day it is
20. Look at the mountains and the sky

Extra Practice, page 24

WRITING APPLICATION A Travelogue

With your class, write a travelogue describing the adventures of mountain climbing. Circle the end punctuation in each sentence.

SUBJECTS IN SENTENCES

When you write a sentence, you express a complete thought. You name the person or thing you are talking about. The **subject** of a sentence tells what or whom the sentence is about. The subject can be one word or more than one word.

The book describes Marco Polo.
Marco Polo explored China.
China is a busy place.

These books are about explorers.

Guided Practice

Tell the subject of each sentence.

Example: Jennifer went to the library.   *Jennifer*

1. Jennifer read a book about Marco Polo.
2. Marco Polo visited China.
3. The group searched for riches.
4. Marco Polo discovered many spices.
5. Spices were not expensive.

THINK

- How do I decide what the subject of a sentence is?

REMEMBER

■ The **subject** of a sentence tells whom or what the sentence is about.

More Practice

Write each sentence. Draw a line under the subject of each sentence.

Example: Marco Polo lived in the 1400s.
Marco Polo lived in the 1400s.

6. Bill read a book about Marco Polo.
7. Marco Polo traveled to China.
8. The men faced rough seas.
9. The wind made the water rough.
10. The sun came out later.
11. The sea became calm.
12. Bill read about spices and silk.
13. Marco Polo brought many spices home.
14. The silk was very colorful.
15. Marco Polo wrote a book.
16. The book was printed in 1477.
17. Many people bought the book.
18. The people learned about China.
19. China is an interesting place.
20. Many people traveled to China.

Extra Practice, page 25

 WRITING APPLICATION A Letter

Imagine that you traveled with Marco Polo to China. Write a letter to a relative about your adventures. Draw a line under the subject of each sentence.

5 PREDICATES IN SENTENCES

You know that the subject of a sentence names a person, a place, or a thing. A sentence also has a part that tells what the subject does or is. This part is called the **predicate.** The predicate can be one word or more than one word.

Many birds live in the trees.
Amy sees a bluejay.

Birds  eat worms.

Guided Practice

Tell the predicate of each sentence.

Example: Amy reads about birds.
reads about birds

1. Amy bought a new camera.
2. Colorful birds sing in the woods.
3. Amy takes pictures of birds.
4. A robin sits in a tree.
5. Amy takes its picture.

?! THINK

■ How can I decide which words make up the predicate?

REMEMBER

■ The **predicate** tells what the subject does or is.

More Practice

Write the sentences. Draw a line under the predicate of each sentence.

Example: The nest is in the oak tree.
The nest is in the oak tree.

6. Amy spots two more birds.
7. One bird is a robin.
8. The other bird is a blue jay.
9. Amy looks for more birds.
10. Amy finds an owl.
11. The owl hoots.
12. Amy snaps its picture.
13. Another owl is in the tree.
14. Amy takes its picture, too.
15. The zoo is an interesting place.
16. The birds are colorful.
17. Sam likes the ostrich.
18. The ostrich has strong legs.
19. Two flamingos stand in the water.
20. Two children laugh.

Extra Practice, Practice Plus, pages 26–27

WRITING APPLICATION An Article

Write an article for a nature magazine telling about the birds that live in your neighborhood. Exchange papers with a classmate. Underline the predicate of each sentence.

6 MECHANICS: Punctuating Sentences

You have learned about the four kinds of sentences. Every sentence begins with a capital letter. A statement and a command end with a **period**. A question ends with a **question mark**. An exclamation ends with an **exclamation mark**.

COMMAND: Watch the sky.
EXCLAMATION: I see a shooting star!
QUESTION: Did you see it?
STATEMENT: I like the night sky.

period   exclamation mark   question mark

Guided Practice

Tell whether each sentence is a **statement, question, command,** or **exclamation.** Then, tell the correct end punctuation for each sentence.

Example: I bought a telescope.   *statement   period*

1. Look at the sky.
2. It is a clear night.
3. The stars are so bright!
4. Can you see the Milky Way?
5. Where is the Big Dipper?

?! THINK

■ How do I decide which end punctuation to use?

REMEMBER

- A **statement** and a **command** end with a **period**.
- A **question** ends with a **question mark**.
- An **exclamation** ends with an **exclamation mark**.

More Practice

Write each sentence correctly.

Example: Put the telescope by the window.

6. Can you find the North Star
7. It is the brightest star in the sky
8. Wow, there it is
9. Some people use it to tell directions
10. That is a great idea
11. Point north
12. Now, point south
13. Can you find east and west
14. How many planets are there
15. Look through your telescope
16. Do you see any planets
17. Wow, the moon looks so big
18. Look at Saturn
19. I can even see the rings
20. Saturn has seven rings

Extra Practice, page 28

WRITING APPLICATION A Travel Poster

COOPERATIVE
LEARNING

Write a travel poster with your class that persuades people to visit a planet you discovered. Describe what life on that planet might be like. Check to make sure that you have used the correct punctuation.

7 VOCABULARY BUILDING: Using Word Clues

As you read, you may come across words you do not know. One way you can find the meaning of a word is to look it up in the dictionary. Another way is to look at the other words in the sentence for clues.

Helen picked an **iris** from the field of flowers.

The words *field of flowers* tell you that an *iris* is a kind of flower.

Sometimes you will need to read the sentence before or after to figure out the meaning of a word.

field of flowers

iris

Guided Practice

Tell which clues in each sentence help to define the underlined word.

Example: The bird book showed an <u>eagle</u>.   *bird*

1. Eagles are <u>symbols</u>, or signs, of strength.
2. We saw an eagle <u>soar</u> high in the sky.
3. Helen <u>gazed</u> at the eagle with a look of wonder.
4. Its <u>huge</u> claws are big enough to carry a rabbit.
5. The mother takes food to her young <u>eaglets</u>.

?! THINK

■ How can I find out the meaning of new words in a sentence?

REMEMBER

■ Use **word clues** in a sentence to figure out the meaning of new words.

More Practice

Write each sentence. Draw a line under the word clues that help you define each underlined word.

Example: Interesting <u>wildlife</u> lives in the woods.
> *Interesting <u>wildlife</u> <u>lives in the woods</u>.*

6. That small, furry animal by the lake is an <u>opossum</u>.
7. The opossum came out of the empty space in the <u>hollow</u> log.
8. An opossum hangs from a branch <u>suspended</u> by its tail.
9. Joel was <u>amazed</u> and surprised at its length.
10. When afraid, it becomes <u>motionless</u> and will not move.
11. It <u>trembles</u>, or shakes, with fear.
12. Joel <u>viewed</u> the opossum and saw it in the tree.
13. Its large eyes looked <u>huge</u> at night.
14. The babies were in a <u>pouch</u>, or pocket.
15. The <u>dozing</u> babies slept soundly.

Extra Practice, page 29

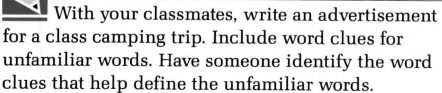

WRITING APPLICATION An Advertisement

COOPERATIVE
LEARNING

With your classmates, write an advertisement for a class camping trip. Include word clues for unfamiliar words. Have someone identify the word clues that help define the unfamiliar words.

GRAMMAR —AND WRITING CONNECTION

Combining Sentences

Sometimes you can make your writing more interesting by combining two sentences. When you want to connect two similar ideas, join the sentences with *and*. Use a comma before *and* when you join sentences.

SEPARATE: Sarita stepped off the train.
Uncle Jim greeted her.

COMBINED: Sarita stepped off the train, and Uncle Jim greeted her.

Working Together

COOPERATIVE LEARNING

With your classmates, discuss how to combine each pair of sentences.

Example: Sarah sat in the wagon.
She held the reins.
Sarah sat in the wagon, and she held the reins.

1. Mr. Hunter snapped the reins.
   The oxen moved forward.
2. Sarah peeked out of the covered wagon.
   The onlookers waved.
3. Sarah smiled bravely at the people.
   She waved back.

Revising Sentences

Teddy is writing a story about traveling across the country. Help Teddy with his story by combining each pair of sentences.

4. The wagons traveled quickly.
   They reached the river.
5. It was early summer.
   The weather was warm.
6. It was a long journey to California.
   Anything could happen on the way.
7. The nights were quiet.
   The travelers slept soundly.
8. Sarah saw some coyotes.
   She saw a bear.
9. A blizzard slowed them down.
   They stopped for a week.
10. They crossed a huge desert.
    Finally, Sarah saw California.

WRITER AT WORK

Imagine what it would be like to cross the country in a covered wagon. Write a journal entry describing a day in a covered wagon. Use *and* to combine any sentences that you can. Place a comma before *and* when you join the sentences.

UNIT CHECKUP

LESSON 1

What Is a Sentence? (page 2) Write each group of words that is a sentence.

1. Sara likes the sailboat.
2. Sailed on the water.
3. Dad fishes in the lake.
4. Outside in the woods.
5. The fish swim.
6. The sun feels warm.

LESSONS 2-3

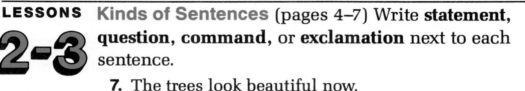

Kinds of Sentences (pages 4–7) Write **statement, question, command,** or **exclamation** next to each sentence.

7. The trees look beautiful now.
8. Have you ever seen a fox?
9. Is that your backpack?
10. Look at the butterfly.
11. It is so colorful!
12. Is that your dog?
13. Bring me his bone.

LESSON 4

Subjects in Sentences (page 8) Write the sentences. Draw a line under each subject.

14. Our friends visit the mountains.
15. John surprised me.
16. Robert fell over a rock.
17. Many animals live in the woods.
18. Three rabbits ran past us.
19. Two girls picked flowers.
20. The flowers looked pretty.

LESSON 5

Predicates in Sentences (page 10) Write the sentences. Draw two lines under each predicate.

21. The flowers are lavender.
22. Jasmine smells lovely.
23. Harry has a flower garden.
24. Tropical plants grow in the jungle.
25. Dale waters the soil carefully.

LESSON 6

Mechanics: Punctuating Sentences (page 12) Write the sentences using the correct end punctuation.

26. Molly saw a bear
27. How scared we were
28. Don't move, Molly
29. What should we do now
30. Wild animals are everywhere

LESSON 7

Vocabulary Building: Using Word Clues (page 14) Write each sentence. Draw a line under the word clues that help define the underlined word.

31. <u>Loggers</u> cut down the trees of the forest.
32. A bird's nest is <u>upset</u> and falls to the ground.
33. The trees <u>float</u> down the river like a raft.
34. Logs are cut into lumber in the <u>sawmill</u>.
35. The lumber is <u>shipped</u> in trucks to far-off places.

Writing Application: Sentence Usage (pages 2–12) The following paragraph contains 10 sentence errors. Rewrite the paragraph correctly.

36.–45.   dad and I went camping? the camping trip was fun, we chopped down a tree. then, we built a crackling fire? we cooked dinner and toasted marshmallows, dad found a raccoon.

Story Chain

Play this game with a friend. Begin a story about a favorite outdoor activity. Tell your friend the first sentence of the story. Then, have your friend continue the story. Take turns adding sentences until the story is complete.

WORD DETECTIVE

Read the sentences below. Choose one underlined word and write it on a sheet of paper. Then, have a friend find the word in the sentence that gives a clue to the meaning of the underlined word. Take turns finding clue words.

1. The ghost town was <u>vacant</u>, or empty.
2. We heard the sound of the <u>squeaky</u> door opening.
3. My knees shook and <u>trembled</u> with fear.

Trailblazers

Think of a place that you would like to explore. It might be a cave or the bottom of the ocean. Cut out pictures from magazines that show this place. Make a poster. Think of three sentences that describe your place. Write these on the poster.

CREATIVE EXPRESSION

A Good Play

We built a ship upon the stairs
All made of the back-bedroom chairs,
And filled it full of sofa pillows
To go a-sailing on the billows.
We took a saw and several nails,
And water in the nursery pails;
And Tom said, "Let us also take
An apple and a slice of cake;"
Which was enough for Tom and me
To go a-sailing on, till tea.
We sailed along for days and days,
And had the very best of plays;
But Tom fell out and hurt his knee,
So there was no one left but me.

          —Robert Louis Stevenson

Try It Out! "A Good Play" is a poem about two children who imagine they are sailing to far-off places. Notice the lines that end with words that sound alike, or rhyme. Write a poem of your own in which you imagine that you are exploring a new land. Have the lines end with words that rhyme.

GRAMMAR

Three levels of practice
What Is a Sentence? (page 2)

LEVEL A. Write the group of words in each pair that is a sentence.

1. A trip to the beach. Ted went to the beach.
2. Ted saw the ocean. The salty ocean water.
3. Ed found a seashell. Seashells by the shore.
4. A sand castle. Ted built a sand castle.
5. The waves knocked it over. By the waves.
6. The bright sun. The sand felt warm.

LEVEL B. Write **sentence** if the group of words is a sentence. Write **not a sentence** if the group is not a sentence.

7. Uncle Robert is a pilot.
8. Has a small plane.
9. Robert lives in Arizona.
10. Robert flew over the desert.
11. Will learn to fly.
12. Many hours.
13. I will fly my own plane.

LEVEL C. Add a subject or a predicate to each group of words.

14. The top of the mountain _____ .
15. _____ hiked and climbed.
16. The climbers _____ .
17. _____ a map and a compass.
18. The steep trail _____ .
19. _____ is cool.
20. The wet rocks _____ .

EXTRA PRACTICE

Three levels of practice
Statements and Questions (page 4)

LEVEL
A. Write each sentence. Write **statement** next to each sentence that tells something. Write **question** next to each sentence that asks something.

1. Rosa packed a suitcase.
2. Will Rosa leave now?
3. Did Rosa pack a gift for her friend?
4. Rosa will take the bus.
5. Rosa will meet her friend at the station.
6. Is the bus on time?

LEVEL
B. Write the sentences. Add the correct end punctuation.

7. Pete and his family visit the lake
8. Did you ever visit a lake
9. Where did Pete go last summer
10. Pete stayed in a large log cabin
11. How many fish did Pete catch
12. Were the fish big
13. This lake is very deep

LEVEL
C. Change each question into a statement.

14. Could the canoe hold three people?
15. Will Liz paddle the canoe?
16. Are there many boats on the river?
17. Should we wear life preservers?
18. Is it time for lunch?
19. Should we swim first?
20. Can we eat later?

EXTRA PRACTICE

Three levels of practice

Commands and Exclamations (page 6)

LEVEL A. Write each sentence. Write **command** next to the sentences that give an order. Write **exclamation** next to the sentences that show strong feeling.

1. Put your backpack in the tent.
2. How big this tent is!
3. What a perfect place this is for a campsite!
4. Look up at the sky.
5. How many stars there are!
6. Bring me the telescope.
7. Wow, this is heavy!

LEVEL B. Complete each command.

8. Richard, wear _____ .
9. Do not forget your _____ .
10. Please take _____ with you.
11. Give the _____ to the scout leader.
12. _____ , draw a map of the park.
13. Please _____ the path.

LEVEL C. Write the sentences. Add the correct end punctuation.

14. Look at the deer
15. What beautiful spotted fur it has
16. Do not scare the deer
17. It is so close to us
18. Notice how graceful it is
19. You must be quiet
20. How fast it runs

EXTRA PRACTICE

Three levels of practice
Subjects in Sentences (page 8)

LEVEL
A. Write the sentences in which the subject is underlined.

1. The <u>path</u> is covered with pine needles.
2. <u>Stan</u> heard an owl hoot in the darkness.
3. Our teacher <u>likes adventure</u>.
4. The <u>ranger</u> pointed at the waterfall.
5. Pools of hot water <u>are scattered over the park</u>.
6. The <u>mountains</u> are so close.
7. Our guide <u>has climbed them</u>.

LEVEL
B. Write each sentence. Underline each subject.

8. The family is in Yellowstone National Park.
9. A guide led a tour of the pine forest.
10. Two porcupines waddled through the grass.
11. Dad took a picture of them.
12. Golden eagles flew across the sky.
13. The trail went through the forest.
14. Leaves covered the path.

LEVEL
C. Add a subject to each group of words. Write each complete sentence.

15. _____ planned a bicycle trip.
16. _____ helped Kathie choose a route.
17. _____ filled the tires with air.
18. _____ met Kathie on the road.
19. _____ was about ten miles long.
20. _____ took us into a park.

GRAMMAR

Three levels of practice
Predicates in Sentences (page 10)

LEVEL A. Write the sentences in which the predicate is underlined.

1. Our parents went on a trip.
2. A narrow road cut through the mountains.
3. Big snowflakes fell everywhere.
4. Karla played in the snow.
5. Karla built an igloo.
6. The cold wind blew the snow.
7. The drifts were high.

LEVEL B. Write each sentence. Underline each predicate.

8. The town held a kite contest.
9. Joel made a kite.
10. The kite was blue and yellow.
11. He sewed a blue cloth on the tail.
12. The judges gave him first prize.
13. Joel thanked the judges.

LEVEL C. Add a predicate to each group of words. Write each complete sentence.

14. The sandy beach _____ .
15. Gentle waves _____ .
16. The lifeguard _____ .
17. Many seagulls _____ .
18. All the swimmers _____ .
19. Many children _____ .
20. The sea breeze _____ .

PRACTICE + PLUS

Three levels of additional practice for a difficult skill
Predicates in Sentences (page 10)

LEVEL
A. Write the sentences that are complete.

1. Columbus discovered new lands.
2. After one month at sea.
3. A sailor saw land ahead.
4. This news made Columbus happy.
5. Green trees and sparkling water.
6. The clear water.

LEVEL
B. Write each sentence. Underline the predicate.

7. Columbus and his men explore the land.
8. They find many new things.
9. The sailors discover unusual fruit.
10. A sailor eats a banana.
11. He is surprised at its taste.
12. Monkeys chatter in the trees.
13. The crew gathers food.

LEVEL
C. Add a predicate to each group of words. Write each complete sentence.

14. Columbus _____ .
15. The people _____ .
16. Three sailors _____ .
17. The ships _____ .
18. The men _____ .
19. The forest _____ .
20. Some sailors _____ .

GRAMMAR

Three levels of practice
Mechanics: Punctuating Sentences (page 12)

LEVEL
A. Write the sentences. Circle the end punctuation. Then, tell whether each sentence is a **statement, question, command,** or **exclamation.**

1. Carl had a great time last summer!
2. Tell me what he did.
3. He visited a ranch in Nevada.
4. Did he go alone?
5. Carl went with his family.
6. Please read his post card.
7. When did he come home?

LEVEL
B. Write the sentences that begin and end correctly.

8. Lee visited the Empire State Building.
9. Have you ever been to the top?
10. take the elevator to the top
11. you can see the Statue of Liberty
12. How tiny the people look
13. What a beautiful view!

LEVEL
C. Write the sentences. Add the correct end punctuation to each sentence.

14. Did you ever see a paddle boat
15. Paddle boats go up and down the Mississippi River
16. Stand on the top deck
17. How loud the steam whistle is
18. Look at the captain wave to us
19. Is the boat very old
20. Wow, the water is muddy

EXTRA PRACTICE

Three levels of practice
Vocabulary Building: Using Word Clues (page 14)

LEVEL
A. Read each sentence. Write the word in ( ) that means the same as the underlined word.

1. Pat <u>discovered</u> a new path all by herself. (drew, found)
2. She walked through the <u>glen</u>, or narrow valley. (valley, gate)
3. She heard rushing water at a <u>cascade</u>. (cabin, waterfall)
4. <u>Boulders</u>, or rocks, lay along the path. (logs, rocks)
5. The shiny rocks <u>glisten</u> in the sunlight. (drop, shine)

LEVEL
B. Read each sentence. Write the word or words that help you find the meaning of each underlined word.

6. Margy went on an <u>expedition</u>, or trip, to the desert.
7. She gathers the fossils and <u>collects</u> them in a bag.
8. A scientist who <u>conducts</u> many tours led this one, too.
9. Margy also found an old <u>shard</u>, or piece, of pottery.
10. The <u>glaze</u> gave it a hard, shiny covering.

LEVEL
C. Write the meaning of each underlined word.

11. The climbers <u>hesitated</u> before climbing again.
12. The <u>difficult</u> path was hard for the climbers.
13. The top of the mountain, which had seemed so <u>distant</u>, was now in view.
14. Larry breathed in deeply to <u>inhale</u> the cold mountain air.
15. The climbers were <u>impatient</u> and could not wait to continue.

UNIT

Writing Paragraphs

Read the quotation on the opposite page. The quotation was written by a famous writer. Why does Jane Yolen think that a reader is a friend of hers?

When you write a paragraph about yourself, you will want your reader to learn something about you. You will want your reader to become a friend of yours.

Focus A story about yourself tells about something that happened in your life.

What would you like to write about? On the following pages you will find a story and some photographs. You can use them to find ideas for writing.

Any reader is a friend of mine, a friend and companion on a wonderful, wonder-filled journey.

—Jane Yolen

LITERATURE

Reading Like a Writer

AWARD WINNING SELECTION

How did you feel when you did something for the first time? Eva Padlyat was about to walk on the seabed alone for the very first time. She had to hurry and collect the mussels before the tide came back in. How do you think Eva felt as she lowered herself through the hole in the ice to begin her mission?

from

VERY LAST FIRST TIME

by Jan Andrews

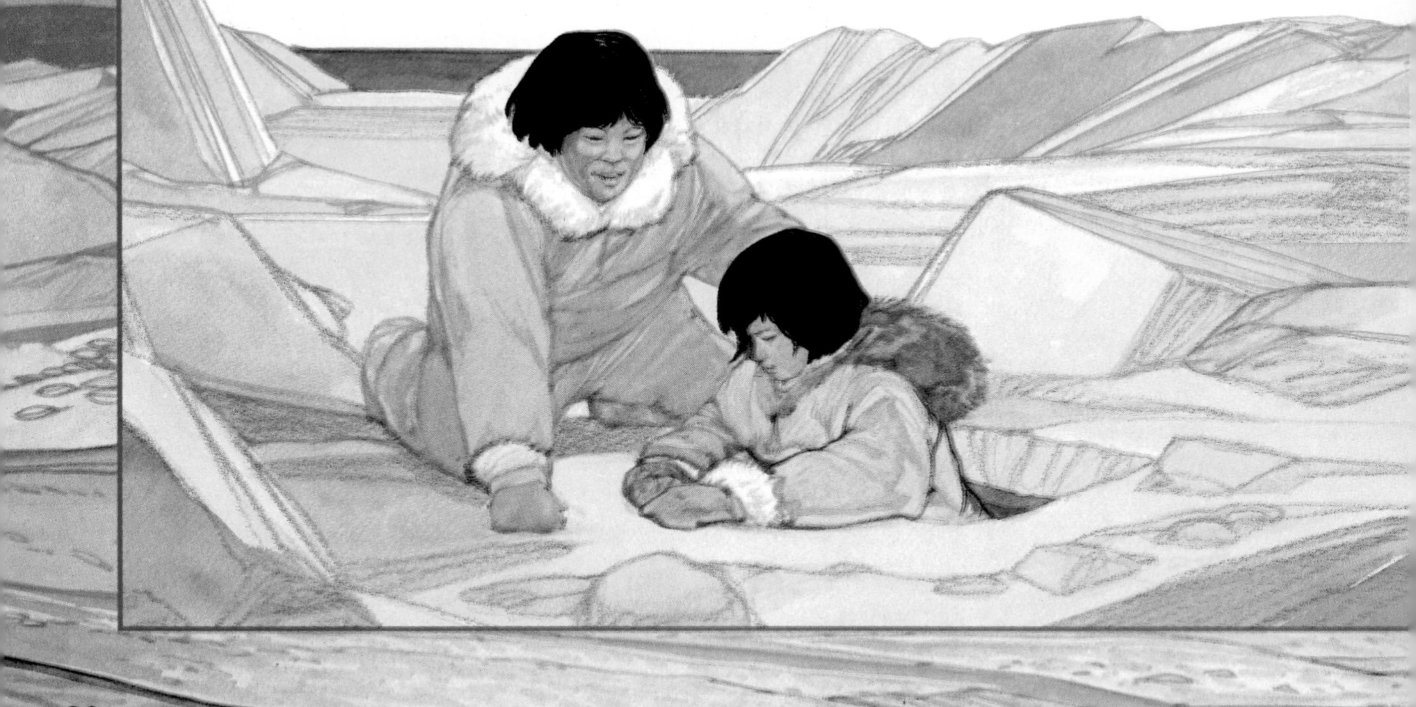

*T*hey had come at the right time. The tide was out, pulling the sea water away, so there would be room for them to climb under the thick ice and wander about on the seabed.

Eva and her mother walked carefully over the bumps and ridges of the frozen sea. Soon they found a spot where the ice was cracked and broken.

"This is the right place," Eva said.

After shoveling away a pile of snow, she reached for the ice-chisel. She worked it under an ice hump and, heaving and pushing with her mother's help, made a hole.

Eva peered down into the hole and felt the dampness of the air below. She breathed deep to catch the salt sea smell.

"Good luck," Eva's mother said.

Eva grinned. "Good luck yourself."

Her eyes lit up with excitement and she threw her mussel pan into the hole. Then she lowered herself slowly into the darkness, feeling with her feet until they touched a rock and she could let go of the ice above. . . .

She held her candle and saw strange shadow shapes around her. The shadows formed a wolf, a bear, a seal sea-monster. Eva watched them, then she remembered.

"I'd better get to work," she said.

Lighting three more candles, she carefully wedged them between stones so she could see to collect mussels. Using her knife as a lever, she tugged and pried and scraped to pull the mussels off the rocks. She was in luck. There were strings of blue-black mussel shells whichever way she turned. . . .

*S*oon her mussel pan was full, so she had time to explore.

She found a rock pool that was deep and clear. Small shrimps in the water darted and skittered in the light from her candle. She stopped to watch them. Reaching under a ledge, she touched a pinky-purple crab. The fronds of the anemones on the ledge tickled her wrist.

Beyond the rock pool, seaweed was piled in thick, wet, shiny heaps and masses. Eva scrambled over the seaweed, up and onto a rock mound. Stretching her arms wide, tilting her head back, she laughed, imagining the shifting, waving, lifting swirl of seaweed when the tide comes in.

*T*he tide!

Eva listened. The lap, lap of the waves sounded louder and nearer. Whoosh and roar and whoosh again. Eva jumped off the rock, stumbled—and her candle dropped and sputtered out. She had gone too far. The candles she had set down between the stones had burned to nothing. There was darkness—darkness all around.

"Help me!" she called, but her voice was swallowed. "Someone come quickly."

Eva closed her eyes. Her hands went to her face. She could not bear to look.

She felt in her pockets. She knew she had more candles there, but she could not seem to find them.

The tide was roaring louder and the ice shrieked and creaked with its movement.

Eva's hands groped deeper. She took a candle out at last and her box of matches, but her fingers were shaking and clumsy. For a long, forever moment, she could not strike the match to light the candle.

The flame seemed pale and weak.

Eva walked slowly, fearfully, peering through the shadows, looking for her mussel pan.

At last, she found it and ran stumbling to the ice-hole. Then, looking up, Eva saw the moon in the sky. It was high and round and big. Its light cast a circle through the hole onto the seabed at her feet.

Eva stood in the moonlight. Her parka glowed. Blowing out her candle, she slowly began to smile.

By the time her mother came, she was dancing. She was skipping and leaping in and out of the moonglow circle, darkness and light, in and out.

"Eva," her mother called.

The details are told in the order in which they happened.

"I'm here," she called back. "Take my mussel pan." Eva scrambled onto a rock and held the pan up high to her mother. Then her mother's hands reached down and pulled her up, too, through the hole.

Squeezing her mother's hand, Eva saw the moon, shining on the snow and ice, and felt the wind on her face once more.

"That was my last very first—my very last *first* time—for walking on the bottom of the sea," Eva said.

Thinking Like a Reader

1. If you had been Eva, would you have been eager or afraid to walk alone under the ice? Why or why not?

Write your response in your journal.

Thinking Like a Writer

2. How does the author let you know how Eva felt when she was lost under the ice?
3. Which details tell you this?
4. Which details let you know how Eva felt when she found her way back?
5. Which details did you like best?

Write your responses in your journal.

LITERATURE

Brainstorm *Vocabulary*

Look back at the story about Eva. Make a list of any words that you do not know. Some words you could choose might be *heaving*, *explore*, and *scrambled*. Find the meanings of these words. Include these words in a personal word list. You might want to use some words from your list when you write.

Talk It Over
Act Out a Scene

Imagine that Eva goes back under the sea to look for mussels. This time she goes with a group of friends. With your classmates, act out a scene in which Eva and her friends explore the bottom of the sea.

Quick Write
Write a Safety Rule

Think of something Eva could do to make sure she doesn't lose her way under the ice again. Write a safety rule she could follow. For example: Leave markers along the way so I can find my way back.

Idea Corner
Think of an Event

Many exciting things happened to Eva while she walked under the ice. Make a list of some interesting things that happened to you in the last two weeks. Write your list in your journal. Your list might look like this:

Started music lessons
Went on a picnic
Rode my bike in the country
Began a hobby
Made a new friend

Finding Ideas for Writing

Look at the pictures. Think about what
you see. What ideas for writing a paragraph
about yourself do the pictures give you?
Write your ideas in your journal.

1 GROUP WRITING: A Paragraph About Yourself

When you write, think about your reason for writing. That is your **purpose.** Think about who will read your writing. That is your **audience.**

What will make a paragraph clear?

- Main-Idea Sentence
- Detail Sentences
- Order of Details

Main-Idea Sentence

Every paragraph has a **main-idea sentence** that tells what the paragraph is about. Often, it is the first sentence in the paragraph. Maria wrote the following paragraph about herself.

> <u>Last summer Dad took my sister and me on a camping trip.</u> We pitched our tent near a lake. All day long we swam and splashed. At night we sat by our campfire and told stories.

The first sentence in a paragraph begins a few spaces in from the margin, or is indented.

Guided Practice: Writing a Main-Idea Sentence

With your classmates, write a main-idea sentence. Choose a topic below, or make one up. Use your journal to find ideas.

- a breathless race
- a strange animal

Detail Sentences

You know that the main-idea sentence in a paragraph tells what the paragraph is about. The other sentences give more details about the main idea. These sentences are called **detail sentences.**

Look back at Maria's paragraph about the camping trip with her family.

- Which sentences provide details about her camping trip?
- How does each detail sentence give more information about the main idea?

Order of Details

Look back at Maria's paragraph. Notice that the details are told in the order in which they happened. When you write a paragraph about yourself, put the detail sentences in order from beginning to end.

- What does Maria tell about first?
- What does she tell about next?
- What does she tell about last?
- Why is this the best order for these sentences?

Guided Practice: Writing Detail Sentences In Order

Reread the main-idea sentence you wrote with your class. Think of details to go with that main-idea sentence. Place those details in the order in which they happened.

Putting a Paragraph Together

With your class you have written a main-idea sentence and detail sentences. Now think more about your **purpose** and **audience**. Keep in mind that a paragraph is a group of sentences about one main idea. Are there any details that you would like to add? What would be the best order for your details? Think about a good title for your paragraph.

Maria added the following title to her paragraph.

Camping Adventures

Guided Practice: Writing a Paragraph About Yourself

Write a paragraph using the main-idea sentence and the details that you wrote with your class. Be sure to keep the details in the correct order. Think about your purpose and audience as you write. Write a title for your paragraph.

Share your paragraph with a friend. Ask your friend to think of any details that would make your paragraph better.

Checklist: A Paragraph

You have learned some important points to keep in mind when you write a paragraph. It is a good idea to make a checklist to help you remember these points. This checklist will help you whenever you write.

Look at this checklist. Some points need to be added. Make a copy of the checklist and complete it. Keep the copy in your writing folder.

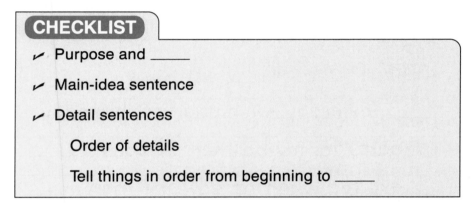

CHECKLIST

✓ Purpose and _____

✓ Main-idea sentence

✓ Detail sentences

　Order of details

　Tell things in order from beginning to _____

2 THINKING AND WRITING: Stating the Main Idea

You know that the **main idea,** or topic, is what the paragraph is about. The main idea of a paragraph is stated in the main-idea sentence. A good main-idea sentence should sum up the topic clearly. It should tell the reader what the whole paragraph is about.

Look at the following paragraph from a student's notebook. The main-idea sentence can be the first sentence of the paragraph.

> Yesterday, we had a first birthday party for my brother. He got very excited when he saw the many colorful presents that we had for him. His eyes grew big when he saw his birthday cake. He clapped his hands as we sang "Happy Birthday." Then, I helped him blow out his candle.

Thinking Like a Writer

- What is the topic of the paragraph?
- Does the main-idea sentence sum up the topic?

THINKING APPLICATION Stating the Main Idea

COOPERATIVE
LEARNING

Four third-grade students are writing paragraphs. They are having trouble with their main-idea sentences and their detail sentences. Help them with their paragraphs. Discuss the paragraphs with your classmates.

1. Add a main-idea sentence as the first sentence in Penny's paragraph.

   First, we went to see the seals. They jumped and swam in the pool. They balanced balls on their noses. Then, we saw the lions and tigers. They are scary, even in cages.

2. Write three detail sentences for Jody's main-idea sentence.

   My first day in third grade was fun.

3. Put Scott's notes in the correct order.
   - now ride easily
   - got on again
   - tried to ride right away
   - fell off
   - got my first bike

4. Add a main-idea sentence as the first sentence in Chuck's paragraph.

   First, I did three laps across the pool. Next, I practiced my backstroke. Finally, I practiced diving into the water.

WRITING TOGETHER

INDEPENDENT WRITING:
A Paragraph

Prewrite: Step 1

You are ready to use what you have learned about paragraphs. A student named Tanya wanted to write a paragraph about herself for her classmates. This is how Tanya chose a topic.

Choosing a Topic

1. First, she made a list of possible topics.
2. Next, she thought about each topic on her list.
3. Last, she decided on the best topic.

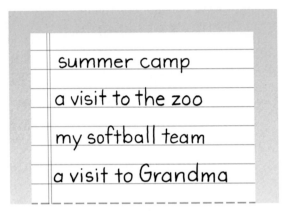

summer camp

a visit to the zoo

my softball team

a visit to Grandma

Tanya chose the first topic on her list. She decided to narrow her topic, and write only about her first day at camp. Tanya explored her topic by making a cluster.

Exploring Ideas: Clustering Strategy

had lunch before going

my first day at camp

had fun

said good-bye to Mom

Tanya decided that her audience might like to know how she felt when she said good-bye to her mother. She added some more details to her cluster.

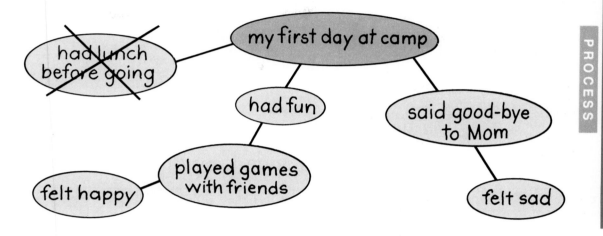

Thinking Like a Writer
- What did Tanya add?
- What did she decide to cross out?
- Why do you think she crossed out that detail?

YOUR TURN

Think of something that has happened to you that you would like to write about. Look in **Pictures** or in your journal to find ideas. Follow these steps.

- Make a list of ideas.
- Choose the one you like best.
- Narrow your topic if it is too broad.
- Think about your purpose and audience.

Make a cluster. Remember, you can add to or take away from the cluster at any time.

Write a First Draft: Step 2

Tanya used a checklist to help her remember what to include in her paragraph. Now, Tanya is ready to write her first draft.

Tanya's First Draft

My first day at summer camp turned out well. First, We unloaded my things. then we sed good-bye for a little while I felt sad. I had fun. Then, I went swimming with my new friend, Gail.

Tanya wrote her first draft quickly. She did not worry about making mistakes. She knew she could correct any errors later.

YOUR TURN

Write your first draft. Ask yourself these questions.

- What will my audience want to know?
- What is my main idea?
- How can I improve my detail sentences?

TIME-OUT You might want to take some time out before you revise. That way you will be able to revise your writing with a fresh eye.

Planning Checklist
- Purpose and audience
- Main-idea sentence
- Detail sentences
- Order of details

Revise: Step 3

When Tanya finished her first draft, she read it over to herself. Then, she shared her paragraph with a classmate. Her friend had a good suggestion.

I like your writing. You really had fun at camp! I think that one part is out of order, though.

You're right! Thanks for noticing that. I'll fix it when I revise.

Tanya looked back at her planning checklist. She had forgotten one point. She checked off *Order of details* so that she would remember this step when she revised. Tanya now has a revising checklist.

Tanya made some changes in her paragraph. She did not stop to correct small errors. Tanya knew she could correct them later. Turn the page. Look at Tanya's revised draft.

Revising Checklist
- Purpose and audience
- Main-idea sentence
- Detail sentences
- Order of details

Tanya's Revised Draft

My first day at summer camp turned out
well. First, We unloaded my things ,and then we
sed good-bye for a little while I felt sad.
I had fun. Then, I went swimming with my
new friend, Gail. I told myself that I could
not do this at home.

Thinking Like a Writer

WISE
WORD
CHOICE

- Which sentences did she combine?
- How does combining them improve the paragraph?
- Which sentence did she add? Do you like the sentence?

YOUR TURN

Read your first draft. Ask yourself these questions.

- How can I improve my main-idea sentence?
- How can I change the order of my details to make my paragraph clearer?
- Which details should I add?

Before you revise your paragraph, you can ask a classmate to read it and make suggestions.

Proofread: Step 4

Tanya knew her paragraph was not complete until she proofread it. Tanya used the proofreading checklist below to correct the small errors in her paragraph.

Part of Tanya's Proofread Draft

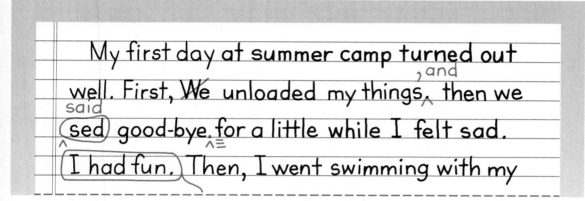

YOUR TURN

Proofreading Practice

Before you proofread your own paragraph, practice your proofreading skills. Find the mistakes in the paragraph below. Then, write the paragraph correctly on a separate piece of paper.

> Our famly just moved to a new town It is far awaay from hour old town. I like our house, but I really miss my best frend. do you think I will make new friends here. I hope so. Maybe I will make friends in my new school. I start on Monday. I am excited about going into the third grade.

Proofreading Checklist
- Did I indent my paragraphs?
- Which words do I need to capitalize?
- Which punctuation errors do I need to correct?
- Did I spell all words correctly?

Applying Your Proofreading Skills

Now proofread your paragraph. Read your checklist before you begin. Also review **The Grammar Connection** and **The Mechanics Connection**. Use the proofreading marks to make changes.

THE GRAMMAR CONNECTION

Remember these rules about sentences.

■ A sentence expresses a complete thought.
■ Every sentence has a subject and a predicate.

Sara played tennis at camp.

Check your paragraph. Is every sentence complete?

THE MECHANICS CONNECTION

Remember how to punctuate the four kinds of sentences.

■ A statement and a command end with a period.
■ A question ends with a question mark.
■ An exclamation ends with an exclamation mark.
■ Remember that a sentence begins with a capital letter.

I will swim in the lake.   Put on your swimsuit.
Will you swim with me?   We will have such fun!

Have you punctuated your sentences correctly? Does every sentence begin with a capital letter?

Proofreading Marks

¶ Indent
∧ Add
⅃ Take out
≡ Make a capital letter
/ Make a small letter

Publish: Step 5

Tanya shared her writing with her classmates. First, she made a neat copy of her paragraph. Then, she made a tape recording of the paragraph so that everyone in her class could listen to it. Her classmates enjoyed hearing about her first day in camp.

YOUR TURN

Copy over your paragraph about yourself. Be sure to write neatly. Then, think of a way to share your paragraph. You might want to use one of the **Sharing Suggestions** in the box below.

SHARING SUGGESTIONS		
Have several classmates help you act out your story.	Read your paragraph aloud to your classmates. Answer any questions that they may have.	Draw pictures to illustrate your paragraph. Post your pictures and paragraph on the bulletin board.

4 SPEAKING AND LISTENING: Making Introductions

You have written a paragraph that tells something about you. When you introduce people to each other, you tell each person something about the other.

Here is how Tanya introduces her friend Gail to her cousin Brad.

> Gail, I'd like you to meet my cousin Brad. He's visiting us from Phoenix.

> Brad, this is my friend Gail. I met her last summer at camp. She goes to my school.

Notice that Tanya uses both Gail's and Brad's names in her introduction. She also tells Gail and Brad a little about each other so that they can begin talking. Follow these speaking guidelines when you introduce two people to each other:

SPEAKING GUIDELINES: Making Introductions

1. Say the name of each person clearly.
2. Tell something interesting about each person you are introducing.
3. Look at the people you are introducing.

- Why is it important to say clearly the names of the people I am introducing?
- Why is it a good idea to say something about each person I am introducing?

SPEAKING APPLICATION Making Introductions

Work with a small group of classmates to act out the following introductions.

1. Anna wants her mother, Mrs. Gomez, to meet her new friend Steve. Steve's family has just moved into the neighborhood.
2. Dana has just joined a collecting club because she likes to collect seashells. She comes to her first club meeting with her friend Ed. Ed introduces Dana to Tim, who likes to collect rocks.
3. Heidi wants to introduce her brother Barry to her new friend Susan. Susan is in Heidi's class. Both Barry and Susan like to play tennis.
4. Sally wants her sister Dana to meet her teacher, Mrs. White. Mrs. White is Sally's favorite teacher. Dana will be in Mrs. White's class next year.

Use the following listening guidelines when you are introduced to someone.

LISTENING GUIDELINES: Making Introductions

1. Look at the person to whom you are being introduced.
2. Listen carefully to the name of the person you are meeting.
3. Repeat the name of the person you are meeting. For example, "It's nice to meet you, Gail."

5 WRITER'S RESOURCES: A Writer's Journal

You have written a paragraph about yourself. How did you think of the idea for your paragraph?

One way to get ideas is to look in your writer's journal. In your journal you have probably written about adventures you had or interesting things that happened to you. Your journal can be more than a record of what happens to you. You can jot down ideas, feelings, or thoughts. Here are some of the things you might want to write down.

1. conversations
2. thoughts
3. dreams
4. ideas for stories
5. opinions
6. feelings

Here is a page from a student's journal.

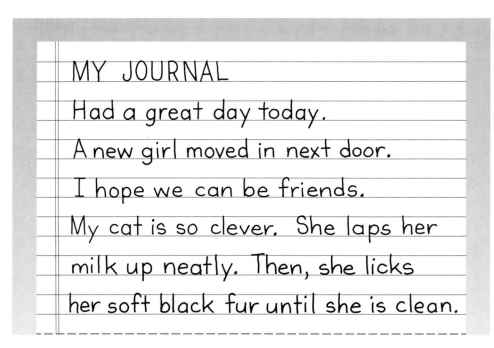

MY JOURNAL
Had a great day today.
A new girl moved in next door.
I hope we can be friends.
My cat is so clever. She laps her
milk up neatly. Then, she licks
her soft black fur until she is clean.

You don't have to worry about writing complete sentences in your journal. Sometimes you will write only a word or two. Sometimes you will want to write more about something that happened or about how you feel.

When you are getting ready to write, look in your journal. You will probably find some ideas to write about.

Practice

1. Imagine that you are a squirrel getting ready for winter. Make an entry in your journal. Write notes about what you do, see, or feel.

2. Imagine that you have to take care of a sick brother or sister. Write some journal entries about what you do during the day. Write about how you feel and what you think.

WRITING APPLICATION A Journal Entry

Practice writing in your journal every day, or as often as you can. Try adding some different entries in your journal, such as feelings and opinions. Use your journal to begin stories or just to jot down ideas. Use your journal to find ideas for writing.

THE CURRICULUM CONNECTION

Writing About Social Studies

In social studies, you will read about people and places from our country's past. You will read about people who have explored this country. You will even read about people who have explored oceans and outer space.

ACTIVITIES

Picture a Place   Think of a place you would like to explore. Imagine how that place looks. Then, draw a picture of it. Below the picture write a few sentences telling why you would like to explore that place.

Describe a Photograph   Look at the photograph on the next page. Write a journal entry describing what you see. You might want to write about what the astronauts have discovered.

Respond to Literature   In 1969 the United States made history by sending three astronauts to the moon. One of the astronauts, Michael Collins, wrote a book called *Flying to the Moon and Other Strange Places.* The paragraph on the next page describes how the moon looked to Collins.

Flying to the Moon and Other Strange Places
The moon I had known all my life, that small
flat yellow disk in the sky, had gone somewhere,
to be replaced by the most awesome sphere I
had ever seen. It was huge, completely filling
Columbia's largest window . . . I felt that I could
almost reach out and touch it . . . Its surface was
lighted by earthshine, which was sunshine that
had bounced off the surface of the earth onto the
surface of the moon. It cast a bluish eerie glow
by which we could see large craters and the
darker flat areas known as maria, or seas.

Write a response to this description. Your response
may be a description of the moon or a paragraph
telling why you would like to be an astronaut.

UNIT CHECKUP

LESSON

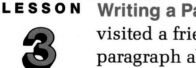

Group Writing: A Paragraph About Yourself
(page 42) Write the following sentences in the correct order.

> We dug up the earth with shovels.
> This spring Mom and I planted a garden.
> Then, we put the seeds in the ground.

LESSON

2

Thinking: Stating the Main Idea (page 46) Read Tim's notes. Write a main-idea sentence. Then, write three detail sentences.

- rode white horse on merry-go-round
- Ferris wheel took us high in air
- got scared on roller coaster

LESSON

3

Writing a Paragraph (page 48) Imagine that you visited a friend who lives far away. Write a paragraph about your trip.

LESSON

4

Speaking and Listening: Making Introductions (page 56) Introduce to each other two friends who are good swimmers.

LESSON

5

Writer's Resources: A Writer's Journal (page 58) Imagine that it is a rainy Saturday and you have to amuse yourself indoors. Write a journal entry about what you do and how you feel.

THEME PROJECT  *Balloon Travels*

People explore in many different ways. Look at the picture below.

This picture shows people floating in hot-air balloons. They are exploring the sky and seeing how the earth looks from above. Discuss the picture with your classmates. Then, talk about what it would be like to float over your town or city in a balloon.

Imagine what it would be like to float in a balloon from your house to your school. How would you feel soaring above the earth? What would you see?

- Draw a picture of the view from your balloon.
- Label your picture.
- Write a sentence or two telling about your experience.

UNIT
3

Nouns

In this unit you will learn about nouns. Nouns name people, places, or things. Think of how often you use nouns when you speak and write.

Discuss Read the poem on the opposite page. The poem mentions a very important person. Who is it?

JOURNAL

Creative Expression The unit theme is *Friends.* What do you like to do with your friends? Do you like to talk on the telephone or have a game of catch? Write a list of things you like to do with your friends. Write your list in your journal.

THEME: *FRIENDS*

*When you can't think of things to do
and the rain won't ever end,
it's nice to have a telephone
to share things with your friend.*

—Jack Prelutsky
from "The Telephone Call"

1 WHAT IS A NOUN?

A noun is a word that names a person, place, or thing.

The **girl** picks a **flower.**

Look at this group of words.

The _____ will plant a _____ .

Any word that makes sense in the blanks is a noun. How many nouns can you think of to fill each blank?

neighbor
garden

Guided Practice

Tell which words in each sentence are nouns.

Example: A girl ties her sneaker. *girl   sneaker*

1. A girl jogs down the street.
2. Two boys meet near the park.
3. The friends run together.
4. The joggers pass a neighbor.
5. The neighbor waves to the girls.

 THINK

■ How do I know if a word is a noun?

REMEMBER

■ A noun names a person, place, or thing.

More Practice

A. Write the sentences. Underline each noun.

Example: The <u>bus</u> drove into the <u>city</u>.

 6. The family visited the city.
 7. The girls went to the circus.
 8. Two brothers visited the library.
 9. The family saw the new play.
10. The play had lively music.
11. The father went to the museum.
12. The mother went to the opera.
13. The family had a picnic in the park.
14. Two sisters bought new clothes.
15. The brothers bought clothes, too.
16. The family liked the city.

B. Write the sentences. Use a noun in each blank.

Example: The city had large _____ .
            The city had large buildings.

17. The family saw a _____ in the city.
18. The _____ had a great time at the play.
19. The play had many _____ .
20. A _____ made the girls laugh.

Extra Practice, page 88

WRITING APPLICATION An Advertisement

COOPERATIVE LEARNING

With your classmates, write an advertisement for a class baseball game. Identify the nouns.

2 SINGULAR NOUNS AND PLURAL NOUNS

A **singular noun** names one person, place, or thing. A **plural noun** names more than one person, place, or thing.

Add *s* to most singular nouns to make them plural.

Add *es* to singular nouns that end in *s*, *sh*, *ch*, and *x* to make them plural.

book**s**   watch**es**   fox**es**   kiss**es**   bush**es**

Some nouns have special plural forms.

man men	woman women	child children

tooth teeth	foot feet

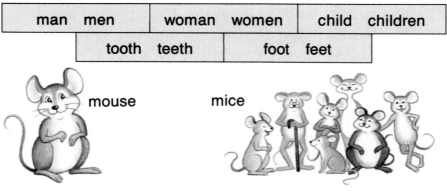

mouse   mice

Guided Practice

Tell whether each word is singular or plural.

Example: children *plural*

1. sun
2. friend
3. baskets

4. sandwiches
5. women
6. feet

7. mouse
8. windows

**THINK**

■ How can I decide if a word is a singular noun or a plural noun?

REMEMBER

- Add *s* to form the plural of most singular nouns.
- Add *es* to form the plural of singular nouns that end in *s, ch, x,* or *sh.*
- Some nouns form their plurals in a special way.

More Practice

Write the sentences. Complete each sentence with the correct singular or plural noun in ( ).

Example: Many (flower, flowers) grow in the park.
Many flowers grow in the park.

9. Marc carries the two (baskets, basket).
10. Many (sandwich, sandwiches) are inside.
11. Marc is on a (picnics, picnic).
12. Marc came in a big (bus, buses).
13. The (park, parks) is very pretty.
14. The children swim in a (lakes, lake).
15. Marc throws (stone, stones) into the water.
16. Maria sees two empty (boats, boat).
17. Maria rows with one (oars, oar).
18. Marc puts two (foot, feet) in the water.
19. A (frog, frogs) jumps into the net.
20. Maria makes three (wish, wishes).

Extra Practice, page 89

WRITING APPLICATION A Cartoon

Work with a classmate to create a cartoon strip about a class picnic. Have a classmate point out the singular nouns and plural nouns.

COOPERATIVE
LEARNING

3 PLURAL NOUNS WITH *ies*

When you write about more than one person, place, or thing, you add *s* or *es* to the singular nouns. Sometimes you must form the plural of singular nouns in a different way.

butterf**ly**   butterfl**ies**

The noun *butterfly* ends with a consonant and the letter *y*. To form the plural of *butterfly*, change the *y* to *i* and add the letters *es*.

butterfly

butterflies

Guided Practice

Tell the plural of each noun.

Example: puppy   *puppies*

1. berry
2. fly
3. pony
4. bunny
5. city

6. lady
7. party
8. activity
9. dairy
10. story

?! THINK

■ How do I know when to change *y* to *i* and add the letters *es* to form a plural noun?

REMEMBER

■ To form the plural of nouns ending in a consonant and *y*, change *y* to *i* and add *es*.

More Practice

A. Write the sentences. Underline the plural noun in each sentence.

Example: The bakeries sell fresh bread.
The <u>bakeries</u> sell fresh bread.

11. Grandpa smiles at the babies.
12. Two black ponies take a nap.
13. Purple berries grow wild.
14. Anne finds six pennies on the road.
15. Two ladies walk down the road.

B. Write the sentences. Change each underlined word to a plural noun.

Example: Sue meets the <u>lady</u> on the road.
Sue meets the ladies on the road.

16. Larry visits the <u>family</u>.
17. Anne eats the red <u>cherry</u>.
18. Sue enjoys the summer <u>sky</u>.
19. The girls write in their <u>diary</u>.
20. Sue picks the ripe <u>strawberry</u>.

Extra Practice, page 90

WRITING APPLICATION A Letter

Write a letter to a relative about an afternoon spent with friends. Write about what you saw and what you did. Circle the plural nouns in your letter.

4 COMMON NOUNS AND PROPER NOUNS

Nouns that name any person, place, or thing are called **common nouns.** Some nouns name a special person, place, or thing. They are called **proper nouns.** Each important word begins with a capital letter.

The **girl** walks away.   Aliza lives in a **city.**
Aliza walks away.   Aliza lives in **Chicago.**

Common nouns	Proper nouns
girl	Aliza
city	Chicago

Guided Practice

Tell which words are common nouns and which are proper nouns.

Example: table   *common noun*

1. city
2. Sunday
3. Texas
4. Maggie
5. table
6. Perry Street
7. park
8. Susan
9. Mr. Hall

?! THINK

- How can I decide if a word is a common noun or a proper noun?

REMEMBER

- A **common noun** is a noun that names any person, place, or thing.
- A **proper noun** is a noun that names a special person, place, or thing.

More Practice

A. Read each sentence. Write **common** or **proper** next to each underlined noun.

Example: They are best <u>friends</u>.   *common*

10. <u>Jeffrey</u> lives in <u>Houston</u>, <u>Texas</u>.
11. The <u>neighbors</u> have a <u>daughter</u> named <u>Ivy</u>.
12. <u>Ivy</u> and <u>Jeffrey</u> attend the same <u>school</u>.
13. Both <u>students</u> write for the <u>newspaper</u>.
14. The <u>club</u> meets on <u>Wednesdays</u>.
15. <u>Fred Johnson</u> is the <u>publisher</u>.

B. Complete each sentence with a proper noun.

Example: ＿＿＿ edits the school newspaper.
Aliza edits the school newspaper.

16. The school newspaper is called ＿＿＿ .
17. ＿＿＿ is the editor.
18. The paper comes out every ＿＿＿ .
19. ＿＿＿ wrote about the class election.
20. Ivy hopes ＿＿＿ will win.

Extra Practice, page 91

WRITING APPLICATION A Story

Write a story about a new place you visited with a friend. Tell about the special people and things you saw.

5 SINGULAR POSSESSIVE NOUNS

How do you show that a person owns something? One way to show ownership is to use a **singular possessive noun.** Add an apostrophe (') and an *s* to singular nouns to make them possessive.

The girl**'s** camera is new.
It is David**'s** camera bag.

the girl's camera   David's camera bag

Guided Practice

Tell the possessive form of each singular noun.

Example: David   *David's*

1. teacher
2. Mrs. Boyd
3. Nancy
4. Jim
5. boy

6. mother
7. cat
8. cousin
9. Kate
10. lion

?! THINK

■ How do I make a noun show ownership?

REMEMBER

- A **possessive noun** is a noun that shows who or what owns something.
- Add an **apostrophe** (') and an *s* to a singular noun to make it possessive.

More Practice

Write each sentence. Use the possessive form of the singular noun in ( ).

Example: (Julie) class developed the photos.

Julie's class developed the photos.

11. My (sister) pictures of our family won the most awards.
12. My (friend) pictures are out of focus.
13. All of the (girl) negatives are ruined.
14. Where are the (woman) slides?
15. (Carmen) photos are excellent.
16. Did you see (Frank) pictures?
17. (Carmen) picture won a prize.
18. (Pam) photo was better.
19. (Mr. Roth) favorite photo was of the blue and yellow bird.
20. Carmen studied (Pam) picture.

Extra Practice, page 92

WRITING APPLICATION A Review

Imagine that you are at a photography show. Write a description of what you see. Exchange papers with a classmate. Look for possessive nouns in each other's work.

6 PLURAL POSSESSIVE NOUNS

When you write, you use a singular possessive noun to show that a person owns something. To show that more than one person owns something, you use a **plural possessive noun.**

My brother**s'** bat is heavy.

Most plural nouns end in *s* or *es*. Add an apostrophe after the *s* to show ownership.

When a plural noun does not end in *s*, an apostrophe and an *s* are added to show possession.

Where is the men**'s** locker room?

BROTHERS' BAT

Guided Practice

Tell if each word is a singular possessive noun or a plural possessive noun.

Example: Stan's   *singular*

1. parents'
2. girls'
3. Nancy's
4. Casey's
5. boys'
6. Susan's
7. women's
8. dogs'
9. fathers'
10. Ellen's

?! THINK

■ How can I decide when a word is a plural possessive noun?

REMEMBER

- Add an apostrophe (') to make most plural nouns possessive.
- Add an apostrophe (') and an *s* to make plural nouns that don't end in *s* possessive.

More Practice

Write the sentences. Change each noun in ( ) to a plural possessive noun.

Example: The (man) team wins the game.
The men's team wins the game.

11. Stan parks his (parent) car.
12. The (player) caps are red.
13. The (boy) club is at the game.
14. The (child) parents cheer.
15. The next game is at my (brother) school.
16. Our (friend) bicycles are outside.
17. My (neighbor) uniforms are new.
18. My (sister) uniforms are blue and white.
19. The (woman) lockers are crowded.
20. The (dog) barks are very loud.

Extra Practice, Practice Plus, pages 93–95

WRITING APPLICATION A Paragraph

Write a paragraph about your favorite team sport. Describe an exciting game. Tell about some of the best parts of the game and who won. Exchange papers with a classmate. Circle the plural possessive nouns in each other's work.

7 MECHANICS: Abbreviations

An **abbreviation** is the shortened form of a word. An abbreviation begins with a **capital letter** and ends with a **period.** You can abbreviate titles before a name.

Mr. Alvin Brown   **Ms.** Jane Cook
Mr. Hunt   **Dr.** Sally Young   **Mrs.** Lopez

You can abbreviate days of the week.

Sun. Mon. Tues. Wed. Thurs. Fri. Sat.

You can also abbreviate the months.

Jan. Feb. Mar. Apr. Aug. Sept. Oct. Nov. Dec.

The following words do not have abbreviations.

Miss   May   June   July

SUN.	MON.	TUES.	WED.	THURS.	FRI.	SAT.
	1	2	3	4	5	6

Guided Practice

Tell what each abbreviation stands for.

Example: Apr.   *April*

1. Jan.
2. Sun.
3. Mar.
4. Mr.
5. Feb.
6. Mon.
7. Dr.
8. Wed.
9. Fri.

?! THINK

■ How can I decide which words to abbreviate?

REMEMBER

- An **abbreviation** is the shortened form of a word.
- Abbreviations begin with a capital letter and end with a period.

More Practice

A. Write each abbreviation correctly.

Example: dec   *Dec.*

10. aug		**16.** dr	
11. Sun		**17.** thurs	
12. ms.		**18.** jan.	
13. oct.		**19.** apr.	
14. Mr		**20.** Sept	
15. Mar		**21.** mrs	

B. Write the sentences. Use a word for each underlined abbreviation.

Example: Linda started running in <u>Jan</u>.
            Linda started running in January.

22. Crest School will have a race in <u>Apr</u>.
23. They have not had a race since <u>Mar</u>.
24. Keith will help us <u>Wed</u>.
25. Michael and Aliza practice every <u>Sun</u>.

Extra Practice, page 96

WRITING APPLICATION A Post Card

Write a post card to a friend describing a contest you would like to enter. Be sure to use abbreviations in your post card. Exchange post cards with a classmate. Find abbreviations in each other's work.

8 VOCABULARY BUILDING: Compound Words

A **compound word** is a word made from two or more words joined together. Studying the two smaller words can help you define the new word.

Kate sees a **sunflower.**
Kate finds a **seashell.**

sun   flower   sea   shell

Guided Practice

Tell which word in each pair is a compound word.

Example: basketball, bunch *basketball*

1. dazzle, daytime
2. shoulders, shoelace
3. bedtime, battle
4. ranch, rawhide
5. waterfall, watery

6. cowboy, composer
7. landmark, lawn
8. distant, dishrag
9. grandpa, grand
10. sidewalk, walking

?! THINK

■ How can I recognize a compound word?

REMEMBER

- A **compound word** is a word made from two or more words joined together.

More Practice

A. Write the sentences. Draw a line between the two words that make up each compound word.

Example: Kate walked across the drive|way.

11. Grandfather helps Kate.
12. Grandmother likes pretty flowers.
13. Kate has a skateboard.
14. Kate practices in the backyard.
15. Kate skates in the sunshine.

B. Write the sentences. Complete each sentence with a compound word from the box below.

Example: Kate woke up at <u>sunrise</u>.

| pancakes | volleyball | sunrise |
| notebook | highway | haircut |

16. Kate ate _____ at 8 A.M.
17. They drove on the _____ .
18. Kate bought a green _____ .
19. Kate got a short _____ .
20. Dad played _____ in the park.

Extra Practice, page 97

WRITING APPLICATION A Journal Entry

Imagine that you are an Olympic athlete. Write a journal entry about your events. Circle the compound words in your entry.

GRAMMAR —AND WRITING CONNECTION

Combining Sentences

You can make your writing more interesting by combining sentences. Use the word *and* to join the words. Leave out the words that repeat.

SEPARATE:	**Joanie** played after school. **Irv** played after school.
COMBINED:	**Joanie and Irv** played after school.
SEPARATE:	Joanie played **softball**. Joanie played **kickball**.
COMBINED:	Joanie played **softball and kickball.**

Working Together

COOPERATIVE LEARNING

With your class, discuss combining nouns in sentences. Then, tell how you would combine the following sentences.

Example: I like Len. I like Lou.   *I like Len and Lou.*

1. Simon moved in next door.
   Matthew moved in next door.
2. They had red hair.
   They had freckles.
3. Charles liked Simon.
   Charles liked Matthew.

Revising Sentences

Holly is writing a story about twins. Help Holly with her story by joining each pair of sentences. Use *and* to combine the sentences. Write the new sentences.

4. Mr. Carpenter noticed that the boys looked alike.
   Mrs. Wicher noticed that the boys looked alike.

5. Matthew said they were twins.
   Simon said they were twins.

6. Charles played on the Little League team.
   Matthew played on the Little League team.

7. Simon marched in the band.
   Charles marched in the band.

8. The three boys rode bikes.
   The three boys rode go-carts.

9. They built a tree house.
   They built a fort.

10. The boys washed cars for money.
    The boys washed dogs for money.

WRITER AT WORK

Imagine what it would be like if you were a twin. Write a journal entry describing a day with your twin. Join any sentences you can by combining nouns. Use the word *and* to combine nouns.

UNIT CHECKUP

LESSON 1

What Is a Noun? (page 66) Write each sentence. Underline the nouns.

1. The girl watched the parade.
2. The parade came down the street.
3. A tall clown wore a tiny hat.
4. One dog jumped through a hoop.
5. A woman walked on a wire.

LESSON 2

Singular Nouns and Plural Nouns (page 68) Write the plural form of these singular nouns.

6. bench
7. kite
8. tooth
9. brother
10. wish
11. man

LESSON 3

Plural Nouns with *ies* (page 70) Write the plural form of these singular nouns.

12. berry
13. baby
14. lily
15. puppy
16. family
17. dairy

LESSON 4

Common Nouns and Proper Nouns (page 72) Write the sentences. Draw one line under the common nouns. Draw two lines under the proper nouns.

18. Two men and three women are in the play.
19. Jessica designed all the costumes.
20. The audience clapped for Monica.

LESSON 5

Singular Possessive Nouns (page 74) Draw a line under each singular possessive noun.

21. Sue's records are in the garage.
22. Put on the boy's headphones.
23. Is this Mother's radio?
24. Where are my brother's records?

LESSON 6

Plural Possessive Nouns (page 76) Use the plural form of each possessive noun in ( ).

25. The (runner's) shirts are white.
26. Where are the (child's) tickets?
27. Where are the (boy's) scores?

LESSON 7

Mechanics: Abbreviations (page 78) Write each word. Then, write the abbreviation for the word.

28. January   **31.** Mister   **34.** Monday
29. Friday   **32.** Doctor   **35.** March
30. Tuesday   **33.** August   **36.** Sunday

LESSON 8

Vocabulary Building: Compound Words (page 80) Add a word from the box to each underlined word to make a compound word. Then, write the sentences.

> shells   guard   front   balls

37. We walked down to the <u>water</u> _____ .
38. I found some beautiful <u>sea</u> _____ .
39. The <u>life</u> _____ blew her whistle.
40. No <u>base</u> _____ were allowed.

Writing Application: Noun Usage (pages 66–78) The following paragraph contains 10 errors with nouns. Rewrite the paragraph correctly.

41.–50.

Three women planned a street fair. All the child helped. They carried the piles of sandwichs. They placed the boxs on the benchs. Three man organized the games. The prizes were stuffed beares and puppys. Mrs jones won two animales. She smiled proudly.

Little Riddles

Play this riddle game with a friend. Make up a riddle that describes a compound word. For example, a riddle for the compound word *doghouse* might be this.

It is a dog, but not a pet. It is a house, but not for people. What is it?

Compound Circles

On a large piece of paper, write a common noun. Think of as many compound words as you can using the noun. Write the compound words in a circle around the noun. Then, cut out pictures from magazines to illustrate each word.

Hanging Around

Cut a piece of cardboard into small squares. On the front of each square, write a day of the week or a month of the year. On the back of the square, write the abbreviation. Use string to attach each square to a wire hanger.

CREATIVE EXPRESSION

Puzzle

My best friend's name is Billy
But his best friend is Fred
And Fred's is Willy Wiffleson
And Willy's best is Ted.
Ted's best pal is Samuel
While Samuel's is Paul...
It's funny Paul says
I'm his best
I hate him most of all.

—Arnold Spilka

Try It Out! "Puzzle" is a funny poem about a group of friends. It has a set rhythm, or beat. Write a poem of your own that has a set rhythm. You might want to write about a time spent with a close friend.

EXTRA PRACTICE

Three levels of practice
What Is a Noun? (page 66)

A. Write each sentence. Underline the nouns.

1. The two boys live near the pond.
2. The water turns to ice.
3. The friends take their skates with them.
4. The path to the frozen pond is crowded.
5. The skaters wear warm jackets.
6. A boy loses his gloves.
7. Two girls find the gloves.

LEVEL
B. Write each sentence. Complete each sentence with the correct noun in ( ).

8. Nika made a new (friend, sing) in school.
9. The friend and her (work, family) just moved to town.
10. Georgette and Nika both like (music, often).
11. The girls heard a group of singers in the (rode, park).
12. Nika heard a favorite (song, loudly).
13. The girls sat under a (walked, tree).
14. Nika finished her (lunch, stepped).

LEVEL
C. Write the sentences. Complete each sentence with a noun.

15. The school had a _____ .
16. Two boys ran in a _____ .
17. The boys ran down the _____ .
18. Don won the _____ .
19. Each boy won a _____ .
20. Dave was proud of his _____ .

EXTRA PRACTICE

Three levels of practice

Singular Nouns and Plural Nouns (page 68)

LEVEL A. Write the underlined noun in each sentence. Write **singular** next to each singular noun. Write **plural** next to each plural noun.

1. Carl and Glen made a <u>telephone</u>.
2. The boys used two <u>cups</u> and a string.
3. Glen made <u>holes</u> in each cup.
4. Carl tied a <u>knot</u> at each end of the string.
5. The string carried the sound of their <u>voices</u>.
6. Carl showed the telephone to his <u>friends</u>.

LEVEL B. Write each noun. Write the plural form of each noun next to it.

7. book	**13.** truck	**19.** face
8. bicycle	**14.** parade	**20.** wish
9. fox	**15.** sash	**21.** horse
10. class	**16.** bus	**22.** compass
11. couch	**17.** ditch	**23.** branch
12. cabinet	**18.** tape	**24.** highway

LEVEL C. Write the sentences. Fill in each blank with the correct noun in ( ).

25. All of the _____ planted a garden. (child, children)
26. One _____ brought the seeds. (child, children)
27. Rick asked a _____ to lend him some tools. (man, men)
28. One _____ helped build a fence. (woman, women)
29. Two _____ ran under the fence. (mouse, mice)
30. The small animals have sharp _____ . (tooth, teeth)

GRAMMAR

Three levels of practice

Plural Nouns with *ies* (page 70)

LEVEL A. Complete each sentence with the correct plural noun in ( ).

1. Katie looks at the sunny _____ . (skys, skies)
2. _____ cross the river each day. (Ferries, Ferrys)
3. The two _____ are filled with people. (cities, citys)
4. Many _____ picnic in the park. (familys, families)
5. Gina found a patch of _____ . (strawberrys, strawberries)
6. The _____ smiled for the camera. (babys, babies)
7. Two _____ snapped the picture. (ladys, ladies)

LEVEL B. Write the plural form of each noun in ( ).

8. The (puppy) are only seven weeks old.
9. The (daisy) are in a vase.
10. The kitten chases the yellow (butterfly).
11. Beautiful plants grow in the (nursery).
12. People share (memory) of growing up.
13. Jessie has a large collection of (penny).
14. Sara buys two cartons of (blueberry).

LEVEL C. Write each sentence. Complete each sentence with the plural form of a word from the word box.

cranberry	party	baby	mystery	memory	bakery

15. Joe had two _____ on his birthday.
16. Three _____ supplied the food.
17. Joe liked the muffins with _____ .
18. Jeanne brought two _____ to the party.
19. Joe read some _____ after lunch.
20. Photos captured the many _____ .

EXTRA PRACTICE

Three levels of practice
Common Nouns and Proper Nouns (page 72)

LEVEL
A. Write each noun. Write **common** or **proper** next to each noun.

1. team
2. Mrs. Holmes
3. San Diego
4. street
5. Lake Placid

6. Chicago Cubs
7. woman
8. city
9. Oak Street
10. lake

LEVEL
B. Write each sentence. Draw one line under each common noun. Draw two lines under each proper noun.

11. Katie visited the zoo.
12. Audubon Zoo is in a park.
13. Many animals are from Asia and Africa.
14. Katie took a picture on Monkey Hill.
15. Jan liked the photo of the giraffes.

LEVEL
C. Write each sentence. Fill in each blank with a common noun or a proper noun.

16. The students from _____ visited the _____ .
                                   (proper)   (common)

17. _____ and _____ like to paint.
    (proper) (proper)

18. Lee drew a picture of _____ .
                                      (proper)

19. _____ bought a _____ .
    (proper)   (common)

20. Someday, _____ would like to be a _____ .
                     (proper)   (common)

EXTRA PRACTICE

Three levels of practice
Singular Possessive Nouns (page 74)

LEVEL
A. Write each sentence. Draw one line under each possessive noun.

1. My new friend's name is Carla.
2. Carla's family just moved to Denver.
3. Carla looked at my sister's records.
4. Carla knew each singer's name.
5. Carla played Denise's favorite song.
6. My neighbor's son likes the song, too.

LEVEL
B. Write each sentence with the possessive form of the noun in ( ).

7. We went to the circus on (Jeff) birthday.
8. The (clown) hat made us laugh.
9. We were amazed at the (magician) tricks.
10. Jeff tried to do the (juggler) act.
11. Jeff used my (brother) tennis balls.
12. The (elephant) trunk sprayed water into the air.
13. The (lion) roar was loud.

LEVEL
C. Rewrite each sentence so that it includes a possessive noun.

14. The sister of Hernando was in the play.
15. Jo played the doctor of the town.
16. Jo followed the orders of the director.
17. Everyone liked the voice of the singer.
18. Jo admired the grace of the dancer.
19. I liked the costume of one actor.
20. The acting of Jo was excellent.

EXTRA PRACTICE

Three levels of practice
Plural Possessive Nouns (page 76)

LEVEL
A. Write the plural possessive form of each phrase.

1. coats of the men
2. owner of the dogs
3. shoes of the women
4. crops of the farmers
5. tools of the carpenters
6. toys of the children
7. computers of the students
8. books of the teachers

LEVEL
B. Write each sentence. Change each noun in ( ) to a plural possessive noun.

9. Howie learned about the (worker) jobs.
10. Tara read the (writer) stories.
11. She visited the (editor) offices.
12. The children admired the (artist) pictures.
13. Jim looked at the (printer) machines.
14. Tara wants to start a (child) magazine.
15. The (girl) ideas were interesting.

LEVEL
C. Rewrite each sentence so that it includes a plural possessive noun. Underline the plural possessive nouns.

16. Ben loved the performance of the athletes.
17. The team of women won three gold medals.
18. The team of men broke records, too.
19. The team of Americans won six gold medals.
20. Cheers of the people filled the stadium.

PRACTICE + PLUS

Three levels of additional practice for a difficult skill
Plural Possessive Nouns (page 76)

LEVEL A. Write the sentences. Underline the plural possessive noun in each sentence.

1. The children's clubhouse is in the backyard.
2. Our neighbors' sons helped build it.
3. The girls used their fathers' hammers.
4. The walls were made of the carpenters' boards.
5. The boys' sisters gave us paintings.
6. The girls' pictures hang on the walls.
7. Shelves hold the boys' clay models.
8. Our friends' rugs sit on the floor.
9. One boy brought his cousins' chairs.
10. Their aunts' curtains cover the windows.
11. Our mothers' flowers are in the vases.
12. Birds' songs fill the air.

LEVEL B. Write the plural possessive noun in each pair.

13. dog's collars, dogs' collars
14. girl's coats, girls' coats
15. dogs' bowls, dog's bowls
16. the foxes's den, the foxes' den
17. the tiger's roar, the tigers' roar
18. the man's boat, the men's boat
19. students' books, student's books
20. brothers' games, brother's games

21. uncle's cars, uncles' cars
22. teacher's pens, teachers' pens
23. woman's shoes, women's shoes
24. dentist's drill, dentists' drill
25. goats' milk, goat's milk
26. boys' toys, boy's toys
27. golfer's game, golfers' game

LEVEL C. Write the sentences. Write the plural possessive form of each noun in ( ).

28. The (girl) trip took many days.
29. The sisters traveled to their (grandparent) house.
30. Jill read her (cousin) books.
31. The (neighbor) children gave a party.
32. The two visited their new (friend) houses.
33. The (child) rooms were large.
34. The (boy) baseballs were old.
35. Jill spotted the (cat) toys.
36. The girls heard the (dog) barks.
37. Pam loved the (woman) flowers.
38. The (sister) vacation ended.
39. The (girl) bags were packed.
40. Their (aunt) hugs were warm.

GRAMMAR

Three levels of practice
Mechanics: Abbreviations (page 78)

LEVEL A. Write the name of each day and each month.
Then, write the correct abbreviation.

1. Friday
2. Saturday
3. Tuesday
4. Wednesday
5. Thursday
6. January
7. April
8. October
9. March
10. February
11. August
12. September
13. November
14. December

LEVEL B. Write each title correctly. Be sure to begin each title
with a capital letter.

15. mrs Marie Lang
16. Dr Anne Lee
17. mr. Troy Hamilton
18. Miss. Amy Winters
19. Mr Ben Lauro
20. Mrs Dina Smart
21. dr Bob Silks
22. Ms Wendy Cooper
23. DR Charles Hill
24. miss Georgia Johnson
25. Mrs Rebecca Ortiz
26. mr Vincent Myers
27. mrs Emilia Rose
28. ms Ellen Flora

LEVEL C. Write the abbreviation of each day of the week or
month of the year correctly.

29. Septm.
30. Febr.
31. sund.
32. Apri.
33. Mun.
34. wednesd.
35. tuesd.
36. Fr.
37. Janua.
38. Satur.
39. Novr.
40. augus.

EXTRA PRACTICE

Three levels of practice

Vocabulary Building: Compound Words (page 80)

LEVEL A. Draw a line between the two words that make up each compound word.

1. flashlight	**5.** barnyard	**9.** hairbrush
2. footprint	**6.** backyard	**10.** earthquake
3. rosebud	**7.** sailboat	**11.** airplane
4. sunshine	**8.** sandbox	**12.** headlight

LEVEL B. Write the sentences. Complete each sentence with a compound word from the box.

> lumberyard   doghouse   doormat   paintbrush   handsaw

13. Ted made a _____ for the puppy.

14. He went to a _____ to buy the wood.

15. Ted's father used a _____ to cut the wood.

16. Ted bought a can of red paint and a _____ .

17. He found an old _____ to put in front.

LEVEL C. Write a compound word to answer each question.

18. What is a pack that you carry on your back?

19. What is the light that comes from the moon?

20. What do you call the shore that is near the sea?

21. What do you call a ball that you kick with your foot?

22. What do you call the end of the week?

23. What do you call the time when you have dinner?

24. What do you call the house a farmer lives in?

25. What do you call the print your finger leaves?

MAINTENANCE

What Is a Sentence? (page 2)

Write the groups of words that are sentences.

1. Molly has a wagon and two horses.
2. The wagon is filled with hay.
3. Always loves riding in the back.
4. Stops for dinner.

Statements and Questions (page 4), Commands and Exclamations (page 6)

Write each sentence correctly.

5. show me how to make a whistle
6. i can carve a whistle, too
7. how well my whistle works
8. do you want to hear a song

Subjects in Sentences (page 8), Predicates in Sentences (page 10)

Write each sentence. Draw one line under the subject.
Draw two lines under the predicate.

9. The horses are tired.
10. One horse lost a shoe.
11. The wagon will stop for a while.
12. Molly feeds the horse.

Unit 3   Understanding Nouns
What Is a Noun? (page 66)

Read each pair of words. Write the noun in each pair.

13. along, trail
14. warm, coat
15. gallop, horse

16. move, girl
17. around, city

Singular Nouns and Plural Nouns (page 68)

Write **singular** or **plural** next to each noun.

18. children
19. baby

20. woman
21. berry

Common Nouns and Proper Nouns (page 72)

Write each sentence. Draw one line under the common nouns. Draw two lines under the proper nouns.

22. The wagons go to Texas.
23. Uncle Jake sings a song.
24. Molly sings another song.
25. Jim sings and plays the guitar.

Singular Possessive Nouns (page 74), Plural Possessive Nouns (page 76)

Write the singular and the plural possessive form of each noun.

26. girl
27. woman

28. brother
29. children

Mechanics: Abbreviations (page 78)

Write the correct abbreviation for each word below.

30. Mister
31. Doctor

32. January
33. Monday

34. August
35. Friday

Vocabulary Building: Compound Words (page 80)

Write each sentence. Draw a line between the words that make up each compound word.

36. Willis writes a letter in his backyard.
37. He drops the letter in the driveway.
38. Willis daydreams about his friend.
39. There is a letter in his mailbox.
40. This afternoon he will write again.

UNIT 4

Writing Stories

Read the quotation and look at the picture on the opposite page. Susan Saunders wrote the story you will read in this unit. She thinks there is a magic to books. Talk about a book that you liked very much.

When you write a story, you will want your reader to find some magic in it. You will want your reader to enjoy what you have written.

Focus A story has a beginning, a middle, and an end. The writer introduces the characters and a possible problem in the beginning. Then, the writer tells what happens to the characters.

What kind of story would you like to write? On the following pages you will find a story and some photographs that may give you some ideas for writing.

THEME: *FRIENDS*

I have always loved children's books.
There is a magic to them....

—Susan Saunders

LITERATURE

Reading Like a Writer

AWARD WINNING SELECTION

Have you ever done something with your family that you looked forward to doing again? Edith Hughes was a real girl from the small East Texas town of Chandler. Every year Edith and her family joined their neighbors for a fish fry. How do you think Edith felt about this event? How does the author let you know about Edith's feelings?

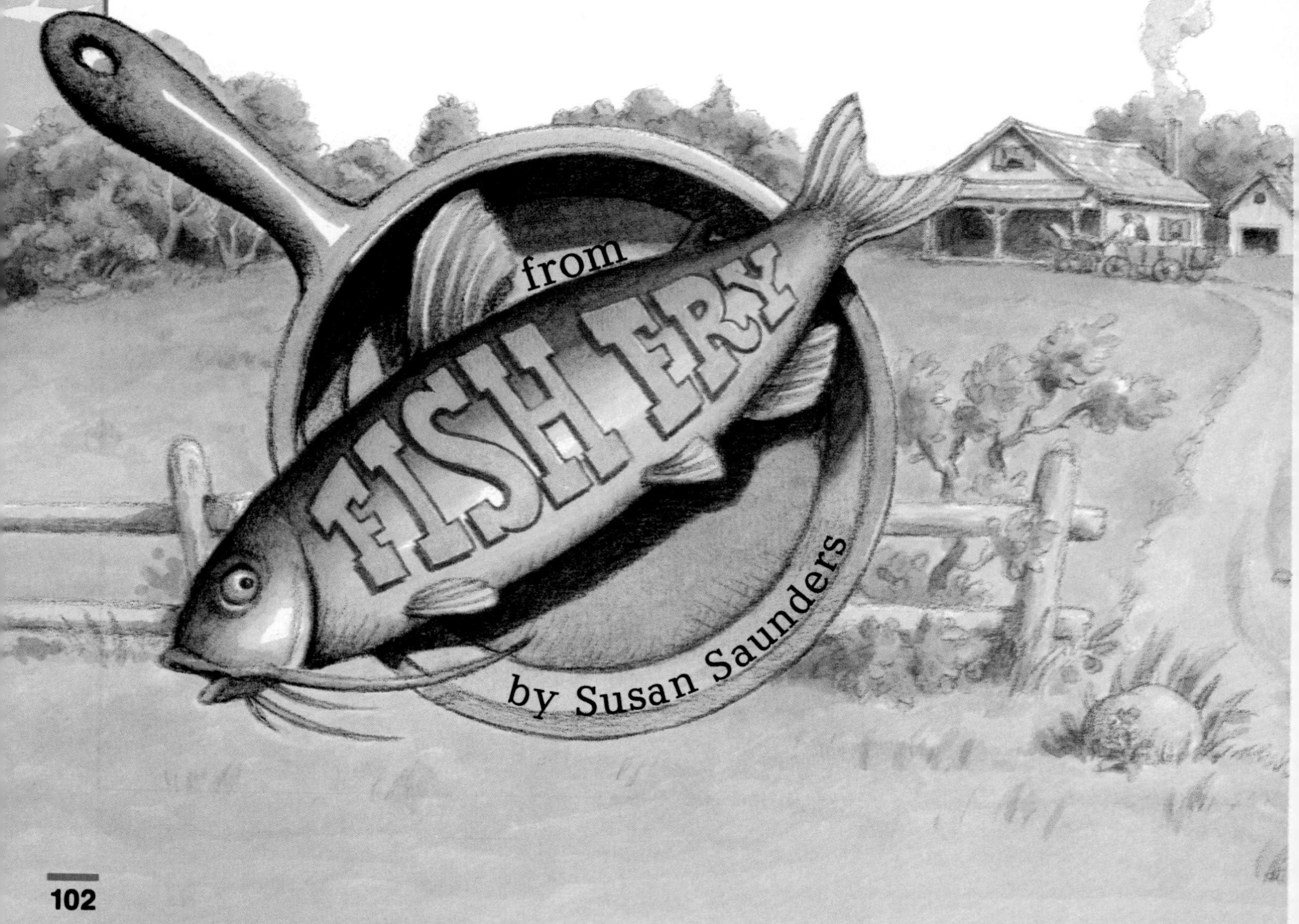

from
FISH FRY
by Susan Saunders

The wagon had two wide seats for the grown-ups. Mama sat up front with Jake, the hired man. But Edith and Katie, who was her best friend, liked to sit in the back and let their legs hang down.

The wagon rolled down Main Street past the courthouse and the drugstore to the edge of town. They stopped at the railroad tracks to let the morning train pass, and Edith and Katie waved to the engineer.

Then they headed down a broad dirt road. Edith and Katie took turns jumping out of the wagon and running alongside. When they got good and dusty, they played games, like who could count the most spotted cows. Sometimes they just lay back and looked up at the clouds.

"When are we going to get there?" Edith asked.

"Oh, it's a way yet," Mama said.

Katie is the main character in the story.

Now there were wagons in front of them and in back of them, a winding line of wagons and horses and mules.

Edith could smell the river long before she could see it, hidden among pine trees and hickories and persimmons. Finally their wagon rolled to a stop.

And from the branches of every tree hung sleek, whiskered catfish!

Daddy stood at a high table skinning fish with his long knife while Mr. Greene tended the fires.

Mama set right to work with an iron fork and a big black skillet. "Run along," she said to the girls. "But keep your bonnets on, and stay away from that river."

So Edith and Katie played hopscotch, and then tag with some of the boys, until Eugene Greene said, "I'm so hungry I could eat an alligator."

And then it was time for dinner on the ground. There were butter beans and potato salad, deviled eggs and hush puppies, and more fried catfish than even Eugene Greene could eat. For dessert there were all those cookies, cakes, and pies, and watermelon cooled in the river.

Edith was so full she sat still for a minute. Until Eugene Greene whispered, "Sssst.

Come on. I'll show you the biggest old alligator in the river."

"I don't believe you," Edith said. But she went anyway. First they stopped at a sweet gum tree to get something to chew on. Then Eugene led Edith around a blackberry patch. The river swirled lazily around rocks and tree trunks in the still of the afternoon.

It was so quiet that Edith heard a turtle slide down the bank and plop into the water.

"See those bubbles," Eugene said, "rising near that stump?"

Edith nodded.

"Well, if you lean way over, you'll see that old alligator on the river bottom, fat and sleepy and bigger than both of us.". . .

Daddy and Jake went down to the river to pull out the last net. And what did they find? Just about the biggest alligator anyone had seen that far up the river. It was dark green and bumpy, with a big thick tail and great rows of teeth.

Eugene was as surprised as everyone else. . . but only for a second. Then he grinned. "See?" he said to Edith.

Until Katie spoke up. "Still hungry enough to eat an alligator, Eugene Greene?"

The alligator gave a loud hiss that made them all jump. Then it lashed its tail and tottered

Time-order words help make the sequence clear.

back down to the water. There would be plenty to tell the folks in town about this fish fry.

On the way home Daddy and Jake sat up front. Edith and Katie sat in the second seat, next to Mama, and counted fireflies until they both fell asleep.

Thinking Like a Reader

1. If you were Edith, would you have gone with Eugene Greene to see an alligator in the river? Why or why not?

Write your response in your journal.

Thinking Like a Writer

2. How does the author let you know that Eugene Greene was only joking when he told Edith that he would show her an alligator?

Write your response in your journal.

LITERATURE

Brainstorm *Vocabulary*

A sentence in "Fish Fry" reads: "The river swirled lazily . . . in the *still* of the afternoon." Look up the word *still* in the dictionary. Which meaning is used in the sentence from the story? Find three more words from the story. Look these words up in a dictionary. Do they have more than one meaning? Add these words to your personal word list.

Talk It Over
Interviewing

Imagine that you are a newspaper reporter. Have a classmate play the part of one of the people at the fish fry. Interview your classmate. Ask questions about where the alligator was found and what happened.

Quick Write *Make a Poster*

Create a poster advertising a fish fry. Provide a menu for the food that will be served. Describe some of the games that will be played. Include the date, the time, and the place. You might want to provide directions explaining how to get to the fish fry from the center of town. Illustrate your poster with colorful pictures of the food that will be served and the games that will be played.

Idea Corner
Think of a Place

Stories can happen in more than one place. The story, "Fish Fry," takes place near a river. Where else might the story take place? Make a list of possible places. Write the list in your journal.

PICTURES

Finding Ideas for Writing

Look at the pictures. Think about what you
see. What ideas for a story do the photographs
give you? Write your ideas in your journal.

PICTURES: Ideas for Writing a Story

1 GROUP WRITING: A Story

COOPERATIVE
LEARNING

Stories can be make-believe or real. They can be funny, exciting, scary, or silly. They can entertain or teach an audience. All good stories have these things in common:

- Beginning, Middle, and End
- Sequence
- Characters and Setting

Beginning, Middle, and End

The beginning of the story tells what the story will be about.

> Nina and Ned planted a maple tree in autumn. First, they placed it in a deep hole in their yard.

The middle of the story tells what happens. This part can have a lot of action.

> Winter came and the tree stood bravely in the cold. High winds whipped around the bare branches. Then, a blanket of snow covered the tree.

The end of the story tells how everything turns out. A good ending completes the story in a way that makes sense. The events can turn out as expected or be a surprise.

> Finally, spring arrived and new leaves burst from the tree. Nina and Ned noticed that the new leaves were a strange shape. It was not a maple tree after all.

Guided Practice: Planning a Beginning, a Middle, and an End

As a class, plan the beginning, the middle, and the end of a story. Choose a topic below, or make up one of your own. Look in your journal to find other ideas.

A Trip to the Moon   The Forgetful Computer

Sequence

In a story, events happen in a certain order called a **sequence.** One event should lead to another. **Time-order words,** such as *first, then, next, last,* and *finally,* help make the sequence of events clear. Look back at the story about Nina and Ned.

- Which details are told first, next, and last?
- Which time-order words help make the sequence clear?

Characters and Setting

The people in a story are called **characters.** The place where the story happens is called a **setting.** When you write a story, describe your characters and setting so that your reader sees them clearly.

Look back at the story about the tree. Who are the characters? Where is the setting?

Guided Practice: Choosing Characters and a Setting

Add characters and a setting to the story you planned with your class. Make sure that you can see your characters clearly.

Putting a Story Together

With your classmates, you have planned the beginning, the middle, and the end of a story. You have chosen characters and a setting for your story. Now think about the details of your story. What details would you like to add to your story?

One student added more details to the sample story in the following way.

> Nina and Ned planted a maple tree in autumn. First, they placed the tree in a deep hole in their yard. Then, they watered the tree carefully.
>
> Winter came and the tree stood bravely in the cold. High winds whipped around the bare branches. Then, a blanket of snow covered the tree and the yard. Nina and Ned brushed the snow from the bare branches.
>
> Finally, spring arrived and new leaves burst from the tree. Nina and Ned noticed that the new leaves were a strange shape. It was not a maple tree after all! They were still proud of their tree, however.

Guided Practice: Writing a Story

Write a story based on the beginning, the middle, and the end that you created with your classmates. Check to see that your details are in the correct sequence.

Have a classmate read your story and suggest any details that would make your story more interesting.

Checklist: A Story

Writing a story can be fun. There are many things to think about and to remember. A checklist can help you to remember some of the basic points about writing a story.

Look at the checklist below. It is missing some important points. Copy the checklist and add the missing points. You will then have a checklist that you can use when you write your stories. Keep your checklist in your writing folder.

CHECKLIST

- ✓ Purpose and audience
- ✓ _____ , middle, and end
- ✓ Sequence
- ✓ Time-order words
- ✓ Characters and _____

2 THINKING AND WRITING: Putting Events in Order

You know that the order of events in a story is called the **sequence.** A correct sequence of events makes sense to the audience. One event leads to the next.

Jared is planning a story about a visit to Ocean World. Jared has not yet put the events in order. Here is a page from Jared's notebook:

> 1. Danny the dolphin jumps and leaps.
> 2. We watch the dolphin show.
> 3. My family visits Ocean World.
> 4. Danny splashes me.

Thinking Like a Writer

■ What is the best order for these events?

Jared begins with his family visiting Ocean World, and ends with getting splashed by Danny.

Here is the best order for the story.

> 1. My family visits Ocean World.
> 2. We watch the dolphin show.
> 3. Danny the dolphin jumps and leaps.
> 4. Danny splashes me.

COOPERATIVE
LEARNING

Four students want to write stories. Help these students put their details in order. Write on a separate piece of paper. Share your thoughts about the stories with your classmates.

1. Hannah is writing an adventure story about a ski trip. What is the best order for these events?

   - They reach the bottom breathless.
   - They race down the icy slope.
   - The skiers face a dangerous slope.
   - They anxiously wait to begin.

2. Mario is writing a funny story about clowns in a circus. What is the best order for these events?

   - A clown throws confetti at the audience.
   - Eight clowns tumble from the tiny car.
   - A tiny car zigzags around the arena.
   - It stops in the middle ring.

3. Ellen wants to write a story about the natural history museum. Write three details that Ellen could include in her paragraph. Put the details in order.

4. Davis wants to write about his visit to an aquarium. What would be the best order for his story?

   - visited the blue whale at 10:00 A.M.
   - arrived as the aquarium opened
   - had lunch in the cafeteria
   - stayed until the aquarium closed
   - saw the stingrays at 2:00 P.M.

3 INDEPENDENT WRITING: A Story

Prewrite: Step 1

Before you begin to write a story, you need to think about your **purpose** and **audience.** Margie chose a topic this way.

Choosing a Topic

1. First, she wrote a list of topics for her story.
2. Next, she thought about each topic.
3. Last, she chose her favorite topic.

a Halloween party

a school picnic

how to swim

the circus

Margie decided to write about learning how to swim. She narrowed her topic to write about how her brother, Billy, learned to swim.

Exploring Ideas: Note-taking Strategy

Margie wrote notes in her journal.

Everyone in family can swim.

Billy wants to swim, too.

Billy asks lifeguard to teach him.

Margie was sure her cousins would want to know all about her brother's latest adventure.

Margie put her ideas in a sequence that made sense. She numbered her ideas and added a new one.

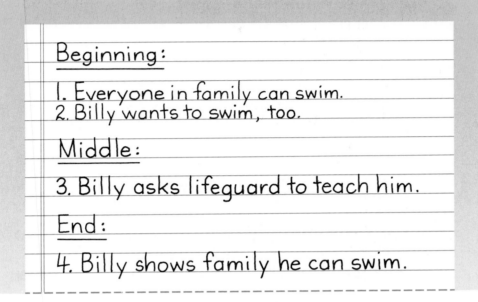

Beginning:

1. Everyone in family can swim.
2. Billy wants to swim, too.

Middle:

3. Billy asks lifeguard to teach him.

End:

4. Billy shows family he can swim.

Thinking Like a Writer

- What did Margie add?

Now it is your turn to plan a story. Use **Pictures** or your journal for ideas. Follow these steps:

- Write some topics. Remember purpose and audience.
- Choose the topic you like best.
- Narrow your topic if it is too broad.
- Make a list of some ideas.
- Put the ideas in order. Number them.

You can add to or take away from your list at any time.

Write a First Draft: Step 2

Margie made a planning checklist so she would not forget any of the important details of her story.

Then, Margie wrote the first draft of her story. She followed her planning checklist as she went along.

Margie's First Draft

Everyone in Billys family could swim. Billy wanted to swim, too. He askd the Lifeguard to teach him. "Guess what my friend the lifeguard taught me," Billy said to his family. Then, he started to swim. Everyone cheered.

Planning Checklist
■ Purpose and audience
■ Beginning, middle, and end
■ Sequence
■ Time-order words
■ Characters and setting

YOUR TURN

Write your first draft. Ask yourself these questions:

■ What will my audience want to know?
■ How can I make my sequence of events clear?

Remember to make and use a planning checklist.

TIME-OUT You might want to take some time out before you write. That way you will be able to revise your writing with a fresh eye.

Revise: Step 3

Margie showed her first draft to a classmate named Marc. They talked about the story. Marc really liked the story about Margie's brother learning how to swim. Marc made a suggestion.

I liked your story a lot. I think it would even be better if you told where Billy learned how to swim.

That's a good idea. I'll add a setting when I revise. Thank you.

Margie looked back at her checklist. She checked *Characters and setting*. This would help her to remember Marc's suggestion. Margie now has a revising checklist to use as she revises.

Next, Margie revised her draft. Notice that she did not correct small errors. Margie knew she could fix them later. Turn the page, and look at Margie's revised draft.

Revising Checklist
- Purpose and audience
- Beginning, middle, and end
- Sequence
- Time-order words
- Characters and setting

Margie's Revised Draft

One year Billy's family spent the summer at the beach.

Everyone in Billys family could swim, ¸and

Billy wanted to swim, too. He askd the

Lifeguard to teach him. "Guess what my

friend the lifeguard taught me," Billy said

to his family. Then, he started to swim.

Everyone cheered.

Thinking Like a Writer

WISE
WORD
CHOICE

- What did Margie add to give her story a setting?
- Which two sentences did she combine?
- How does this improve her story?

YOUR TURN

Read the first draft of your story. Make a checklist. Ask yourself these questions:

- What is the best sequence for my story?
- How can I describe my characters and setting more clearly?

You may want to ask a classmate for suggestions. Then, revise your story.

Proofread: Step 4

It was now time to proofread Margie's story. She used the proofreading checklist below to help as she proofread.

Part of Margie's Proofread Draft

One year Billy's family spent the summer at the beach. Everyone in Billy's family could swim, and Billy wanted to swim, too. He asked the Lifeguard to teach him. "Guess what my

YOUR TURN

Proofreading Practice

You can use the paragraph below to practice your proofreading skills. Copy the paragraph onto a separate piece of paper. Find the errors.

It was a brite spring day. Suddenly toby heard sirens. A big red fire engine pulled up in front of tobys house. "What's going on?" she asked.

"A cat is stuck in a tree?" said a neighbor. Suddenly, three fire fighters dashed from their truck. they quickly brought the cat down from the tree. Everyone cheered.

Proofreading Checklist
- Did I indent my paragraphs?
- Did I capitalize letters correctly?
- Did I use punctuation correctly?
- Did I spell all words correctly?

Applying Your Proofreading Skills

Proofread your own story. Look back at the proofreading checklist. Review **The Grammar Connection** and **The Mechanics Connection**.

THE GRAMMAR CONNECTION

Remember these rules about possessive nouns.

- For singular nouns, add an apostrophe and an *s*.

- For plural nouns ending in *s*, add only an apostrophe.

- For plural nouns that don't end in *s*, add an apostrophe and an *s*.

    Billy**'s** family   girls**'** toys   men**'s** boat

Proofreading Marks

¶ Indent
∧ Add
⸜ Take out
≡ Make a capital letter
/ Make a small letter

THE MECHANICS CONNECTION

- Use quotation marks to show that somebody is speaking.

- Quotation marks come at the beginning and end of a person's exact words.

    "Look at me," said Sally.
    "Will you help me?" Sally asked.
    "It would make me happy!" she added.

Publish: Step 5

Margie gave a copy of her story to her cousins. She read the story aloud when her cousins came for a visit. Margie drew pictures of the main events in the story. She held these pictures up as she read.

YOUR TURN

Make a final copy of your story. Think of a way to share your story. You might want to use one of these **Sharing Suggestions.**

SHARING SUGGESTIONS

| Put on a play based on your story. | Draw a comic strip based on your story. | Act out your story without using any words. |

4 SPEAKING AND LISTENING: Conducting an Interview

Sometimes another person can give you information to use in your writing.

Margie wanted to find out more about swimming. She decided to interview the swimming coach at the local pool. An **interview** is a kind of meeting. She thought her classmates would be interested in what she found out.

Margie and the coach agreed to meet at the pool after school. Margie made a list of questions.

How many people swim in the United States?

When do most people learn how to swim?

How many swimming competitions are there?

How do people train for a swimming competition?

What are some of the basic swimming strokes?

Margie asked these questions and others that came to mind. She copied down what the coach said so that she could quote her correctly.

Margie wrote her report immediately after the interview. She wanted to do this while the information was still fresh in her mind. In an interview, keep these speaking guidelines in mind.

SPEAKING GUIDELINES: An Interview

1. Ask exact questions in order to get the information you need.
2. Ask your questions clearly.
3. Look at the person you are interviewing.
4. Thank the person after the interview.

- Why should I plan and write out my questions in advance?
- Why should I write my report soon after the interview?
- Why should I ask the person that I am interviewing specific questions?

SPEAKING APPLICATION An Interview

Now you are ready to conduct an interview of your own. Talk to someone who has an interesting job or an unusual hobby. You might want to interview a police officer, a firefighter, or a bus driver. Be sure to ask exact questions in order to get the information that you need. Write a report based on your interview. Read the report to your class. Use the following listening guidelines as you conduct your interview.

LISTENING GUIDELINES: An Interview

1. Listen carefully to what the person is saying.
2. Take notes so that you will remember exactly what was said.
3. Think of other questions to ask the speaker.

5 WRITER'S RESOURCES: The Dictionary

Alphabetical Order

When you write a story, you may need to know how to spell a word correctly. Sometimes you may want to know the exact meaning of a word. You can find both the spellings and the meanings in a dictionary.

Each word explained in a dictionary is called an **entry word**. The entry words are listed in **alphabetical order,** or in the same order as the letters of the alphabet.

> **a**im, **b**oy, **c**at, **d**og

When words begin with the same letter, the second letter is used to put them in alphabetical order.

> a**b**out, a**c**tor, a**d**d, a**f**ford

When words begin with the same two letters, the third letter is used to put the words in alphabetical order.

> be**a**t, be**l**ieve, be**s**t, be**t**ter

Suppose you want to check on the spelling and meaning of the word *cloth*. You can use the **guide words** found at the top of each page in the dictionary. Guide words are the first and last entry words on the page. All the other entry words on the page come between them in alphabetical order.

cloth 1. Material made by weaving or knitting fibers. Cloth is made from cotton, wool, silk, linen, or other fibers. 2. A piece of cloth used for a particular purpose. Use this *cloth* to dust the living room. **cloth** (klôth) *noun, plural* **cloths.**

clothe To put clothes on someone; dress; provide with clothes. I *clothed* the baby warmly because it was cold outdoors.
clothe (klōth) *verb,* **clothed** or **clad, clothing.**

clown A person who makes people laugh by playing tricks or doing stunts. A clown in a circus often wears funny clothing and makeup. *Noun.*
—To act like a clown. Don't *clown* around when you are supposed to be doing your homework. *Verb.*
clown (kloun) *noun, plural* **clowns;** *verb,* **clowned, clowning.**

The last word on the page is *clump.*

Practice

1. Put the words in each group into alphabetical order.

    a. fish, ball, zero, silly
    b. boat, bad, bed, break
    c. home, house, hobby, holiday

2. Which of these words will also be found on the dictionary page with the guide words *cloth/clump*?

cloud, client, clever, clover, clue, close

WRITING APPLICATION Guide Words

Put the following words in alphabetical order. Then, use a dictionary to find the guide words for each word. Write the guide words next to each word.

a. simple
b. lighten
c. forget
d. listen
e. intelligent
f. saxophone

WRITING EXTENSION

6 WRITER'S RESOURCES: The Dictionary Entry

A dictionary tells you the **definition,** or the meaning, of a word. Often, there is more than one meaning for a word. Each meaning of a word is numbered in a dictionary.

---

golden **1.** Made of or containing gold. This pair of *golden* earrings was given to me by my grandparents. **2.** Having the color or shine of gold; bright or shining. The field of *golden* wheat swayed in the wind. The baby's hair is soft and *golden.* **3.** Very good or valuable; excellent. If you join that team, it will be a *golden* opportunity for you to train with an excellent coach. **4.** Very happy, with much success, wealth, or good fortune. That was the *golden* age of Roman history when the empire was at peace. **gold·en** (gōl′ dən) *adjective.*

An **example sentence** sometimes follows each definition in a dictionary. This shows you how to use the word. The example sentence also gives you a clue to the meaning of the word.

---

128 WRITER'S RESOURCES: The Dictionary Entry

Practice

1. What are two meanings of the word *golden*? Write a sentence for each meaning.

2. Look up the word *horn* in the dictionary. How many definitions can you find for the word *horn?* Write the definitions. Next to each definition, write an example sentence using that meaning for the word *horn*.

3. Write the definition of each underlined word below as it is used in the sentence. Then, write two other definitions for the word.
   a. I jumped over the <u>low</u> wall.
   b. My two socks do not <u>match</u>.
   c. I made a <u>model</u> of our house out of wood.
   d. I had a free <u>pass</u> for the movies.

WRITING APPLICATION A Story

Use a dictionary to find three words that have more than one meaning. Write a story using the words. Be sure to use the words more than once to show the different meanings.

Writing About Music

There are many kinds of music. There is classical music, popular music, folk music, and jazz. You probably enjoy listening to different types of music. Maybe you like to sing or play a musical instrument.

Songwriters set their ideas to music. They follow many of the steps that you do when you write a story. Songs can tell about someone's experience or feelings. A song can be funny, sad, or even silly.

ACTIVITIES

Create a Musical Sketch Draw a picture of somebody playing a musical instrument. Write a few sentences about what is happening in the picture.

Describe a Photograph Look at the photograph on the top of the next page. Describe what is happening. Imagine the song that the children in the photograph are playing. Write the first stanza of the song.

Respond to Literature George Antheil was a famous pianist and composer. He wrote a book called *Bad Boy of Music*.

Bad Boy of Music

When I was eight years old a lot of kids in our neighborhood formed a club...We continued this club under many names until I was thirteen: "Easy Going Club," "The Seneca Detective Agency," "101 Ranch." On the outside, so to speak, I commenced the study of the violin, then the piano. None of the kids thought any the worse of me for it. Most of them had to learn to play one instrument or another, too. The only difference between them and me was that I enjoyed practicing. They didn't know this until, one day, I invited them all into our front parlor and played for them a new piano "sonata" which I had written....

I became the club's official composer.

Imagine that you were a member of the "Easy Going Club." Write a letter to a friend about the day when George played for the club.

UNIT CHECKUP

LESSON 1

Group Writing: A Story (page 110) Write a beginning, a middle, and an end for one of the following topics.

Exploring a Haunted House

The Special Birthday Present

LESSON 2

Thinking: Putting Story Events in Order (page 114) Kevin is planning a story about a boy who goes to clown school. Put these events in the correct sequence.

- graduates from clown school
- learns to put on clown makeup
- enters clown school

LESSON 3

Writing a Story (page 116) Write a story about a Halloween party. Describe the costumes, the food, and the decorations. Tell about something exciting that happened at the party. Make sure your story has a beginning, a middle, and an end.

LESSON 4

Speaking and Listening: An Interview (page 124) Why should you ask specific questions to the person you are interviewing?

LESSONS 5-6

Writer's Resources: The Dictionary (pages 126-129) Use a dictionary to find a word that would appear on the same page as each set of guide words below.

1. fight/filings
2. scant/schedule
3. mail/manage
4. found/fragment
5. satin/sawmill
6. mayor/measure

THEME PROJECT

A SCENE

Groups of friends are playing together in the park. Notice the many activities that are taking place. Discuss the picture with your classmates. What are the different groups of friends doing? What do you think they might be saying? What beginning, middle, and end would you write for a scene about one of the children's activities?

Think of a story that you can turn into a scene. You might want to develop some of the characters you see in the picture above.

- Write a scene for the children in the park to play in.
- Give each of the children a name.
- Talk about the personality of each child and what she or he likes. You might even describe some of the hobbies the children have.
- Act out the scene with your classmates. Assign a different part to each child.

Action Verbs

In Unit 5 you will learn about action verbs. Action verbs are words like *crawled* and *jumped*.

Discuss Read the poem on the opposite page. What does the poem describe? What have the children made?

Creative Expression The theme of this unit is *Inventions.* Have you ever invented or made anything? Perhaps you have made a poster or a model car. Draw a picture of something that you have made. Write a name for your invention. Draw your invention in your journal.

THEME: *INVENTIONS*

We stretched a rope between two trees
And hung a blanket over it.
We pegged the bottom down with stones
And then we crawled inside to sit.

— Margaret Hillert
from "The Funny House"

1 WHAT IS AN ACTION VERB?

An action verb is a word that shows action.

When you speak or write, the words that show actions are called **action verbs**. In a sentence, action verbs tell what the subject of a sentence does.

The machine **sews** the shoe.
A worker **glues** the heel.

A man polishes a shoe.

Guided Practice

Tell which word is the action verb in each sentence.

Example: The factory produces many shoes. *produces*

1. A cobbler makes a pair of shoes.
2. He stretches the leather.
3. He draws a shape.
4. A machine sews the pieces together.
5. It stitches a design on the shoe.

?! THINK

- How can I decide which word is an action verb?

REMEMBER

- An **action verb** is a word that shows action.

More Practice

A. Write the sentences. Underline each action verb.

Example: One man <u>polishes</u> the shoes.

6. Many people work in the factory.
7. They make different kinds of shoes.
8. One man starts a machine.
9. He places the leather inside.
10. The machine cuts the leather.
11. John works, too.
12. Two workers cut the rubber.
13. They glue two pieces together.

B. Write the sentences. Choose the correct action verb in ( ).

Example: One man (designs, folds) the sneakers.
   One man designs the sneakers.

14. My class (visited, obeyed) a sneaker factory.
15. Hundreds of people (make, sing) sneakers.
16. Wally and Kira (work, sing) there.
17. They (wear, pile) the cloth onto a table.
18. A sharp tool (hangs, walks) over the table.
19. The tool (faces, traces) a pattern.
20. A big machine (holds, likes) the leather.

Extra Practice, page 158

 WRITING APPLICATION An Advertisement

COOPERATIVE LEARNING

With your classmates, write an advertisement for sneakers that could make people fly. Circle the action verbs in your advertisement.

2 VERBS IN THE PRESENT

A verb can show action. The **tense** of a verb tells when the action takes place. A verb in the **present tense** tells that something is happening now. Follow these rules when you use verbs with singular subjects.

- Add *s* to most verbs.

  The magnet stick**s** to metal.

- Add *es* to verbs that end in *sh, ch, ss, s, zz,* or *x.*

  Joe watch**es** the compass.

- Change *y* to *i* and add *es* to verbs that end with a consonant and *y.*

  Joe carr**ies** his compass on hikes.

Do not add *s* or *es* when you use verbs with plural subjects.

Guided Practice

Tell whether a singular subject or a plural subject is used with each underlined verb.

Example: A compass <u>shows</u> direction.   *singular*

1. The magnet <u>attracts</u> a nail.
2. Kira <u>teaches</u> us about magnets.
3. Magnets <u>turn</u> inside compasses.
4. The children <u>watch</u> her carefully.
5. Barney <u>uses</u> a compass.

?! **THINK**

- How do I know when to add *s* or *es* to a verb?

REMEMBER

- Add *s* or *es* to most present-tense verbs when you use them with singular subjects.
- If a verb ends with a consonant and *y*, change the *y* to *i* and add *es*.

More Practice

Write the verb in each sentence. If the sentence has a singular subject, write **singular**. If it has a plural subject, write **plural**.

Example: The men move the box.   *move   plural*

6. The doghouse needs a ramp.
7. A man carries a long board.
8. The workers lean it against the steps.
9. One man lifts the heavy box.
10. Two workers slide the box down the ramp.
11. One worker catches the box.
12. Two men put the box into a truck.
13. Gary fixes the ramp for the doghouse.
14. He finds the hammer.
15. Tom passes him a nail.
16. Jan carries a short board.
17. She hurries toward the doghouse.
18. The dogs watch from under a tree.
19. The children put the ramp in place.
20. The boys finish the job.

Extra Practice, page 159

WRITING APPLICATION An Article

Write an article about a simple machine. Describe how it makes your everyday life easier. Check that you have correctly added *s* or *es* to the verbs.

3 VERBS IN THE PAST

A verb can tell about an action that has already happened. Use these rules for **past-tense verbs.**

- Add *ed* to most verbs.   look**ed,** talk**ed**
- Drop the *e* and add *ed*   smil**ed,** danc**ed** to verbs that end with *e.*
- Change *y* to *i* and add   carr**ied,** stud**ied** *ed* to verbs that end with a consonant and *y.*
- Double the consonant   dra**gged,** sto**pped** and add *ed* to verbs that end with one vowel and one consonant.

Guided Practice

Tell how each past-tense verb is formed.

Example: fill   *add ed*

1. learn
2. look
3. try
4. use
5. plan

?! THINK

- How can I decide if I have spelled a past-tense verb correctly?

REMEMBER

■ Add *ed* to most verbs to show past tense.

More Practice

A. Write the sentences. Underline the past-tense verbs.

Example: The sky <u>twinkled</u> with stars.

6. Galileo watched the night sky.
7. He wondered about the stars.
8. Galileo stared at the tiny lights.
9. The stars filled the sky.
10. People laughed at Galileo.
11. Galileo continued his work.
12. Galileo never stopped his search.
13. He invented the telescope.
14. He studied the Milky Way.

B. Write the sentences. Complete each sentence by changing the verb in ( ) to the past tense.

Example: Galileo (explain) his ideas.
Galileo explained his ideas.

15. Galileo (figure) the distance to the stars.
16. He (worry) when people laughed at him.
17. Soon they (stop) laughing.
18. Galileo (discover) moons around Jupiter.
19. He (prove) that the Milky Way was a group of stars.
20. Many people (cheer) Galileo.

Extra Practice, Practice Plus, pages 160–162

WRITING APPLICATION A Biographical Sketch

Write a biographical sketch about an inventor. Have a classmate identify the past-tense verbs in your sketch.

VERBS IN THE FUTURE

4

You know how to show an action that happens now or in the past. Verbs can also show an action that will happen in the **future.** To write about the future, use the special verb *will.*

One day we **will live** on another planet.
We **will travel** in a rocket.

Guided Practice

Tell whether each action verb is in the **past, present,** or **future.**

Example: Astronauts will visit Pluto.   *future*

1. Astronomers discovered new planets.
2. They studied the stars.
3. Many people watch the solar system.
4. They see stars and planets.
5. A scientist will plan space travel.
6. Soon families will walk on the moon.

?! THINK

■ How can I decide if an action verb tells about the future?

REMEMBER

■ A verb in the **future tense** tells about an action that is going to happen.

More Practice

Write the sentences. Then, write whether the underlined verbs tell about an action in the **past, present,** or **future.**

Example: I will visit many planets.

I will visit many planets.   future

7. Rocket ships <u>carry</u> people far away.
8. We <u>counted</u> the stars.
9. Many people <u>traveled</u> in space.
10. Our planet <u>moves</u> in space.
11. The earth <u>looked</u> like a giant ball.
12. Planets <u>circle</u> the sun.
13. A comet <u>will come</u> close to the earth.
14. We <u>will see</u> asteroids that day.
15. I <u>will take</u> photographs.
16. Rockets <u>carry</u> satellites into space.
17. Two astronauts <u>boarded</u> the rocket.
18. The satellites <u>will take</u> pictures.
19. Scientists <u>will use</u> these photos.
20. Some instruments <u>will send</u> coded messages.

Extra Practice, page 163

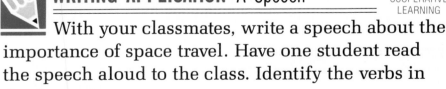

WRITING APPLICATION A Speech

COOPERATIVE LEARNING

With your classmates, write a speech about the importance of space travel. Have one student read the speech aloud to the class. Identify the verbs in the future tense.

G R A M M A R

5 HELPING VERBS

You use the verbs *has, have,* and *had* to help other verbs to show an action in the past. These verbs are called **helping verbs.** Add the letters *ed* to most verbs that have a helping verb.

Rule	Example
Use *has* with a singular subject and with *he, she,* or *it.*	The chef **has** cooked the dinner.
Use *have* with a plural subject and with *I, you, we,* or *they.*	The assistants **have** helped.
Use *had* with a singular or a plural subject.	The customers **had** waited patiently.

Guided Practice

Tell the helping verb in each sentence.

Example: I have ordered food.   *have*

1. The chef has explained about the food.
2. He has described the many spices.
3. He had sailed to India for the spices.
4. The customers have tasted the bread.
5. Daryl has finished all the bread.

?! THINK

- How can I decide if a word is a helping verb?

REMEMBER

■ A **helping verb** helps to show an action. *Have, has,* and *had* are often used as helping verbs.

More Practice

A. Write each sentence. Underline the helping verb.

Example: We <u>have</u> tasted the delicious food.

6. The chef has invented a new recipe.
7. She has learned the names of the spices.
8. The helpers had washed the vegetables.
9. They have peeled the vegetables, too.
10. The chef had created the secret sauce.
11. The helpers have watched and learned.
12. They have followed the instructions.

B. Write each sentence with the correct helping verb.

Example: Taylor (has, have) finished the meal.
    Taylor has finished the meal.

13. Taylor (have, had) surprised his friends.
14. He (has, have) cooked dinner.
15. Taylor (have, had) chopped carrots.
16. He (had, have) boiled the vegetables.
17. He (have, had) added the spices.
18. Taylor (has, have) tasted the soup.
19. Taylor's friends (has, have) arrived.
20. They (have, has) finished the soup.

Extra Practice, page 164

WRITING APPLICATION A Review

Imagine that you are a food taster. Write a review of a new food that you have tasted. Identify the helping verbs in your review.

6 IRREGULAR VERBS

Some verbs form the past tense in a special way. Some verbs also have a special spelling when used with a helping verb.

Present	Past	Past with *have, has,* or *had*
begin	began	begun
come	came	come
do	did	done
eat	ate	eaten
give	gave	given
go	went	gone
grow	grew	grown
run	ran	run
see	saw	seen
sing	sang	sung

Guided Practice

Tell the verb in each sentence.

Example: We went to a concert last week.   *went*

1. The show had begun early.
2. We saw the new group.
3. They have given a great performance.
4. We have sung with them.
5. We ran home with our friends.

?! THINK

■ How can I decide if a verb is irregular?

REMEMBER

- Some verbs have special spellings to show the past tense.

More Practice

Write the sentences. Change each present-tense verb in ( ) to the past tense.

Example: The band has (do) a good job.

The band has done a good job.

  6. We (go) to a concert.
  7. The concert (begin) at 7:00 P.M.
  8. We (come) early for good seats.
  9. The crowd (grow) quiet.
 10. The band had (go) to the stage.
 11. The band has (begin) the show.
 12. Two singers have (come) down the aisle.
 13. The band has (see) the smiling audience.
 14. The audience has (sing) along.
 15. Karla (sing) along with the music.
 16. She (do) a good job.
 17. The band has (give) a great show.
 18. Karla (give) the band flowers.
 19. Karla and Kim (eat) after the show.
 20. We had (eat) after the show, too.

Extra Practice, page 165

WRITING APPLICATION A Post Card

Write a post card to a relative describing the kind of music you enjoy. You might want to tell about specific songs. Be sure to include irregular verbs in your post card. Circle the irregular verbs.

7 MECHANICS: Using Commas

When you read, **commas** tell you where to pause. Commas should be used in the following ways:

- Use commas to separate three or more words in a series.
- Use a comma after the name of a person being spoken to.
- Use a comma between the name of a city and a state.

Bob played baseball with Staci, Tab, and Joe.
Bob, did Joan play?
Bob Adams was born in Toledo, Ohio.

Guided Practice

Tell where a comma is needed in each sentence.

Example: Bob moved to Dallas Texas.   *after Dallas*

1. Pam moved from Las Vegas Nevada.
2. She now lives in Austin Texas.
3. Pam did you watch the baseball game?
4. Joel Pam and Bob played baseball.
5. Pam did you hit a home run?

 **THINK**

- How can I decide where to place commas in a sentence?

REMEMBER

- **Commas** separate three or more words in a series.
- A **comma** is used after the name of the person being spoken to.
- A **comma** is used between the name of a city and a state.

More Practice

Write the following words and sentences. Add commas where needed.

Example: Ames Iowa   *Ames, Iowa*

6. Mexico City Mexico
7. Joseph Tammy and Sandy
8. St. Louis Missouri
9. Mr. Dunn Mrs. Lurt and Ms. Hines
10. Seattle Washington
11. Marc Smith Helen Graham and Sally Winters
12. Cooperstown New York
13. Hoboken New Jersey
14. Joel Pam and Barbara
15. Joel when was baseball invented?
16. Barbara was it invented in 1839?
17. Brooklyn New York
18. Joel Peter and Pam
19. Did you catch the fly ball Peter?
20. Pam did you score two runs?

Extra Practice, page 166

WRITING APPLICATION A Scene

Write a scene about the first baseball game. Have classmates act out the scene. Identify the commas in your work.

8 VOCABULARY BUILDING: Prefixes

You can change the meaning of a word by adding a prefix to the base word, or main part of the word. A **prefix** is a word part added to the beginning of a base word.

Study the following chart of prefixes and their meanings.

Prefix	Meaning	Example
dis	not, the opposite of	**dis**like
re	again, back	**re**read
un	not, the opposite of	**un**able

dislike   like

Guided Practice

Name the prefix in each underlined word. Tell its meaning.

Example: I <u>repacked</u> the gym bag.   *re packed again*

1. The crowd was <u>unfriendly</u>.
2. We <u>reentered</u> through the gate.
3. My friends <u>disobeyed</u> the guards.
4. Dad <u>disapproved</u> of their behavior.
5. I <u>restated</u> the rules of the game.

 **THINK**

■ How can I decide if a word begins with a prefix?

REMEMBER

■ A **prefix** is a word part that is added to the beginning of a base word.

More Practice

A. Write the sentences. Draw a line under the word in each sentence that has a prefix.

Example: I <u>reviewed</u> the rules of the game.

6. Some people dislike tennis.
7. Many fans still recall the great games.
8. The game on Saturday was unpleasant.
9. Some players never recover from a loss.
10. The court was unsafe that day.
11. Tanya wants a rematch.
12. Tanya unties her sneakers.
13. She is dissatisfied.

B. Add a prefix to each underlined word.

Example: We were <u>happy</u>.   *unhappy*

14. This helmet was <u>built</u> for protection.
15. Knee pads can be <u>comfortable</u>.
16. Our team <u>agreed</u> with the fans.
17. A player was <u>prepared</u> for the serve.
18. The coach <u>played</u> the tape of the match.
19. Tennis teams <u>hire</u> the best players.
20. The owner is <u>comfortable</u>.

Extra Practice, page 167

WRITING APPLICATION A Letter

Write a letter to a friend about a tennis match or other sports event that you have seen. Circle any words with prefixes.

GRAMMAR ——AND—— WRITING CONNECTION

Combining Sentences

If you find you have written two sentences with similar subjects, you can join the sentences by combining the predicates. Use the word *and* to combine the predicates.

SEPARATE: Jason saw the ship. Jason liked the ship.
COMBINED: Jason saw and liked the ship.

Working Together

COOPERATIVE
LEARNING

With your classmates, discuss how you would join each pair of sentences by combining the predicates.

Example: Terry watched the stars.
Terry studied the stars.
Terry watched and studied the stars.

1. Terry loved spaceships.
   Terry studied space science.
2. Mr. Smith built spacecrafts.
   Mr. Smith needed a helper.
3. Terry took the job.
   Terry worked hard.

Revising Sentences

Dana wrote this story about a spacecraft. Help Dana combine her sentences by joining the predicates. Use the word *and* to combine the predicates. Write the new sentences.

4. The spaceship sat on the ground.
   The spaceship would not start.
5. Terry invented a new starter.
   Terry showed it to Mr. Smith.
6. Mr. Smith was surprised.
   Mr. Smith thanked Terry.
7. Terry put in the new starter.
   Terry flicked a switch.
8. The spaceship started.
   The spaceship soared upward.
9. Terry guided the spacecraft.
   Terry landed it safely.
10. Mr. Smith cheered.
    Mr. Smith shook Terry's hand.

WRITER AT WORK

Think about an invention that would make space travel easier. Write a paragraph describing the invention. Reread your paragraph. Join sentences by combining the predicates. Use the word *and* to combine the predicates.

UNIT CHECKUP

LESSON 1

What Is an Action Verb? (page 136) Write the sentences. Underline each action verb.

1. John holds the bat.
2. Tyrone throws a fast ball.
3. The children jump up and down.
4. Some players sit on the bench.
5. Marsha steals second base.

LESSON 2

Verbs in the Present (page 138) Write the sentences. Use the correct form of the present-tense verb in ( ).

6. My sister (hurry) on stage.
7. The conductor (lead) the band.
8. Crystal (fix) her violin.
9. Mother (watch) the recital.
10. Max (toss) flowers to Crystal.

LESSON 3

Verbs in the Past (page 140) Write the sentences. Change each verb in ( ) to the past tense.

11. Tina (work) on her invention.
12. She (hurry) to finish.
13. Tina (drag) the heavy equipment.
14. She (race) through the steps.
15. Bob (like) Tina's invention.

LESSON 4

Verbs in the Future (page 142) Change each verb to the future tense.

16. I build a special computer.
17. We win an award.
18. People use it for work and play.
19. Many businesses need computer programs.
20. Computers store many files.

LESSON 5

Helping Verbs (page 144) Write the sentences. Complete each sentence with the correct helping verb.

21. An airship (has, have) entered the sky.
22. It (had, have) moved through the air.
23. A scientist (has, have) studied air travel.

LESSON 6

Irregular Verbs (page 146) Write the sentences. Change each verb in ( ) to the past tense.

24. Our class has (go) to the planetarium.
25. We have (see) stars and asteroids.
26. Guides have (give) a talk on the atmosphere.

LESSON 7

Mechanics: Using Commas (page 148) Write the sentences. Add commas where needed.

27. Henry did you see that balloon?
28. It landed in Austin Texas.
29. Do you want to see it Jack?
30. Julie Gail and Martin will go.

LESSON 8

Vocabulary Building: Prefixes (page 150) Write the prefix in each word.

31. unlucky   **34.** unbutton   **37.** unhappy
32. distrust   **35.** repay   **38.** disagree
33. refinish   **36.** distaste   **39.** redo

Writing Application: Verb Usage (pages 136–144) The following paragraph contains 6 errors with action verbs in the past. Rewrite the paragraph correctly.

40.–45.   The tailor sew a pair of pants. He has stitch the material carefully. The tailor had carry the pants to the ironing board. He press the pants swiftly. He whistle as he pressed. The tailor has finish on time.

Switcheroo

Play this game with a friend. Tell your friend a sentence that has an action verb. Have your friend change the action verb. Take turns making up sentences and replacing verbs. For example, you might say: I played in the park yesterday. Your friend might say: I will dance in the park tomorrow.

Prefix Pick

Play this game with a group of friends. Have each person act out a word. The word must begin with the prefix *un, dis,* or *re.* For example, to act out the word *redial*, you might pretend to dial a telephone. Then, you dial the telephone again. Take turns acting out and guessing words.

Tomorrow's Toys

Invent a game to play with your class. Draw a picture of it. Describe what it will be like. Be sure to use verbs in the future. Explain your game to your class.

Shopping Spree

You just won $100 to spend at the mall, but you must spend it in 15 minutes. Write a story about your shopping spree. Use different verbs to tell how you get from one store to the other. If you like, you can act out your story for your friends.

Easy Does It

Think of an invention that would make your life easier. Make a poster showing the special features of your invention. Think of six action verbs to describe your invention. Write these words on your poster.

Menu Makers

Make a menu with a partner. Decide what you will serve. Then, tell how you will cook each item. Finish your menu by drawing some colorful foods and adding the price for each item. Now you are ready for business!

$8.00

EXTRA PRACTICE

Three levels of practice
What Is an Action Verb? (page 136)

LEVEL
A. Write each sentence. Underline the verb.

1. Some inventors work alone.
2. Many inventors learn from each other.
3. One scientist tells another an idea.
4. They walk to the laboratory.
5. They plan an experiment together.
6. This scientist teaches a class.
7. The students listen carefully.

LEVEL
B. Choose the correct word in ( ) to complete each sentence.

8. Some scientists _____ new machines. (science, invent)
9. People in factories _____ these machines. (use, cities)
10. We _____ machines for our homes. (buy, easy)
11. Machines _____ our work easier. (make, new)
12. Some machines _____ in hospitals. (nurse, help)
13. One machine _____ oxygen. (pumps, mouth)

LEVEL
C. Write the sentences. Complete each sentence by adding an action verb.

14. Alice _____ through the telescope.
15. She _____ the stars and the moon.
16. Hundreds of stars _____ brightly.
17. A large cloud _____ in front of the moon.
18. Suddenly, a comet _____ through the sky.
19. Alice _____ to her helper.
20. The helper _____ up the stairs.

EXTRA PRACTICE

Three levels of practice
Verbs in the Present (page 138)

LEVEL
A. Write each sentence. Choose the correct verb in ( ).

1. Debby _____ Sal her sewing machine. (show, shows)
2. Sal _____ the machine. (start, starts)
3. They _____ some cloth. (find, finds)
4. Debby _____ two kites. (sew, sews)
5. The kites _____ in the wind. (flutter, flutters)
6. The strings _____ against the kites. (pulls, pull)

LEVEL
B. Write each sentence. Use the correct present-tense form of the verb in ( ).

7. Carlos (watch) a movie about airplanes.
8. Jet engines (roar) loudly.
9. A plane (fly) through a cloud.
10. The plane (carry) 300 passengers.
11. Pilots (control) the plane.
12. The flight crew (talk) about safety.
13. The plane (cross) the ocean.

LEVEL
C. Write the sentences. Use the correct form of a verb from the word box to complete each sentence.

> study   choose   use   direct   write   teach   watch

14. Mrs. Reese _____ the students about computers.
15. Al _____ very hard.
16. He _____ his computer often.
17. Mark _____ Al work.
18. Mark _____ a play about computers.
19. The students _____ the parts they want.
20. Mark _____ the play.

EXTRA PRACTICE

Three levels of practice
Verbs in the Past (page 140)

LEVEL A. Write each sentence. Draw a line under the verb.

1. Mr. Judson loved machines.
2. His inventions included the zipper.
3. People tried the new invention on boots.
4. Customers liked the boots.
5. Soon, stores carried clothing with zippers.
6. Customers hurried to buy the new styles.

LEVEL B. Write each sentence. Complete each sentence by writing the past tense of the verb in ( ).

7. Pony Express riders (hurry) from town to town.
8. Riders (carry) mail over the mountains.
9. Samuel Morse (create) the telegraph.
10. The telegraph (tap) messages through wires.
11. The Pony Express (stop) its service.
12. Many people (learn) Morse code.
13. Telegraph wires (stretch) from city to city.

LEVEL C. Change each verb to the past tense. Write each new sentence.

14. Henry Ford tries a new idea.
15. Workers produce cars on assembly lines.
16. Millions of cars roll out of Ford's factory.
17. The assembly line never stops.
18. Ford supplies the country with many cars.
19. Other factories follow this idea.
20. Many people work on assembly lines.

Three levels of additional practice for a difficult skill
Verbs in the Past (page 140)

LEVEL
A. Write the sentences. Underline the past-tense verb.

1. Benjamin Franklin showed great talent.
2. Franklin invented many things.
3. He tried experiments many times.
4. People shivered in the winter.
5. The cold air chilled them.
6. They used their fireplaces.
7. The fireplaces worked poorly.
8. The rooms filled with smoke.
9. Franklin created a stove.
10. Franklin named the stove.
11. The Franklin stove heated rooms well.
12. People warmed their hands.
13. They removed their coats.
14. Many families tried the Franklin stove.
15. People thanked Benjamin Franklin.

LEVEL
B. Write the correct past-tense verb for each sentence.

16. Franklin also _____ with eyeglasses.
    a. worked   b. works
17. Bad eyesight _____ many people.
    a. bother   b. bothered
18. Franklin _____ their problem.
    a. share   b. shared
19. His eyes _____ help.
    a. need   b. needed
20. Franklin _____ a pair of special eyeglasses.
    a. created   b. creates

GRAMMAR

21. He _____ these glasses *bifocals*.
    a. named   b. names
22. The glasses _____ different problems.
    a. solved   b. solves
23. The bottom _____ close objects.
    a. magnify   b. magnified
24. The top _____ people to see far away.
    a. help   b. helped
25. The lenses _____ very well.
    a. worked   b. work
26. Benjamin Franklin _____ a pair.
    a. used   b. uses
27. People _____ to enjoy life more.
    a. learn   b. learned

LEVEL
C. Complete each sentence. Write the past tense of the verb in ( ).

28. Franklin also _____ a printing press. (own)
29. Metal plates _____ the words quickly. (print)
30. Franklin _____ words. (love)
31. He _____ a newspaper. (start)
32. His paper _____ many new ideas. (describe)
33. Franklin _____ America to rule itself. (want)
34. Some people _____ differently. (believe)
35. They _____ his writing. (dislike)
36. Others _____ to buy his newspaper. (hurry)
37. Franklin's ideas _____ many followers. (gain)
38. The news _____ to England. (travel)
39. Franklin's articles _____ the king. (worry)
40. The king _____ a war. (fear)

EXTRA PRACTICE

Three levels of practice
Verbs in the Future (page 142)

LEVEL
A. Write each sentence. Write whether each underlined verb is in the **present, past,** or **future** tense.

1. We <u>will visit</u> the science museum.
2. Richard <u>looked</u> at pictures of the moon.
3. Large craters <u>cover</u> the moon.
4. The guide <u>will explain</u> the pictures.
5. We <u>will learn</u> about space travel.
6. Dee <u>walked</u> through the spaceship model.
7. We <u>will touch</u> some moon rocks.

LEVEL
B. Write the sentences. Change each verb in ( ) to the future tense.

8. The ranger (show) us a compass.
9. We (use) the compass on our hike.
10. The needle (point) north.
11. Our group (travel) north.
12. We (find) our way back.
13. Tony (swim) across the stream.
14. The breeze (cool) us.

LEVEL
C. Write each sentence in the future tense.

15. The astronauts explore the solar system.
16. They pass Jupiter.
17. They fly near Saturn.
18. Scientists study the planets.
19. The instruments measure the temperature.
20. Special suits protect the astronauts.

EXTRA PRACTICE

Three levels of practice

Helping Verbs (page 144)

A. Write each sentence. Draw a line under the helping verb.

1. People have invented many machines.
2. Machines have solved many problems.
3. Farmers had cut wheat by hand.
4. The reaper has helped farmers.
5. The farmer has produced better crops.
6. Special pipes have watered the farmland.
7. The farmers had fed the cows.

B. Write the sentences. Complete each sentence with the helping verb *has* or *have*.

8. People _____ dreamed about air travel.
9. Two brothers _____ invented a balloon.
10. They _____ watched the balloon.
11. A hot-air balloon _____ crossed the ocean.
12. I _____ traveled in a hot-air balloon.
13. My balloon _____ carried six people.
14. My uncle _____ filled the balloon.

C. Write each sentence. Use the helping verb *has* or *have* and the correct past tense of the verb in ( ).

15. I _____ the carnival. (visit)
16. I _____ my friends on the Ferris wheel. (watch)
17. Ferris wheels _____ hundreds of passengers. (carry)
18. Alice _____ to me. (wave)
19. Alice _____ the ride. (enjoy)
20. My sisters _____ for Alice. (wait)

EXTRA PRACTICE

Three Levels of practice
Irregular Verbs (page 146)

LEVEL A. Write the sentences. Underline the irregular verbs.

1. The school play had begun at 9:00 P.M.
2. We came one hour early.
3. We have seen our seats in the first row.
4. We sang along with the actors.
5. The actors have given us a great show.
6. They have gone to the dressing rooms.
7. We ran to the stage door.

LEVEL B. Write the sentences. Change each present-tense verb in ( ) to the past tense.

8. The scientist has (grow) new vegetables.
9. She has (give) us her book.
10. She (begin) her talk about the book.
11. We (see) the pictures of her vegetables.
12. We even (eat) some of them.
13. She had (come) to our school before.
14. We (go) to her laboratory.

LEVEL C. Write the sentences. Complete each sentence with an irregular verb from the box.

grew	came	given	eaten	gone	saw

15. Inventors have _____ people new ideas.
16. Settlers _____ better crops.
17. People have _____ to far-away places.
18. They _____ many new things.
19. Many have _____ different foods.
20. They _____ with new ideas.

GRAMMAR

Three levels of practice
Mechanics: Using Commas (page 148)

LEVEL A. Write the sentences. Underline the commas.

1. Come to the library with me, Anne.
2. I want to read about Buffalo, New York.
3. Will Kathy, Hal, and Donna be there?
4. Anne, do not forget your library card.
5. We can meet Jack, Bart, and Beth later.
6. This room has tapes, records, and videos.
7. The books are downstairs, Hal.

LEVEL B. Underline the sentences that use commas correctly.

8. Margie do you know about bicycles?
9. Steve the early bicycles had no pedals.
10. Jerry, how did those bicycles work?
11. Gail, Willis, and Tara have pictures.
12. They were in Portland, Maine.
13. I saw a bike race in Nutley, New Jersey.

LEVEL C. Add commas where they are needed.

14. Alan have you seen my new camera?
15. Leslie come and look at the camera.
16. Karen Jill and Candy have the same one.
17. It was made in Seattle Washington.
18. John may I take your picture?
19. Should I smile Paul?
20. I need film batteries and a case.

EXTRA PRACTICE

Three levels of practice
Vocabulary Building: Prefixes (page 150)

LEVEL A. Write the word in each sentence that has a prefix. Next to each word, write the prefix.

1. Kathy rebuilt the broken table.
2. It is hard to untangle the yarn.
3. The driver disobeyed the rules.
4. The door was unlocked when I arrived.
5. The gardener replanted the tulips.
6. His phone was disconnected.
7. Please rewrite this message.

LEVEL B. Write the word from the box next to its definition below.

unclear	disappear	repaint	dishonest
unsafe	unfair	reheat	

8. paint again
9. opposite of safe
10. not appear
11. opposite of clear
12. not honest
13. heat again
14. not fair

LEVEL C. Complete each sentence with a word from the box.

unable	readjusted	unclear
displeased	unlocked	retied

15. Arthur was _____ with the problem.
16. He was _____ to use his bicycle.
17. The problem was _____ .
18. Arthur _____ his shoelaces.
19. He _____ his sister's bike instead.
20. Then, he _____ the seat.

GRAMMAR

UNIT 6

Writing Instructions

Read the quotation on the opposite page. Look at the picture, too. What is enthusiasm? How could enthusiasm help a person get what she or he wants?

When you write instructions, you explain how to do something step-by-step.

Focus Instructions explain how to do something in a clear and sensible way.

What do you know how to do or build? What could you write instructions about? In this unit, you will read about a famous inventor, Ben Franklin. You will find some photographs, too. You can use the story and the photographs to get ideas for writing.

Nothing great was ever achieved without enthusiasm.

—Ralph Waldo Emerson

LITERATURE

Reading Like a Writer

Have you ever made music by blowing across the top of a bottle or plucking a rubber band?

Many of the musical instruments that you know are made of simple, everyday items. Ben Franklin made the glass armonica out of ordinary glass bowls. He created a sound different from any heard before.

As you read, notice how the author explains how Ben Franklin made his invention.

from *Ben Franklin's* GLASS ARMONICA

by Bryna Stevens

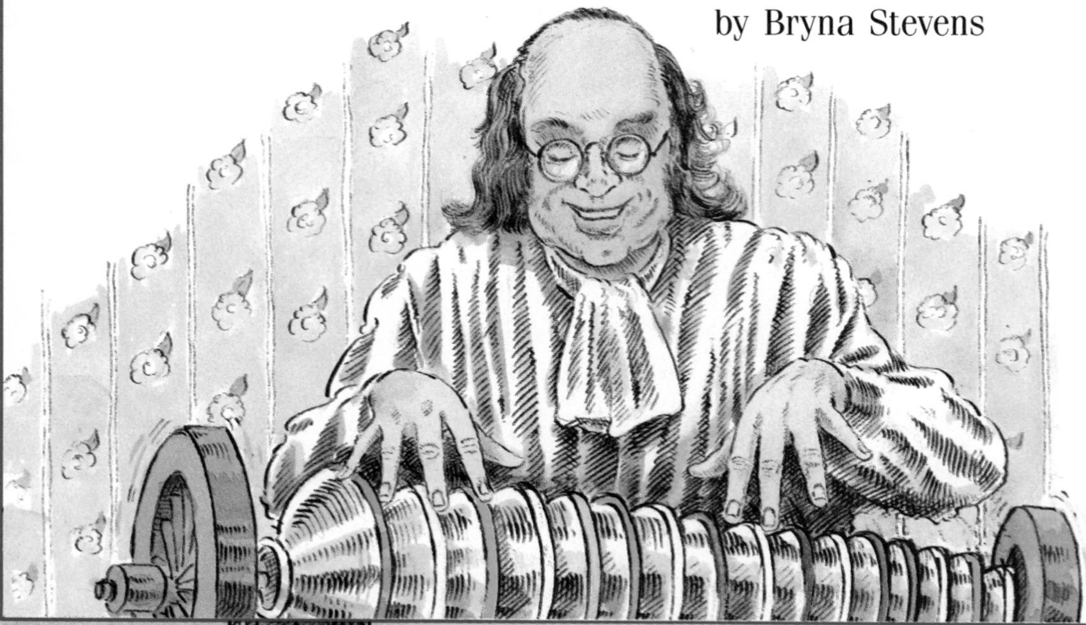

What do you think of when you hear the name Benjamin Franklin? The Declaration of Independence? Flying a kite in a thunderstorm? Many things come to mind, but music usually doesn't.

Actually Ben Franklin was a very fine musician. He knew how to play the harp, the guitar, and the violin. Once he even invented a new musical instrument. This is the story of that invention.

It all began in China. A clever Chinese girl had an idea. She tapped a glass with a stick.

"What a pretty sound," she said.

She filled the glass with water and tapped it again. Now the sound was lower.

Then she drank some of the water. She tapped the glass once more. The sound was higher.

The Chinese girl put a few glasses together. Each glass held a different amount of water. By tapping different glasses, she could play tunes.

All of her friends loved the glass music. So did some travelers who were in China. When the travelers went home to Europe, they told everyone about the Chinese girl's music. Soon people all over Europe were playing musical glasses.

One of those people was Edmund Delaval. Around 1761, he gave a musical-glass concert in London, England. Ben Franklin was staying in London at the time. He went to Delaval's concert.

Franklin loved music. He loved to play his harp,

his guitar, and his violin. He especially liked to play Scotch folk songs, but sometimes he played music that he had written himself.

Franklin watched Delaval carefully. Delaval stood in front of several crystal glasses. Each glass held a different amount of water.

Mr. Delaval wet one of his fingers. He rubbed it around the rim of a glass. It made a clear, beautiful sound. Then he rubbed the rim of another glass. It made a different sound. Mr. Delaval played many songs on his crystal glasses.

Franklin liked the tunes that Delaval played. "This music is so sweet and clear," he thought. "But Mr. Delaval plays so slowly. I like my music fast. Delaval can play only one note at a time. I like lots of notes played together. Chords and harmonies make music interesting."

The next day Franklin sat at his desk. He thought about the concert. Then he drew something on a piece of paper.

"I think I can improve the musical glasses," he said.

Franklin ran outside. He called for a hansom cab.

"Take me to Charles James's," he said to the driver. "He lives on Purpool Lane."

Franklin entered Charles James's glass shop. James was making a bowl.

"I want to order 37 glass bowls," Franklin said to James. "Each bowl must have a hole in its center."

"Holes in their centers?" said Charles James. "Then the bowls will leak."

"It doesn't matter," said Franklin. "The bowls are not for holding anything. They are for playing music."

Charles James was puzzled, but all he said was, "Oh." He didn't want to question the famous Dr. Franklin.

When the bowls were ready, Franklin tuned them. He wanted each one to sound like a musical note. When a bowl didn't sound right, he ground off some glass. When he finished, each bowl sounded like a different note. Then he painted their rims different colors.

"Colors will make each note easier to pick out," he said.

He painted all the Cs red. He painted all the Ds orange. All the Es were yellow. All the Fs were green. He painted the Gs blue. The As were dark blue. The Bs were purple.

He painted some bowls white. The white bowls sounded like the black keys on a modern piano.

Franklin laid all the bowls on their sides. He arranged them from the largest bowl to the smallest. Then he ran a long iron rod through their centers. He attached the rod to a wheel. The wheel was attached to a foot pedal.

Specific details help make instructions clear.

Franklin pressed the foot pedal. The rod began to turn. The bowls began to spin. So far, everything was working.

Franklin sat down at his instrument. He kept the bowls spinning. He wet his fingers. Then he rubbed them with chalk. The chalk would help "catch" the glass.

Franklin touched the rim of a bowl. What a beautiful sound it made! Then he touched another and another. Soon Franklin could play tunes with one hand. He played chords and harmonies with the other hand.

Franklin loved his instrument. The music was sweet and clear. He called it an *armonica*. Armonica means "harmony" in Italian. But many people came to call it Franklin's glass harmonica.

Thinking Like a Reader

1. Ben thought the first tunes he heard were too slow. How did he solve this problem with his glass armonica?
2. What do you think of his solution?

Write your responses in your journal.

Thinking Like a Writer

3. Which details did the author use to let you know the steps Franklin followed in making his glass armonica?
4. What questions would you ask Ben Franklin about how the glass armonica worked?

Write your responses in your journal.

Brainstorm *Vocabulary*

In the story, "Ben Franklin's Glass Armonica," there are many words that have to do with music. Look back at the story and find some of these words. Then, think of other music words. The words can tell how music sounds or can describe a musical instrument. Add these words to your personal word list. You can use this list when you write.

Talk It Over
Tell a Friend

Imagine that you went to a glass armonica concert. Describe the concert to a friend. Be sure to explain what the glass armonica is and how it sounds. Answer any questions your friend may have.

Quick Write *Music Lessons*

Imagine that you are taking glass armonica lessons. Explain to a friend how to play the glass armonica. Be sure that you write the steps in step-by-step order. Remember, your friend does not know a thing about glass armonicas. Write the steps in your journal.

Idea Corner
Teach a Friend

Make a list of things that you know how to do. Write the list in your journal. You might want to include some of the following in your list.

- play checkers
- plant seeds
- ride a bicycle
- make a sandwich
- build a model
- write a recipe
- fly a kite

Finding Ideas for Writing

Look at the pictures. Think about what you
see. What ideas for writing instructions do the
pictures give you? Write your ideas in your journal.

1 GROUP WRITING: Instructions

COOPERATIVE LEARNING

When you write instructions, you need to be clear. Your **audience** needs to understand your **purpose**. How can you make instructions easy to understand?

- Topic Sentence
- Step-by-step Details
- Specific Details

Topic Sentence

A paragraph is a group of sentences about one main idea. Read the paragraph that Anne wrote.

> <u>Making a telephone is easy</u>. First, punch a small hole in the bottom of two paper cups. Next, tie a knot in a long piece of string. Pull the unknotted end through the hole in the cup. Then, pull the string through the hole in the second cup. Last, tie a knot in the other end of the string. Your telephone is ready to use!

The underlined sentence is the **topic sentence.** The topic sentence tells the main idea of the paragraph.

Guided Practice: Writing a Topic Sentence

With your classmates, write a topic sentence for a set of instructions. Choose a topic from the list below, or think of one of your own. Look in your journal for ideas.

basket   pot holder   toy boat   kite

Example: Making a fishing pole is simple.

Step-by-step Details

When you write instructions, the details need to be in step-by-step order. The details should follow each other in the order in which the instructions need to be carried out. Time-order words help to make the steps easier to follow. Some **time-order words** are *first, next, then,* and *last.* Look back at the paragraph that Anne wrote.

- What are the steps in making a telephone?
- Why did Anne put the steps in this order?
- Which time-order words help you to follow the order?

Specific Details

When you write instructions, it is important to make your details exact. This helps your audience to follow your instructions easily. Look back at Anne's paragraph about making the telephone. Anne told what kind of cups to use. She also told exactly where to make the small holes. These details make her instructions clear. They tell exactly what needs to be done.

Guided Practice: Writing
Specific Details

Look back at the topic sentence you wrote with your class. Add specific details that clearly state what needs to be done. Try picturing each detail to make sure it is clear. Check that your details are in time order.

Putting Instructions Together

You and your classmates have written a topic sentence for a set of instructions. You have added specific details and made sure that each detail was clear.

When Anne reread her instructions, she decided that she needed to add another specific detail. Read Anne's final instructions for making a telephone.

Making a telephone is easy. First, punch a small hole in the bottom of two paper cups. Next, tie a knot in one end of a long piece of string. Pull the unknotted end through the hole in the first cup. Then, pull the string through the hole in the second cup. Last, tie a knot in the other end of the string. Your telephone is ready to use!

How did Anne change her paragraph? How does this change make Anne's paragraph clearer?

Guided Practice: Writing Instructions

Write a set of instructions for the topic you chose with your class. Make sure your details are specific and are in step-by-step order. Be sure to include time-order words.

Have a friend read your instructions. Does your friend think that he or she could follow your instructions? See if your friend can think of any other details that would make your paragraph clearer.

Checklist: Instructions

When you write instructions, you must keep certain points in mind. Make a checklist to help you remember these points.

Look at the checklist below. Some points have been left out. Add those points. Keep the completed checklist in your writing folder.

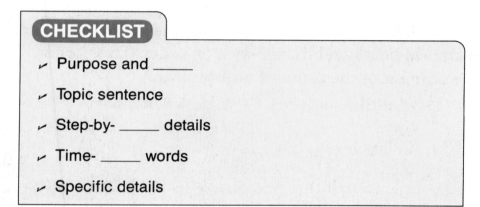

CHECKLIST

- ✓ Purpose and _____
- ✓ Topic sentence
- ✓ Step-by- _____ details
- ✓ Time- _____ words
- ✓ Specific details

2 THINKING AND WRITING: Solving Problems

Writing a set of instructions is like solving a problem. Instructions tell how to solve a problem step-by-step.

A writer must find the easiest way to explain how to solve the problem. The topic sentence should state the problem clearly. The details that follow should be placed in step-by-step order. Time-order words make the order of events clear.

Look at this page from a writer's notebook.

I made sock puppets last Saturday. First, I got two long socks. Then, I glued paper eyes, a nose, and a mouth on each sock. Next, I attached hair, made out of string. Last, I decorated the body of the puppet with bits of string and colored paper.

Thinking Like a Writer

- What is the topic sentence?
- Which time-order words help you to know the order of the steps?

THINKING APPLICATION Solving Problems

COOPERATIVE
LEARNING

Three third-grade students want to write instructions. Help them write their instructions. Explain your thinking to your classmates.

1. Diane gave her younger brother written instructions on how to do a cartwheel. She forgot to add a topic sentence. Write a topic sentence for Diane's instructions.

   ■ First, bring your right hand down to the floor.
   ■ Next, balance your weight on your hands.
   ■ Then, bring your legs up until they go over your body in a circle.
   ■ Finally, stand up after your legs touch the ground.

2. Taylor's instructions will describe how to make a boat. Write his details in step-by-step order.

   ■ Then, put a toothpick on one end of the soap.
   ■ First, get a bar of soap.
   ■ Last, glue the paper sail on the toothpick.
   ■ Next, cut out a paper sail.

3. Hope wants to teach her friend Heidi how to make a kite. Hope's details are in the wrong order. Put Hope's details in step-by-step order.

   ■ Then, make a wooden frame.
   ■ Last, add a tail to the body of the kite.
   ■ Next, glue paper onto the wooden frame.
   ■ First, buy the materials.

3 INDEPENDENT WRITING: Instructions

Prewrite: Step 1

You have learned many things that will help you to write instructions. Now you are ready to write your own instructions. First, you must choose a topic. Gene, a student your age, chose a topic in this way.

Choosing a Topic

1. First, Gene made a list of possible topics.
2. Next, he thought about each topic on his list.
3. Last, he decided on the best topic.

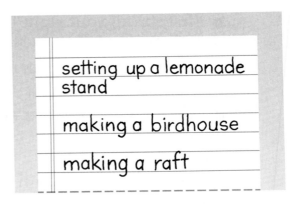

setting up a lemonade stand

making a birdhouse

making a raft

Gene liked his first choice best. He thought it would be fun to explain how to set up a lemonade stand. He could share the instructions with his friend Bart. Gene explored his topic by making a **cluster** like this one.

Exploring Ideas: Clustering Strategy

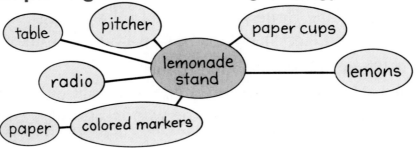

table   pitcher   paper cups

radio   lemonade stand   lemons

paper   colored markers

Before starting to write, Gene thought about each step involved in setting up a lemonade stand. He added more details to his cluster.

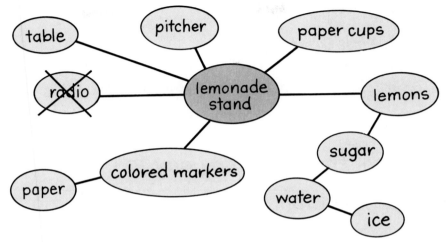

Thinking Like a Writer

- What did he add?
- What did he cross out?
- Why do you think he crossed out that part?

YOUR TURN

JOURNAL

Think of something you could explain how to make. Look in **Pictures** or in your journal for ideas. Follow these steps.

- Make a list of ideas.
- Decide who your audience will be.
- Choose the idea you like best.
- Narrow your topic if it is too broad.

Make a cluster. Think of the materials you will need. Remember, you can add to or take away from the cluster at any time.

Write a First Draft: Step 2

Gene used a checklist to help him remember what to include in his instructions. Gene is now ready to write his first draft.

Gene's First Draft

> You can builds a Lemonade Stand easily. Wait for the first sunny day to begin. first, set up the table. Next, make the lemonade. Then, make a sign. Write how much a glass of lemonade will cost. Last, put the lemonade and the cups on the table.

While Gene was writing his first draft, he did not worry about errors. He just put his ideas on paper.

Planning Checklist

- Purpose and audience
- Topic sentence
- Step-by-step details
- Time-order words
- Specific details

YOUR TURN

Write your first draft. Ask yourself these questions.

- What will my audience need to know?
- What is the best order for my details?

TIME-OUT You might want to take some time out before you revise. That way you will be able to revise your writing with a fresh eye.

Revise: Step 3

After he wrote his first draft, Gene let a classmate read it. Gene wanted to make sure that his instructions were clear and that they were in the correct order. He wanted some suggestions for improving his instructions.

I like your instructions, but shouldn't you make the lemonade last?

You're right! I wouldn't want all the ice to melt. Thanks for catching that.

Gene then looked at his planning checklist. He checked off *Step-by-step details* so that he would remember to change the order of his steps when he revised. Gene now has a checklist to use as he revises.

Gene made some changes in his paragraph. He did not correct the small errors yet. He would fix them later.

Turn the page. Look at Gene's revised draft.

Revising Checklist
- ■ Purpose and audience
- ■ Topic sentence
- ✔■ Step-by-step details
- ■ Time-order words
- ■ Specific details

> You can builds a Lemonade Stand easily.
> Wait for the first sunny day to begin. first,
> set up the table. Next, make the lemonade.
> Then, make a sign, ,and Write how much a glass of
> lemonade will cost. Last, put the lemonade
> and the cups on the table. Wait for people to
> buy your delicious lemonade.

Thinking Like a Writer

WISE
WORD
CHOICE

- Why did Gene take out the second sentence?
- Which sentences did he combine? How does this improve the paragraph?
- Which sentence did Gene add? How does it help the paragraph?

YOUR TURN

Read your first draft. Make a checklist. Ask yourself these questions.

- What is my main idea?
- Which specific details make my instructions easy to understand?

You may want to ask a friend to read your paragraph and make suggestions. Then, revise your paragraph.

Proofread: Step 4

Gene's next step was to proofread his instructions. He used a proofreading checklist to help him as he proofread his work.

Part of Gene's Proofread Draft

> You can builds a Lemonade Stand easily.
> Wait for the first sunny day to begin, first,
> set up the table. Next, make the lemonade.

YOUR TURN

Proofreading Practice

Use the following paragraph to practice your proofreading skills. Find the errors. Write the paragraph correctly on a separate piece of paper.

A Banana milk shake is an easy and healthful snack to make. all you need are bananas milk ice a blender and a glass. Put all of the ingredients in the blender. Turn it on. Blend until everything is mixed. First, turn off the blender and pour your banana milk shake into a glass. Now, you have a tasty banana shake.

Proofreading Checklist
■ Did I indent my paragraph?
■ Did I spell all words correctly?
■ Did I use punctuation correctly?
■ Did I capitalize letters correctly?

Applying Your Proofreading Skills

Now, proofread your instructions. Reread your checklist before you begin. Review **The Grammar Connection** and **The Mechanics Connection** below.

THE GRAMMAR CONNECTION

- Verbs in the present tense end in *s* or *es*.
  He **wants** a yogurt shake. He **mixes** the shake.
- Add *ed* to most verbs to show past tense.
  Joe **invented** a new milk shake.
- Some verbs change their spelling when *ed* is added.
  Joe **liked** the new recipe. He **tried** to follow it exactly.
  Joe **dropped** an egg on the floor.

THE MECHANICS CONNECTION

- Use a comma between three or more words in a series.
  Jan walked, skipped, and hopped down the road.
- Use a comma to separate the name of a city and state, and after the name of a person spoken to.
  Carl, do you live in Seattle, Washington?

Proofreading Marks

- ¶ Indent
- ∧ Add
- ✗ Take out
- ≡ Make a capital letter
- / Make a small letter

Publish: Step 5

Gene wanted to share his instructions with his friend, Bart. He copied his paragraph neatly and gave it to Bart. Bart suggested that they set up a lemonade stand that weekend.

YOUR TURN

Make a final copy of your paragraph. Use your best handwriting. Think of a way to share your instructions. You may want to use one of the ideas in the **Sharing Suggestions** box below.

SHARING SUGGESTIONS

Make a poster showing instructions. Include art.	Make a copy of your instructions for each member of your family and add drawings.	Make a tape recording of your instructions and play it for your friends.

4 SPEAKING AND LISTENING: Giving Directions

You have just written instructions that tell how to make something. Directions are like instructions.

Suppose a friend needs directions to your house. Your directions will have to be in step-by-step order. They will have to provide specific details about how to get to your house. Time-order words will make your directions clear.

Gene wanted his classmates to see the lemonade stand that he had built. Gene invited his classmates to visit his lemonade stand after school. Gene wrote directions telling his classmates how to get to his house. Look at the directions to his house that Gene gave.

Directions to Gene's House

Address: 1415 Hilltop Drive

1. First, cross the school's playground.

2. Then, make a right turn at the corner.

3. Next, walk straight to the firehouse.

4. Finally, turn left and walk two blocks.

5. My house is the first house on Hilltop Drive.

Keep these speaking guidelines in mind when you give directions. They will help you to give clear directions.

SPEAKING GUIDELINES: Directions

1. Give your directions in step-by-step order.
2. Include specific details.
3. Use time-order words to make your directions clear.
4. Speak clearly.

- Why is step-by-step order important when giving directions?
- How can specific details help someone follow directions?
- Why should you include time-order words in your directions?

SPEAKING APPLICATION Directions

Imagine a place that you would like to visit with a friend. Think about the easiest way to get to that place. Provide your friend with directions. Explain your directions clearly. Make sure that you put your directions in step-by-step order. Include time-order words to make your directions easier to follow. Your friend should follow these listening guidelines as she or he listens.

LISTENING GUIDELINES: Directions

1. Listen for each step.
2. Listen for specific details.
3. Try to picture each step in your mind.

5 WRITER'S RESOURCES: The Library

The library is a good source of information for a writer.

The library has many kinds of books. You can use the **card catalog** to find the books you need. The card catalog lists all the books the library has by author, subject, and title.

Fiction books are made up. The stories in them did not happen. Fiction books are arranged in alphabetical order by the author's name.

Nonfiction books are true. They include facts about real people and events that really happened. Nonfiction books are grouped according to topics.

Reference books contain true information about many topics. Some reference books are the **dictionary, atlas, almanac,** and **encyclopedia.** An atlas is a book of maps. An almanac is a book of facts.

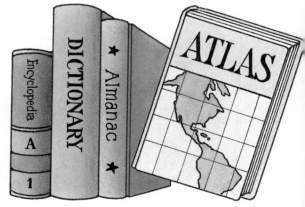

The Encyclopedia

An **encyclopedia** is a set of books that contains information about many subjects. Every **volume,** or book, has articles in alphabetical order.

Each volume includes topics beginning with a letter of the alphabet. Articles about people are listed under their last names.

Practice

1. Write the name of the reference book in which you would find the following information.
   a. Who was Albert Einstein?
   b. How far is China from India?
2. Write the number of the encyclopedia volume above that would have an article about each subject below.
   a. locomotives   c. South Carolina
   b. Benjamin Franklin   d. farming

WRITING APPLICATION Facts About Inventors

Use an encyclopedia to look up information about a machine. Write about the machine and the inventor. Keep your work in your writing folder.

THE CURRICULUM CONNECTION

Writing About Science

When you think about science, you probably think of memorizing many facts. Facts are important to scientists. Scientists use known facts to find new information. Sometimes scientists perform experiments to find new facts.

The word *experiment* means "to test something, using the facts that are already known." Scientists follow a set of steps. You included steps when you wrote instructions. Scientists then write down what they observed during an experiment. If an experiment goes well, a scientist may discover some new facts.

ACTIVITIES

Create a Poster   Make a poster showing how to use the machine you researched in the encyclopedia. Write step-by-step instructions about how to use the machine.

Describe a Photo   Study the picture of Florence Nightingale on the next page. How do you think improvements in the hospital made her job easier?

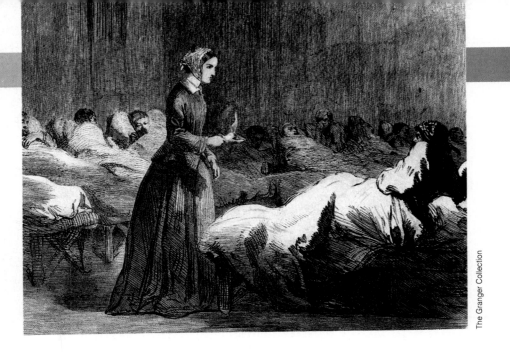

Respond to Literature   During the early 1800s, hospitals were not as clean and as well run as they are now. One woman spent her entire life caring for the sick. She tried to give people the best care possible. This woman was Florence Nightingale.

On her seventy-fifth birthday, Florence Nightingale wrote a letter to a friend. Here is part of that letter. It sums up her feelings about her life spent helping others.

> ### *Florence Nightingale—Nurse to the World*
> I have lost much in failure and disappointments, as well as in grief, but do you know, life is more precious to me now. . . .Life is a special gift!

Write a note to Florence Nightingale, responding to her view that life is a special gift. Explain why you agree or disagree with her.

UNIT CHECKUP

THEME PROJECT AN INVENTION

One hundred years ago many of the items that make your life easier today had not yet been invented. If you had lived at that time, you would not have had radio, televison, or many other helpful items. You would have had to do the work that many machines do for you today. Study the picture below.

This picture shows an old-fashioned kitchen. Talk with your classmates about some of the things you see in the picture.

Think of something you would like to invent to help you with your chores.

- Brainstorm for some ideas with your classmates.
- Choose one invention from those ideas.
- Then, write step-by-step instructions on how to use the item. Describe how it would save you time.
- Draw a picture of your invention.

UNIT

7

More Verbs

In this unit you will learn about the verb *be.* This special verb helps tell about you and your world.

Discuss Read the poem on the opposite page. How do you share your special thoughts with your friends?

Creative Expression The unit theme is *Pen Pals.* Have you ever thought about children in other countries? How are their lives different from yours? How are they the same? Write a list of questions you would like to ask a pen pal from another country. Write your list in your journal.

THEME: *PEN PALS*

On Tuesday
we agreed
to write each other notes
in secret code
that only we could read.

—Beatrice Schenk de Regniers
from "A Week in the Life of Best Friends"

WHAT IS SPECIAL ABOUT THE VERB *BE*?

The special verb *be* does not show action.

You know that action verbs tell what someone or something does. The special verb *be* tells what someone or something is or is like. The special verb *be* has several forms.

Maria **is** my pen pal.
She **was** my pen pal last year.
I **am** happy with my pen pal.
We **are** good friends.
We **were** friends for a long time.

Guided Practice

Tell which underlined verb is a form of the verb *be*. Tell which is an action verb.

Example: Maria <u>is</u> my new friend.   *be*

1. Maria <u>is</u> a good writer.
2. We <u>are</u> both in the third grade.
3. She <u>lives</u> in Puerto Rico.
4. I <u>am</u> three months older than Maria.
5. I <u>visited</u> Puerto Rico with my family.

THINK

■ How can I decide if a verb is a form of the special verb *be*?

REMEMBER

- The special verb *be* does not show action.

More Practice

Write the sentences. Write whether the underlined verb is an **action** verb or a **be** verb.

Example: The water is cold.   *be*

6. We <u>traveled</u> to Puerto Rico by plane.
7. We <u>were</u> guests for a week.
8. The weather <u>was</u> very warm.
9. Puerto Rico <u>is</u> a sunny island.
10. The beaches <u>are</u> beautiful.
11. Flowers <u>grow</u> all year long.
12. My family <u>visited</u> Maria in San Juan.
13. San Juan <u>is</u> the capital of Puerto Rico.
14. Maria <u>is</u> a tall girl with blue eyes.
15. She <u>plays</u> basketball with her friends.
16. Maria <u>introduced</u> me to them.
17. Her friends <u>are</u> very nice.
18. I <u>went</u> to school with them one day.
19. The teacher <u>welcomed</u> me to the class.
20. Maria <u>is</u> my favorite pen pal.

Extra Practice, page 218

WRITING APPLICATION A Post Card

Write a post card to your pen pal about yourself. Describe some of the things that you enjoy doing in your spare time. You might tell about a hobby. Underline the verbs in your post card.

2 VERBS IN THE PRESENT

When you write, use the verbs *is, am*, and *are* to show **present time**. Study the following chart to see which verbs in the present should be used with a singular or a plural subject.

Subject	Verb	Example
Singular noun *he, she, it*	is	Maria **is** very funny. She **is** my pen pal.
I	am	I **am** happy with her.
Plural noun *you, we, they*	are	The girls **are** in the house. We **are** happy to see them.

Guided Practice

Tell which is the correct verb in ( ).

Example: The post office (is, are) crowded. *is*

1. I (am, is) in the post office.
2. The workers (is, are) very busy.
3. They (is, are) behind the counter.
4. A mail carrier (is, are) on the telephone.
5. I (am, is) in a hurry.

?! THINK

- How do I decide which verb to use to tell about the present?

now
are   is
am

present time

REMEMBER

■ The verbs *is, am,* and *are* tell about the present.

More Practice

Write each sentence with the correct verb in ( ).

Example: My letters (is, are) finished.
    My letters are finished.

6. The post office (is, are) near my home.
7. It (is, are) crowded today.
8. We (is, are) in line for stamps.
9. Carol (is, are) with me.
10. She (is, are) my sister.
11. My letters (is, are) in my pocket.
12. They (is, are) long, funny letters.
13. Maria's address (is, are) on them.
14. I (is, am) next in line.
15. Two men (is, are) behind me.
16. We (am, are) also here for a package.
17. It (is, are) from Maria.
18. I (am, is) excited about my package.
19. It (is, are) a book about Puerto Rico.
20. The pictures (is, are) colorful.

Extra Practice, page 219

WRITING APPLICATION A Scene

Write a scene about a post office. Have students play the parts of postal workers and customers. Identify the verbs that are used.

COOPERATIVE
LEARNING

3 VERBS IN THE PAST

The verbs *was* and *were* tell about the **past**. Study the following chart to find out which verbs in the past should be used with a singular or a plural subject.

Subject	Verb	Example
Singular noun *I, he, she, it*	was	The letter **was** from David. He **was** my new pen pal.
Plural noun *you, we, they*	were	Six stamps **were** on the envelope. They **were** beautiful stamps.

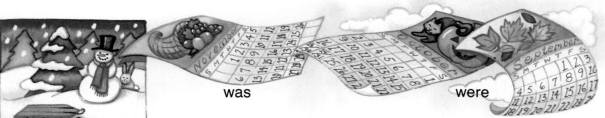

was   were

Guided Practice

Tell which is the correct verb in ( ).

Example: I (was, were) excited about the letter. *was*

1. The envelope (was, were) heavy.
2. Many photos (was, were) inside.
3. You (was, were) curious about them.
4. They (was, were) photos of David's family.
5. He (was, were) one of eight children.

?! THINK

■ How can I decide which verb to use to tell about the past?

REMEMBER

■ The verbs *was* and *were* tell about the past.

More Practice

Write each sentence. Change each underlined verb from the present to the past.

Example: I <u>am</u> a good photographer.
>   *I was a good photographer.*

6. My camera <u>is</u> new.
7. Film <u>is</u> in my camera.
8. It <u>is</u> color film for outdoors.
9. I <u>am</u> excited about these photos.
10. They <u>are</u> for David.
11. My parents <u>are</u> in the yard.
12. They <u>are</u> happy about the photos.
13. My funny cat <u>is</u> in one picture.
14. She <u>is</u> under a soft blanket.
15. We <u>are</u> laughing at the picture.
16. Some photos <u>are</u> of a baby.
17. It <u>is</u> my brother.
18. He <u>is</u> tiny.
19. Two older boys <u>are</u> in the photos.
20. They <u>are</u> my cousins.

Extra Practice, Practice Plus, pages 220–221

WRITING APPLICATION A Paragraph

Write a paragraph about a photo that you have taken or one that you like. Describe who is in the photo and what is happening. Circle the verbs.

MECHANICS: Contractions

A **contraction** is a shortened form of two words. A contraction leaves out one or more letters. Use an **apostrophe (')** to take the place of the missing letters.

Contractions with *not*			
has not	hasn't	cannot	can't
have not	haven't	do not	don't
had not	hadn't	does not	doesn't
is not	isn't	did not	didn't
are not	aren't	would not	wouldn't
was not	wasn't	could not	couldn't
were not	weren't	should not	shouldn't

The word *won't* is a special contraction. It means "will not."

Guided Practice

Tell which words make up each contraction.

Example: The letter wasn't on time.   *was not*

1. This letter isn't what I expected.
2. The handwriting isn't clear.
3. The letter doesn't make any sense.
4. I can't tell what it means.
5. I won't answer it.

THINK

- How can I decide where to place the apostrophe (') in a contraction?

REMEMBER

■ A **contraction** is a shortened form of two words.

More Practice

A. Write the sentences. Write the two words that make up each contraction.

Example: The envelope wasn't closed.   *was not*

   6. I can't understand the letter.
   7. I shouldn't let that stop me.
   8. It isn't an impossible job.
   9. I won't give up.
   10. The letter couldn't be about a sock.
   11. My pen pal doesn't write about socks.
   12. He didn't feel well when he wrote this.
   13. He says he can't go out.
   14. He wasn't in school today.
   15. I haven't seen him in a week.

B. Write each sentence with a contraction in place of the underlined words.

Example: The code <u>should not</u> be hard to break.   *shouldn't*

   16. I <u>have not</u> written in a while.
   17. Jan <u>will not</u> understand this letter.
   18. The words <u>do not</u> have spaces between them.
   19. He <u>will not</u> get my message right away.
   20. This <u>is not</u> the usual get-well card.

Extra Practice, page 222

WRITING APPLICATION A Note

Write a note in code about a favorite after-school activity. Have a friend identify the contractions.

COOPERATIVE
LEARNING

VOCABULARY BUILDING: Suffixes

You can change the meaning of a word by adding a suffix to the base word. A **suffix** is a word part added to the end of a base word.

Suffix	Meaning	Example
er	one who _____	play**er**
or	one who _____	sail**or**
less	without	friend**less**
able	able to be	break**able**
ible	able to be	collect**ible**
ly	in a _____ way	quiet**ly**
ful	full of	color**ful**

Guided Practice

Tell which suffix was added to each word.

Example: teacher   *er*

1. washable
2. farmer
3. hairless
4. actor
5. bravely
6. helpful

 **THINK**

■ How do I decide if a word contains a suffix?

REMEMBER

■ A **suffix** is a word part added to the end of a base word.

More Practice

A. Write the meaning of each word that has a suffix.

Example: I close my eyes tiredly.   *in a tired way*

7. The engine is lifeless.
8. The airline schedule is not flexible.
9. A worker approaches the runway.
10. The people wait patiently.
11. They are hopeful.
12. Colorful mail is loaded on the plane.
13. The mail will arrive quickly by plane.
14. The engine is fixable!
15. We shout happily.

B. Write the sentences. Complete each sentence by adding a suffix to the word in ( ).

Example: We arrive in the city (quick).
         We arrive in the city quickly.

16. The sky is (cloud).
17. The plane runs (smooth).
18. The pilot is (skill).
19. The (visit) see the city.
20. Their trip is (enjoy).

Extra Practice, page 223

WRITING APPLICATION A Letter

Write a letter to a relative, describing a plane trip to a faraway place. Circle the suffixes.

GRAMMAR AND WRITING CONNECTION

Using Contractions Correctly

You know that a contraction is the shortened form of two words. Many contractions are formed with the word *not*. Words with *not* are called **negative words.** When you speak or write, do not use two negative words in one sentence.

> **WRONG:** Nina **didn't** have **no** pen pals.
> **RIGHT:** Nina **didn't** have **any** pen pals.

Words that have *no* in them are also called **negative words.** The following words are negative words.

no	none	nothing
nobody	no one	nowhere

COOPERATIVE
LEARNING

Working Together

With your classmates, discuss negative words. Then, tell which word in each sentence is a negative word.

Example: Nina found nothing in her mailbox.
nothing

1. Nobody had written to her.
2. None of Nina's pen pals had answered her letters.
3. She would write to no one else.

Revising Sentences

John is writing a story about bringing his dog to school for a visit. Help John with his story. Rewrite each sentence so that there is only one negative word

4. My dog, Dizzy, can't not come to school.
5. My teacher doesn't allow no pets in school.
6. Dizzy wouldn't listen to no one, however.
7. I couldn't not keep Dizzy from school.
8. Dizzy wouldn't not stay in the schoolyard.
9. She wouldn't not stop barking.
10. My mother didn't think it was no joke.

Imagine that you have a pen pal. Write a letter to your pen pal about an adventure with your pet or a neighbor's pet. Make sure you use only one negative word in each sentence.

UNIT CHECKUP

LESSON 1

What Is Special About the Verb *be*? (page 202)
Write the sentences. Draw one line under the action verbs. Draw two lines under the *be* verbs.

1. My friend Susan is from France.
2. She lives in a small village.
3. She was a good student.
4. We write often.
5. Her letters were in French last year.

LESSON 2

Verbs in the Present (page 204) Write each sentence. Use the correct form of the verb in ( ).

6. I (is, am) glad I have a pen pal.
7. It (is, are) fun to get his letters.
8. He (is, are) on the soccer team.
9. His letters (is, are) exciting.
10. They (is, are) all about football.

LESSON 3

Verbs in the Past (page 206) Write each sentence with the correct form of the verb.

11. The train (was, were) in the station.
12. It (was, were) on time.
13. Our seats (was, were) comfortable.
14. They (was, were) in the last car.
15. The suitcases (was, were) on the rack.

LESSON 4

Mechanics: Contractions (page 208) Write the contraction for each word or words.

16. does not
17. is not
18. could not
19. would not
20. cannot
21. will not

22. has not
23. had not
24. are not
25. do not
26. did not
27. have not

LESSON 5

Vocabulary Building: Suffixes (page 210) Add *er, or, less, able, ible, ly,* or *ful* to each word.

28. collect
29. arm
30. read
31. eager
32. enjoy

33. near
34. friend
35. fond
36. jump
37. quick

38. swift
39. teach
40. slow

Writing Application: Verb Usage *(be)* (pages 202–208)
The following paragraph contains 10 verb errors. Rewrite the paragraph correctly.

41.–50.
    I is going to write a letter to my pen pal. He does'nt live near me. We was friends for many years. I were thinking of sending him a present. His favorite things is books. He are also interested in sports. I is deciding between a football and a book. The book am about football. I were sure he would like it. The book are the best idea.

A "Be" Song

With your friends, think of song titles that contain the verb *be*. Make a poster of the song titles. Have each person write one song title and draw one picture on the poster.

SUFFIX HUNT

Play this game with a friend. Write down as many words with the suffix *ly* as you can. The person who has the most words at the end of two minutes wins. Repeat the game using the suffixes *ible, ful, less, or, able,* and *er.*

able
er
or
ly
less
ible
ful

CONTRACTION MOBILE

Make a mobile that shows some of the contractions that you know. Get a hanger and string, and cut out shapes of paper. On one side of a shape, write two words such as *will not*. On the other side of the shape, write *won't*, the contraction for the words *will not*. Use string and a hole punch to attach your contraction shapes to the hanger. Add more contractions to your mobile as you learn them.

won't
can't
could not
have not
would not

CREATIVE EXPRESSION

The Birthday Child

Everything's been different
  All the day long,
Lovely things have happened,
  Nothing has gone wrong.

Nobody has scolded me,
  Everyone has smiled.
Isn't it delicious
  To be a birthday child?

—**Rose Fyleman**

TRY IT OUT! Some poems tell a story. They describe events, ideas, or feelings. What story is being told in "The Birthday Child"? Write a story poem of your own. You might want to write about something that you have built or an experience that you have had.

Three levels of practice

What Is Special About the Verb *be*? (page 202)

Write each sentence. Draw one line under the action verbs. Draw two lines under the *be* verbs.

1. My pen pal lives in Spain.
2. Her grandparents are farmers.
3. She mailed me pictures of the farm.
4. The pictures of the farm were beautiful.
5. Soccer is a popular sport in Spain.
6. My uncle was a soccer player.

Write each sentence. Draw a line under the verb. Write whether the verb is an action verb or a *be* verb.

7. My pen pal's name is Melena.
8. We are good friends.
9. A letter arrives every month.
10. I am excited about the last letter.
11. I read the letter eagerly.
12. Melena sent me a picture of her family.
13. There are four children in all.

Write those sentences that have a *be* verb.

14. Melena's favorite sport is tennis.
15. I play tennis, too.
16. Last summer was very hot.
17. The tennis courts were empty.
18. We visited the beach many times.
19. The sand was very hot.
20. The cold water felt wonderful.

EXTRA PRACTICE

Three levels of practice
Verbs in the Present (page 204)

LEVEL A. Write each sentence. Choose the correct form of the verb in ( ).

   1. Mount Fuji (is, are) in Japan.
   2. It (is, are) the highest mountain there.
   3. Melena's parents (is, are) mountain climbers.
   4. Melena (is, are) a mountain climber, too.
   5. Melena's letters (is, are) about climbing.
   6. I (am, is) glad when Melena's letters arrive.
   7. They (is, are) full of interesting facts.

LEVEL B. Write each sentence. Complete each sentence with **is, am,** or **are.**

   8. I _____ fascinated by Japan.
   9. Life in Japan _____ interesting.
   10. Shinji _____ a student in Tokyo.
   11. Her favorite subjects _____ math and art.
   12. I _____ good in math, too.
   13. Tokyo _____ the capital of Japan.
   14. Many people _____ in the city.

LEVEL C. Complete each sentence by joining the words on the left with the correct words on the right. Add a present-tense *be* verb to each sentence.

   15. I   _____ fast and modern.
   16. My pen pal's name   _____ a third-grade student.
   17. Japan   _____ very grassy.
   18. The countryside   _____ a small country.
   19. Japanese trains   _____ Shinji.
   20. Mount Fuji   _____ very steep.

GRAMMAR

Three levels of practice
Verbs in the Past (page 206)

LEVEL A. Write each sentence. Draw a line under the verb. Write whether the verb is an action verb or a *be* verb.

1. My pen pal mailed me a birthday present.
2. I was happy with a book about the Vikings.
3. The Vikings were brave explorers.
4. They sailed across the Atlantic.
5. Their journeys were long and dangerous.
6. They faced many hardships.
7. I finished the book yesterday.

LEVEL B. Write each sentence. Complete each sentence with *was* or *were.*

8. My summer vacation _____ exciting.
9. The best part _____ my trip to Arizona.
10. The Grand Canyon _____ enormous.
11. The guides _____ helpful.
12. Shinji and her family _____ happy.
13. They _____ thrilled with their trip.
14. I _____ glad.

LEVEL C. Write the sentences. Change each verb to the past tense.

15. My pen pal, Max, is a stamp collector.
16. I am a stamp collector, too.
17. Some of my stamps are rare.
18. The stamps on Max's letters are lovely.
19. A lion is on my favorite stamp.
20. That lion is a brave animal.

PRACTICE + PLUS

Three levels of additional practice for a difficult skill
Verbs in the Past (page 206)

LEVEL
A. Write the *be* verb in each pair.

   1. was, hurried
   2. cried, was
   3. were, saddened
   4. jumped, was
   5. were, yelled

LEVEL
B. Write the sentences. Underline the *be* verb in each sentence.

   6. Ted and Lin were pen pals.
   7. Ted was sad that no letter came.
   8. He was worried about Lin.
   9. Lin was now in France.
   10. Ted was happy when he got Lin's letter.
   11. She said France was very exciting.
   12. Lin and her parents were thrilled with the famous sights.

LEVEL
C. Complete each sentence with the correct verb in ( ).

   13. Lin (was, were) interested in art.
   14. Her parents (was, were) artists.
   15. Her mother (was, were) a portrait painter.
   16. Her father (was, were) a sculptor.
   17. Lin (was, were) good at drawing.
   18. She (was, were) excellent at drawing buildings.
   19. Her parents (was, were) proud of her.
   20. Lin's brothers (was, were) talented, too.

GRAMMAR

EXTRA PRACTICE

Three levels of practice
Mechanics: Contractions (page 208)

LEVEL
A. Write each contraction. Then, write the words that form each contraction.

1. Haven't you ever wanted a pen pal?
2. I didn't have a pen pal before.
3. My parents weren't sure I would write.
4. I won't ever disappoint my pen pal.
5. I couldn't do that to him.
6. He wouldn't write anymore.
7. He wasn't disappointed in my last letter.

LEVEL
B. Replace the underlined word or words in each sentence with the correct contraction. Write each new sentence.

8. My pen pal could not write in English.
9. I have not finished my Spanish course.
10. I do not write well in Spanish, yet.
11. My pen pal cannot understand my letters.
12. Some of my sentences did not make sense.
13. My pen pal does not mind, though.
14. He told me I should not stop trying.

LEVEL
C. Rewrite each sentence by using a contraction.

15. Kim has not answered my letter yet.
16. Kim's letters are not a bit dull.
17. I had not known much about Kim's country.
18. Kim is not sure he can visit me.
19. His family cannot take a vacation.
20. They do not have the time.

EXTRA PRACTICE

Three levels of practice
Vocabulary Building: Suffixes (page 210)

LEVEL A. Match each word on the left with its definition on the right. Write each word and its meaning.

1. colorless	in a quick way
2. breakable	someone who directs
3. director	full of peace
4. peaceful	without color
5. quickly	able to be broken
6. teacher	someone who teaches
7. laughable	able to be laughed at

LEVEL B. Write each sentence. Write the meaning of each word that has a suffix.

8. Someone knocked loudly on the door.

9. I saw the gardener in the doorway.

10. He is a helpful man.

11. His lilies were beautiful.

12. His yellow tulips were colorful.

13. The sun rose in the cloudless sky.

14. He quickly cut the grass.

LEVEL C. Complete each sentence with a word from the word box. Write the meaning of the word.

15. My pen pal is a good _____ .

16. I read her letters _____ .

17. Her letters describe Alaska _____ .

18. Two months of the year are _____ .

19. Often, _____ bears slide on the ice.

20. Some areas are _____ only by sled.

playful
writer
eagerly
reachable
sunless
clearly

MAINTENANCE

UNIT 1: Understanding Sentences

Statements and Questions (page 4) **Commands and Exclamations** (page 6) Write each sentence with the correct end punctuation.

1. Is there a puppy in the box
2. Come here, little puppy
3. She will be my new friend
4. Oh, you are adorable

Subjects in Sentences (page 8) **Predicates in Sentences** (page 10) Draw one line under the subject and two lines under the predicate.

5. Rick takes a picture of the dog.
6. The picture looks clear.
7. The dog barks happily.
8. The day is warm and sunny.
9. Rick snaps a picture of the trees.
10. Pink flowers fall from the trees.

UNIT 3: Understanding Nouns

Singular Nouns and Plural Nouns (page 68) **Plural Nouns with *ies*** (page 70) Write **singular** or **plural** next to each underlined noun.

11. My <u>brother</u> is a good cook.
12. He picks <u>cherries</u> from the tree.
13. He will make <u>pies</u>.
14. I cannot wait for <u>dinner</u>.
15. Three <u>ladies</u> will eat with us.

Common Nouns and Proper Nouns (page 72) Draw one line under the proper nouns. Draw two lines under the common nouns.

16. Write a letter to Sara.
17. Sara lives in Hartdale.
18. Jill will go to Camp Tilden this summer.
19. Sara and Jill will swim in Lake Tilden.
20. Many children will go to camp.
21. Marsha will go to tennis camp.

Singular Possessive Nouns (page 74) **Plural Possessive Nouns** (page 76) Write each group of words with the possessive form of each underlined noun.

22. Carmen friend
23. baby toys
24. dogs collars
25. children lunch
26. cats paws
27. boys bikes
28. girls books
29. parent car
30. birds feathers
31. sisters hat

Mechanics: Abbreviations (page 78) Write the abbreviation for each word.

32. Tuesday
33. Saturday
34. January
35. March
36. Doctor
37. December

UNIT 5: Understanding Action Verbs

Verbs in the Present (page 138) Write the sentences with the correct present-tense verb.

38. Julie (buy) a pile of wood.
39. She (bring) the wood to the yard.
40. She (put) nails and a hammer on the table.
41. Joe and Marty (offer) their help.
42. The boys (build) the doghouse with Julie.

Verbs in the Past (page 140) Write each sentence with the correct past-tense verb.

43. What (happen) to Julie's doghouse?
44. Julie (hurry) to finish it.
45. Spot (drop) his leash.
46. He (move) into his new home.
47. Julie (smile) at Spot.
48. Spot (rush) into the doghouse.

Verbs in the Future (page 142) Write each sentence with the correct future-tense verb.

49. Dana (talk) to her teacher.
50. They (discuss) her book report.
51. Dana (write) about Benjamin Franklin.
52. She (read) the report aloud.
53. She (try) to make it interesting.
54. The class (enjoy) the report.
55. Dana (get) a good grade.

Helping Verbs (page 144) Underline the helping verb in each sentence.

56. The new robot has arrived.
57. The boys have unpacked it.
58. The family had watched the robot.
59. I had hoped for a homework helper.
60. Mother has said it would not help.
61. We have thought of games to play.

Irregular Verbs (page 146) Write the sentences. Write the correct past tense of each verb in ( ).

62. Joe (see) his friend, Billy.
63. They had (eat) lunch together.
64. They (run) in the park later.
65. Joe has (give) Billy a tomato.
66. Joe (grow) it in his garden.

Vocabulary Building: Prefixes (page 150) Underline the prefix in each word. Then, write the meaning of the word.

67. disagree
68. redo
69. replace
70. repaint
71. unhappy
72. unfair

UNIT 7: The Special Verb *Be*

What Is Special About the Verb *be*? (page 202) Write the *be* verb in each group of words.

73. are, write
74. am, sing
75. were, like
76. give, is
77. were, talk
78. am, dance
79. laugh, is
80. walk, am

Verbs in the Present (page 204) **Verbs in the Past** (page 206) Write whether the underlined verb is in the **present** or **past**.

81. Grandma is happy when I call.
82. I am her favorite grandchild.
83. She was in her garden.

Mechanics: Contractions (page 208) Write a contraction for each word or group of words.

84. cannot
85. could not
86. had not
87. does not
88. has not
89. would not
90. have not
91. is not
92. will not
93. should not
94. do not
95. are not

Vocabulary Building: Suffixes (page 210) Write the sentences. Write the meaning of each word that has a suffix.

96. Mr. Smith is my instructor.
97. He is very helpful.
98. He teaches quietly.
99. I tried a wonderful trick.
100. He found it laughable.

UNIT

Writing Letters

Read the quotation and look at the picture on the opposite page. Writing in a journal is like writing a letter to yourself. A letter sends information about you and the things you do. A journal is a place to keep this information just for you.

In a letter you will want to include exciting news. The person reading it will want to write back to find out more.

Focus A friendly letter has five parts. Each part gives the reader important information.

What exciting event would you like to write about in a letter to a friend? In this unit you will read several letters. You will look at some photographs, too. You can use the letters and the photographs to get ideas for writing.

Write, write letters. Keep a journal.
Only write something every day.

—Norma Fox Mazer

Have you ever had to write to someone whom you did not know? Joseph's English assignment is to write a letter to a lady in a retirement home. How do you think Joseph feels about writing the letter?

Dear Aunt Helen

by Helen S. Munro

The moment had come. He got out his pencil and paper and looked at the name: *Mrs. Helen Smith.* Might as well get it over with.

Dear Mrs. Smith,

My name is Joseph, and I am nine years old. I am in the third grade. I would like to be your pen pal.

Sincerly,
Joseph Bellini

The body of a letter gives the writer's message.

That says it all. How much more would an old lady want to know about a little kid, mused Joseph. Especially me.

The weekend went quickly, and on Monday Miss Touchin found only one mistake in Joseph's letter. He copied it over in his neatest handwriting, mailed it, and forgot about it.

About a week later, Joseph found a letter in the mailbox, addressed to Master Joseph Bellini. "That's me!" he shouted—and tore it open immediately.

Dear Joseph,

   I am eighty-one years old and not in the third grade. I live in a retirement home with a lot of other ladies. Our building is all on one floor, and my room has a door that goes outside to a small patio. I planted petunias today, and I'm going to invite everyone to a party in my petunia patch.
   The ladies here are nice but a little dull. What do you do for fun?

                     Sincerely,
                     H. Smith

P.S. Please call me Aunt Helen, as my nieces, great-nieces and nephews, and assorted friends do. Mrs. Smith sounds like the name of a pie!

Joseph was excited about his letter and took it to school the next day. What a mistake!

"Well, write her another letter," said Miss Touchin. "Show it to me before you send it, and I'll give you some extra credit in English for it."

Rats and double rats, more writing, thought Joseph. But somehow Aunt Helen sounded better than Mrs. Smith.

Dear Aunt Helen,

  I'm glad you are out of the third grade. I wish I were.

  My baseball team finally won a game. I hit the ball, and a dog grabbed it and ran away. I scored the only run, and without the ball we couldn't play.

  Sincerely, your pen pal,
  Joseph

P.S. That's what I do for fun. Baseball, not school.

Another week went by, and another letter arrived.

Dear Joseph,

I'm glad to hear that your team won, sneaky as it was.

Some of the ladies here feel about this place as you feel about school. Their children put them here. I have passed out all the lipsticks I got for Christmas to try to make them look cheerier.

I feel that I am lucky. My husband and I had no children, and I am here because it is a good place for me. I get three meals a day, and when they have liver, they don't make me eat it.

Love, your friend,
Aunt Helen

This time Joseph got smart and didn't show it to his teacher. But somehow he still felt like writing.

Thinking Like a Reader

1. At first, Joseph feels it's a chore to write. At the end, he wants to write. Have you ever felt as Joseph did about something you were doing? Explain your answer.

Write your response in your journal.

Thinking Like a Writer

2. How does the author let you know what kind of person Mrs. Smith is?
3. Which details does she use?
4. Which details do you like best?

Write your responses in your journal.

Brainstorm *Vocabulary*

In "Dear Aunt Helen" there are a number of compound words. One compound word is *handwriting.* Find six more compound words in the story. Write these words in your personal vocabulary list. When you see other compound words, add them to your list. You can use these words in your writing.

Talk It Over
Talking on the Telephone

Imagine a telephone conversation between Aunt Helen and Joseph. Act out the conversation with a classmate. For example, Aunt Helen might invite Joseph to her party in the petunia patch. Joseph might invite Aunt Helen to watch him play in a baseball game.

Quick Write
Write Directions

Imagine your pen pal is coming to visit you for the first time. Write directions telling your pen pal how to get to your house. Be sure to include your exact address in your directions. Place your directions in an order that makes sense. Keep your directions in your writing folder.

Idea Corner
Letter Ideas

Joseph and Aunt Helen wrote a number of letters to each other. Think of some people you have received letters from. Make a list of topics you would like to write to them about. Your topics might include a hobby or a weekend activity.

PICTURES SEEING LIKE A WRITER

Finding Ideas for Writing

Look at the pictures. Think about what you see.
What ideas for writing letters do the pictures give you?
Write your ideas in your journal.

1 GROUP WRITING: A Letter

A letter is a way to share news, to extend an invitation, or to say thank you. The type of letter you write depends on your reason for writing, or your **purpose.** What do you need to remember about letters?

COOPERATIVE LEARNING

- Correct Letter Form
- Purpose and Audience
- Correct Letter Type

Correct Letter Form

Every letter includes five parts.

17 Mulberry Street Salisbury, North Carolina 28704 December 2, 1990	HEADING
Dear Uncle Ken,	GREETING
My class went on a trip to the airport. We went inside a 747. I got to sit in the captain's seat!	BODY
Your nephew, Adam	CLOSING SIGNATURE

- The **HEADING** is the writer's address and the date.
- The **GREETING** says "hello." It begins with a capital letter and ends with a comma.
- The **BODY** gives the writer's message.
- The **CLOSING** says "good-bye." It begins with a capital letter and ends with a comma.
- The **SIGNATURE** tells who wrote the letter.

Guided Practice: Brainstorming Greetings

As a class, choose a favorite book. Brainstorm greetings to a character in that book and to the author of the book.

Purpose and Audience

Knowing your **purpose** and **audience** will help you decide the type of letter to write. Look back at Adam's letter. Who is his audience? What is his purpose for writing?

Correct Letter Type

The greeting of a letter identifies your **audience.** The body of a letter tells your **purpose** for writing. It also tells what type of letter it is. **Friendly letters** share news. **Invitations** invite people to something. **Thank-you notes** thank others for gifts or favors that you have received.

Reread the letter from Adam to his uncle.

- Which type of letter is it?
- Which part of the letter tells you this?

Guided Practice: Choosing Letter Type

Look back at the author of the book you chose with your class. Decide what type of letter you will write. You might want to write an **invitation** to the author to visit your class. You might want to write a **friendly letter,** telling why your class likes the author. You can look on page 455 to see an invitation and a thank-you note.

Putting a Letter Together

With your classmates you chose an author. You decided on the type of letter to write. Now, think about what you want to say to the author.

Adam decided to write a letter to his favorite author. He wrote this letter to poet Shel Silverstein.

> 17 Mulberry Street
> Salisbury, North Carolina 28704
> December 5, 1990
>
> Dear Mr. Silverstein,
>
> You are my favorite poet. My favorite poem is "Eighteen Flavors." Ice cream is my favorite food.
>
> Yours truly,
> Adam

Guided Practice: Writing a Letter

Write a letter to your favorite author. Explain why you like his or her work. Include the five parts of a letter—**Heading, Greeting, Body, Closing,** and **Signature.**

Make an envelope for your letter. Be sure to place the return address in the upper left-hand corner. Place the receiver's address in the center of the envelope.

Share your letter with a friend. Have your friend suggest ways to make your letter clearer.

Checklist: A Letter

This checklist will help you when you write letters. Make a copy of the checklist and finish it. Keep it in your writing folder.

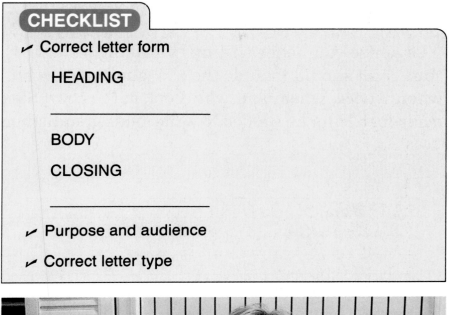

CHECKLIST

✓ Correct letter form

    HEADING

    _____

    BODY

    CLOSING

    _____

✓ Purpose and audience

✓ Correct letter type

2 THINKING AND WRITING: Charting

Letters are a way to share news. Before you write a letter, think about the topics that will interest your reader.

Organize your letter writing by making a chart. Your chart should include the 5 W questions—**who, what, where, when,** and **why.** Look at the chart Sam made for a letter he wanted to write to his grandfather.

Who
Grandpa

What
new piano teacher

Where
my house

When
last Wednesday

Why
to learn how to play the piano

Thinking Like a Writer

■ What other details might Sam include in his letter to his grandfather?

THINKING APPLICATION Charting

COOPERATIVE
LEARNING

Each of these four students wants to write a letter. Make a chart for the students to use as they write their letters. Discuss with your classmates to whom each of these students might write and what he or she might write about.

1. Susan wants to write a letter to her cousin Carol, who is the same age. Susan's hobbies are volleyball and swimming. What should Susan tell Carol?

2. Dale wants to tell someone about his swimming trophy. He has a cousin in Nebraska and a pen pal in Georgia. He also has an uncle in New York, who is a swimming coach. To whom should he write a letter?

3. Nina recently started ballet class and her mother bought her a ticket to see a ballet. Nina cannot wait to write this bit of news in a letter. She has a friend in Texas, who also studies ballet. Nina also has a sister who is away at school, and a grandmother in Canada. To whom should Nina write?

4. Tracy just received a letter from a new pen pal, who lives across the country. Tracy is in the third grade, loves to paint, and plays the guitar. What should Tracy tell her new friend?

WRITING

TOGETHER

3 INDEPENDENT WRITING: A Letter

Prewrite: Step 1

Sharie, a student your age, has a new box of stationery. To whom will she write first?

Choosing an Audience

1. First, Sharie made a list of family and friends.
2. Next, she thought about to whom she most wanted to write.

> My Pen Pals
> 1. Aunt Marie
> 2. Cousin Luis
> 3. Beth

Sharie decided to write to Beth and invite Beth to see her class play. Sharie made a chart to help organize her letter.

Exploring Ideas: Charting Strategy

Who	Beth
What	invitation to school play
Where	school auditorium
When	next Thursday
Why	Beth wants to be an actress

Before beginning to write, Sharie thought more about the school play. Then, she added another detail to her chart.

Who	Beth
What	invitation to school play I have the biggest part
Where	school auditorium
When	next Thursday
Why	Beth wants to be an actress

Thinking Like a Writer

- What did Sharie add?
- Why did she add this item?

YOUR TURN

Think of an activity you could write a pen pal about. Use **Pictures** or your journal for ideas. Follow these steps.

- Make a list of people to whom you would like to write.
- Choose the person to whom you are most eager to write.
- Think about your purpose and audience.

Make a chart of the details you want to include in your letter. Be sure to include the 5 Ws. You can add to or take away from your chart at any time.

Write a First Draft: Step 2

Sharie made a planning checklist to help her remember the parts of a letter. Sharie is now ready to write her first draft.

Sharie's First Draft

> Tinsel Maine
>
> April 15 1990
>
> Dear Beth,
>
> i'm going to be in a schol play. We were doing it next Thursday. my class wrote the play. Everyone tried out. I got the biggest part!

While Sharie wrote her first draft, she did not worry about errors. She just put her ideas on paper.

YOUR TURN

Write your first draft. As you write, ask yourself:

- What does my audience want to know?
- What is the best way to tell what I want to say?

TIME-OUT You might want to take some time out before you revise. That way you will be able to revise your writing with a fresh eye.

Planning Checklist
- Correct letter form
  heading
  greeting
  body
  closing
  signature
- Purpose and audience
- Correct letter type

THE WRITING PROCESS: Writing a First Draft

Revise: Step 3

After Sharie finished her first draft, she read it to herself. Then, she shared her writing with a classmate.

Sharie looked at her checklist once more. She put a check next to *Purpose and audience* so that she would remember it when she revised. Sharie now has a checklist to use as she revises.

Sharie revised her letter. She did not correct the small errors. She will correct them later. Turn the page, and look at her revised draft.

Revising Checklist
■ Correct letter form
  heading
  greeting
  body
  closing
  signature
✔■ Purpose and audience
■ Correct letter type

Tinsel Maine

April 15 1990

Dear Beth,

i'm going to be in a schol play. We were doing it next Thursday. my class wrote the play. Everyone tried out ,and I got the biggest part! I hope you will come to my play!

Thinking Like a Writer

- What information did Sharie add?
- Which sentences did she combine?

WISE
WORD
CHOICE

YOUR TURN

Read your first draft. Ask yourself these questions.

- How can I make my purpose clearer?
- Which details could I add?
- How can I improve my writing?

You might want to ask a friend to read your letter and make suggestions before you revise it.

Proofread: Step 4

Sharie knew that she had to proofread her letter. She used a proofreading checklist.

Part of Sharie's Proofread Draft

> Tinsel, Maine
>
> April 15, 1990
>
> Dear Beth,
>
> i'm going to be in a (schol) *school* play. We were *are*
>
> doing it next Thursday. my class wrote the

YOUR TURN

Proofreading Practice

Below is a letter you can use to practice your proofreading skills. Write the letter correctly on a separate piece of paper.

> Dear Jim,
>
> mom, Dad, susie, and me are in new york City. The hotel were in is big. It has room service. mom lets I call, and they send up anthing we want to eat. its great! Tomorrow we'll go see a play. It's called *Cats*.

Proofreading Checklist
- Did I indent my paragraphs?
- Did I capitalize letters correctly?
- Did I use punctuation correctly?
- Did I spell all words correctly?

Applying Your Proofreading Skills

Now proofread your letter. Read your checklist again. Review **The Grammar Connection** and **The Mechanics Connection**, too.

THE GRAMMAR CONNECTION

Remember these rules about the special verb *be*.

- The special verb *be* shows what someone or something is or is like.
- The special verb *be* has several forms.

  David **is** my favorite pen pal.
  I **was** pleased with his birthday present.
  I **am** happy with his presents.
  We **are** good friends.
  We **were** friends for two years.

Have you used the special verb *be* correctly?

THE MECHANICS CONNECTION

Remember these rules about using commas.

- Use a comma between the day and the year.
- Use a comma between the city and the state.

  January 9, 19--   Brooklyn, New York

Have you used commas correctly?

Proofreading Marks
¶ Indent
∧ Add
ዖ Take out
≡ Make a capital letter
/ Make a small letter

Publish: Step 5

Sharie and her classmates made a post office in their classroom. At the end of each day, the chosen mail carrier delivers the letters to everyone in the class. Stamps are placed on letters for people outside the class. These letters are then mailed.

YOUR TURN

How will you share your letter? You might want to use an idea in the **Sharing Suggestions** box below.

SHARING SUGGESTIONS

Make a mobile of letters and post cards that you have written. Hang your mobile in your classroom.	Create your own stationery by decorating paper. Glue different shapes onto the paper. Share your stationery with your classmates.	Make a box to hold the letters you received. Show your letters and box to your friends and family.

4 SPEAKING AND LISTENING: Speaking on the Telephone

There are many ways to share news. One way is to write a letter. Talking on the telephone is another way. When you take a telephone message for someone, you are also sharing news.

Read the phone conversation between Kim and Emily. Then, read the message Emily left for John.

KIM: Hello. This is Kim. May I please speak to John?

EMILY: John is not home now. May I take a message for him?

KIM: Yes, please. Tell John that I got a letter from my pen pal. Please have him call me at 555-2345.

EMILY: The message is: Kim got a letter from her pen pal. Call her at 555-2345. I'll give John the message. Thanks. Good-bye.

John,

Kim got a letter from her pen pal.

Call her at 555 - 2345.

Emily

When you talk on the telephone, follow these rules.

> **SPEAKING GUIDELINES:** Telephone Messages
>
> 1. Be polite.
> 2. Speak clearly.
> 3. Have the person to whom you are speaking repeat your name, phone number, and message.

- What is a polite way to begin a telephone conversation?
- What is a polite way to end a telephone conversation?

SPEAKING APPLICATION Telephone Messages

Practice these telephone conversations with a friend. Keep the following guidelines in mind.

1. Leave a message for Dad that Mom will be home at 7:00. Have Dad call Mom at 565-9078.

2. The library called your sister. The book she wanted is in. She can pick it up tomorrow morning.

3. Cousin Bill called to invite your sister to play tennis Sunday. She should call him tonight.

> **LISTENING GUIDELINES:** Telephone Messages
>
> 1. Listen carefully to the caller's name, telephone number, and message.
> 2. Be sure to write the caller's name, number, and message correctly.

WRITING

EXTENSION

5 WRITER'S RESOURCES: Newspapers and Magazines

Newspapers and magazines are another way of sharing news. Newspapers share news about what is happening in the world or even in a small part of the world. Magazines often cover many topics. News magazines cover national and international news, science news, and theater and movie news, too. Other magazines are about a single topic.

What do you like to do? What are your hobbies? Whatever you enjoy doing, there is probably a magazine or newspaper that tells all about it. Most newspapers are published every day. Magazines are published once a week or once a month.

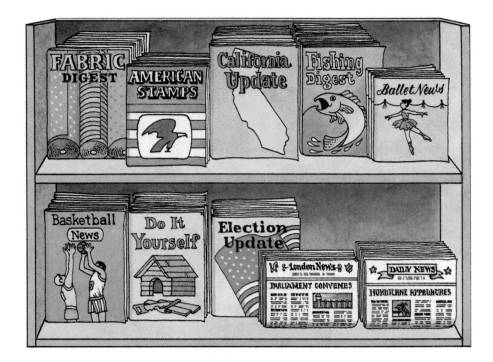

Practice

Look at the newspaper and magazine covers on the opposite page. Think about the kind of information you would find in each. Then, write the name of the magazine or newspaper where you might find the following headlines.

1. Students Sew It Up
2. Record Temperatures Scorch the South
3. Rare Stamp Discovered in Maine
4. Basketball Star of Tomorrow
5. New Ballet Sizzles
6. Where the Fish Bite in Idaho
7. Tourists Tour London
8. New School for Dance Opens in California
9. Carve Your Own Canoe
10. Voter Turnout Up

WRITING APPLICATION A Scrapbook

Begin a scrapbook of articles that interest you. Cut out articles from newspapers and magazines. Add to your scrapbook as you find articles that you like.

THE CURRICULUM CONNECTION

Writing About Communications

Newspapers, magazines, and television are just a few ways people share news, or communicate. Billboards, singing telegrams, and skywriting are a few more. People read signs in order to follow directions and obey laws.

How do you find out about current events? Which newspapers and magazines do you read? What information do you get from reading signs?

ACTIVITIES

Make a Choice   Imagine that you had to give up the telephone. Write a paragraph telling about another kind of communication that you might use instead.

Describe a Photograph   Study the photograph on the top of the next page. Which form of communication do you see? What other means of communication could the woman use?

Respond to Literature   *Sarah, Plain and Tall* by Patricia MacLachlan is based on a true story. Caleb lives with Anna, Papa, and their dogs, Lottie and Nick. Anna and Caleb's Mama has died. Papa is ready to marry again. He advertises in a newspaper. Sarah answers the ad. Papa writes a letter inviting her to visit them. Caleb writes, too. Look at the letter Caleb received.

Sarah, Plain and Tall

Dear Caleb,

My cat's name is Seal because she is gray like the seals that swim offshore in Maine. She is glad that Lottie and Nick send their greetings. She likes dogs most of the time. She says their footprints are much larger than hers (which she is enclosing in return).

Your house sounds lovely, even though it is far out in the country with no close neighbors. My house is tall and the shingles are gray because of the salt from the sea. There are roses nearby.

Yes, I do like small rooms sometimes. Yes, I can keep a fire going at night. I do not know if I snore. Seal has never told me.

Very truly yours,
Sarah Elisabeth

Imagine that you are Caleb. Answer Sarah's letter.

UNIT CHECKUP

LESSON 1 — **Group Writing: A Letter** (page 238) What are the five parts of a letter?

LESSON 2 — **Thinking: Charting** (page 242) Make a chart for a letter that a student wants to write to her aunt. Susan wants to invite Aunt Joby to a concert in Susan's school next Thursday. Susan will play the violin.

LESSON 3 — **Writing a Letter** (page 244) Write a letter to someone who lives in another town. Thank the person for a gift or note you received.

LESSON 4 — **Speaking and Listening: Speaking on the Telephone** (page 252) Why should you write down a telephone message?

LESSON 5 — **Writer's Resources: Newspapers and Magazines** (page 254) Would you find the following information in a newspaper or magazine?

1. the score of last night's baseball game
2. an interview with a musician
3. the five-day weather forecast

THEME PROJECT  A CARD

Greeting cards are sent for many reasons. You can send someone who is sick a get-well card. You can wish someone a happy birthday. You can cheer someone up or even say thank you. There are thousands of cards to choose from for every occasion.

Think of an occasion for which you would like to send a greeting card. Then, think about who will receive the card.

- Design a greeting card.
- Use colored paper and pencils.
- Draw pictures and write the occasion on the outside.
- Write your greeting inside.

UNIT
9

Adjectives

You will learn about adjectives in Unit 9. Adjectives are words that can add extra excitement to your writing.

Discuss Read the poem on the opposite page. Would you carry a pet in your hat? Tell how it might feel?

Creative Expression The unit theme is *Pet Parade.* Think about the smallest pet you have ever seen. Draw a picture of that pet and its owner. Write one or two sentences that tell about your picture. Write your sentences in your journal.

I have a dog,
I had a cat.
I've got a frog
Inside my hat.

—David McCord
"Notice"

1 WHAT IS AN ADJECTIVE?

An adjective is a word that describes a noun.

A noun names a person, place, or thing. When you write, you use adjectives to tell **what kind** of person, place, or thing it is.

Clover wagged his **long** tail.
Clover had a **cold** nose.

In the following sentence any word that makes sense in the blank is an adjective. How many adjectives can you think of to fill each blank?

The _____ girl petted the _____ dog.

happy

tall

Guided Practice

Tell which word in each sentence is an adjective.

Example: Clover is a friendly dog. *friendly*

1. Clover greeted the tall girl.
2. Betsy patted his fluffy head.
3. They ran into the warm house.
4. Betsy put food in a blue bowl.
5. Clover finished his tasty dinner.

?! THINK

■ How can I decide which words are adjectives?

REMEMBER

- An **adjective** is a word that describes a noun.
- An adjective can tell *what kind.*

More Practice

Write the sentences. Draw one line under each adjective. Draw two lines under the noun that the adjective describes.

Example: Clover had <u>brown</u> <u><u>fur</u></u>.

6. Clover lay down in a sunny corner.
7. The corner was behind the big chair.
8. This was Clover's favorite place.
9. Clover liked the yellow carpet.
10. He stretched his short legs.
11. A pink tongue showed as he yawned.
12. His floppy ears hung to the ground.
13. Clover closed his tired eyes.
14. Clover slept in the quiet house.
15. The bright sunlight warmed his fur.
16. Betsy opened the white box.
17. She took out a red leash for Clover.
18. She put it on the brown dog.
19. Betsy took Clover for a long walk.
20. They walked down a quiet street.

Extra Practice, page 280

WRITING APPLICATION A Paragraph

Imagine that you could have any pet you want. Write a paragraph describing the pet. Circle the adjectives.

2 MORE ABOUT ADJECTIVES

You use some adjectives to tell what kind. Adjectives can also tell **how many.** Adjectives that tell how many come before the nouns they describe.

Three birds flew in the store window.

Few, many, and *several* are special adjectives that tell how many.

A **few** children came into the pet shop.
The children saw **many** pets.
They saw **several** parakeets.

Guided Practice

Tell which word in each sentence is an adjective.

Example: Parakeets come in many colors.   *many*

1. Eric saw several birds in the shop.
2. One canary sang a song.
3. It sang for a few minutes.
4. A canary can live for 24 years.
5. They can be pets for many years.

 THINK

■ How can I decide which adjectives tell how many?

REMEMBER

- An **adjective** can tell *how many.*
- *Few, many,* and *several* are special adjectives that tell how many.

More Practice

Write the sentences. Draw one line under each adjective that tells how many. Draw two lines under the noun that the adjective describes.

Example: My neighborhood has <u>many</u> <u>stores</u>.

6. One store had cages of birds.
7. Three girls watched them.
8. Many birds sang in the cages.
9. Two boys talked to the parrots.
10. The parrots said a few words.
11. The store had several finches.
12. Five finches flew around the store.
13. Amy wanted one finch for a pet.
14. The owner showed her two parrots.
15. One man came over and talked to them.
16. Amy bought five goldfish instead.
17. Charles taught two parrots to talk.
18. He repeated three words over and over.
19. At first, the two parrots would not speak.
20. Charles repeated several words.

Extra Practice, page 281

COOPERATIVE
LEARNING

WRITING APPLICATION A List

Make a list of the pets that you and your classmates have. Be sure to tell how many of each pet there are. Underline the adjectives that tell how many.

3 ADJECTIVES THAT COMPARE

When you write, you use adjectives to describe nouns. You can also use adjectives to compare two or more nouns. Add *er* to an adjective to compare two nouns. Add *est* to an adjective to compare more than two nouns.

> The dachshund is a **small** dog.
> The Siamese cat is **smaller** than the dog.
> The gray mouse is the **smallest** pet of all.

small   smaller   smallest

Guided Practice

Tell which is the correct adjective in ( ).

Example: My cat is (smaller, smallest) than my dog.
    smaller

1. My cat is (younger, youngest) than my dog.
2. Tippy is the (cleaner, cleanest) pet in town.
3. He is the (smarter, smartest) pet I know.
4. He is a (faster, fastest) runner than my dog.
5. Tippy is a (slower, slowest) eater than Ralph.

?! THINK

- How can I decide which adjectives to use to compare nouns?

REMEMBER

- Ad *er* to an adjective to compare two nouns.
- Add *est* to an adjective to compare more than two nouns.

More Practice

Write the sentences. Complete each sentence with the correct form of the adjective in ( ).

Example: Gus is _____ than Duke. (smart)
Gus is smarter than Duke.

6. Max is (strong) than Boots.
7. He is the (old) of my three cats.
8. He is the (small) cat I own.
9. Boots is (young) than Max.
10. Nan is the (quick) of my cats.
11. Max is (sweet) than Nan.
12. Gus is (old) than Jan's dog, Duke.
13. His tail is (long) than Duke's.
14. He has the (short) legs in the city.
15. He is the (smart) dog I know.
16. Gus has a (thick) coat than Duke.
17. Duke is the (young) dog on the block.
18. He has the (loud) bark.
19. Duke is (fast) than Gus.
20. He is the (strong) dog of all.

Extra Practice, Practice Plus, pages 282–284

WRITING APPLICATION A Post Card

Write a post card to your cousin or another relative comparing two pets that you know. Underline the adjectives in your post card.

4 USING *A, AN,* AND *THE*

You use adjectives to describe nouns. The words *a, an,* and *the* are special adjectives called **articles.**

➪ Use *an* before singular nouns that begin with a vowel.   **an** egg

➪ Use *a* before singular nouns that begin with a consonant.   **a** bird

➪ Use *the* before singular nouns and plural nouns.
the tree   **the** trees

the tree

the birds

an egg

a fence

Guided Practice

Tell which is the correct article in ( ).

Example: Judy helped pack (the, an) picnic basket.
the

1. Judy's family went on (a, an) outing.
2. They drove to (an, the) country.
3. (A, The) trees were in bloom.
4. Judy brought (a, an) bird book along.
5. She spotted (a, an) bluebird.

?! THINK

■ How can I decide when to use the articles *a, an,* and *the?*

REMEMBER

■ *A, an,* and *the* are adjectives called **articles.**

More Practice

A. Write the sentences. Complete each sentence with the correct article in ( ).

Example: They visited (the, an) lake.
   They visited the lake.

   6. Mr. Hall rented (a, an) rowboat.
   7. The family rowed down (an, the) creek.
   8. Soon, they threw in (a, an) anchor.
   9. They watched (an, the) ducks swim.
   10. One duck had (a, an) orange head.
   11. (An, The) ducklings dove into the water.
   12. Judy saw (a, an) family of swans.

B. Write the sentences with **a** or **an**.

Example: The bird sang ____ song. *a*

   13. Judy heard ____ hoot outside the cabin.
   14. It was the sound of ____ owl.
   15. The sun woke Judy in ____ few hours.
   16. She took ____ bird book outside.
   17. Judy saw ____ oak tree near the cabin.
   18. She saw ____ brown bird in the tree.
   19. The bird had ____ big yellow beak.
   20. Judy found ____ picture of the bird.

Extra Practice, page 285

WRITING APPLICATION A Story

Imagine that you saw a rare bird. Write a story about it. Circle the articles.

5 MECHANICS: Commas in a Series

When you write, you use a **comma** to show a pause. Always use commas to separate the words in a series of three or more words. Commas help make the meaning of a sentence clear.

WRONG: The cow was big spotted and old.
RIGHT: The cow was big, spotted, and old.

Guided Practice

Tell where commas belong in each sentence.

Example: The farmers were busy happy and proud.
busy, happy,

1. The day was warm sunny and clear.
2. The country fair was busy noisy and exciting.
3. People drove cars buses and trucks to the fair.
4. The banners were big bright and colorful.
5. Men women and children rode on the Ferris wheel.

 **THINK**

■ How can I decide where to use commas in a series?

REMEMBER

■ Use **commas** to separate three or more words in a series.

More Practice

Write the sentences. Add commas where they are needed.

Example: Radishes were red round and crisp.

Radishes were red, round, and crisp.

6. Pumpkins were huge heavy and orange.
7. The round red and juicy tomatoes were delicious.
8. The green hard and crisp pickles were sour.
9. The judges were fair eager and experienced.
10. The happy excited and proud people cheered.
11. The pigs sheep and goats ran quickly.
12. One pony was fast small and gray.
13. Its thin weak and wobbly legs were funny.
14. The horse was big strong and healthy.
15. It trotted galloped and jumped the fence.
16. Its coat was smooth brown and shiny.
17. The sheep were fat woolly and fluffy.
18. The pink fat and dirty pigs played.
19. Their tails were short curly and wiggly.
20. We saw brown white and spotted rabbits.

Extra Practice, page 286

WRITING APPLICATION A Letter

Imagine that your pet won a prize at a fair. Write a letter to a friend telling him or her about the event. Describe what your pet looks like. Circle the commas in your work.

6 VOCABULARY BUILDING:
Synonyms and Antonyms

Synonyms are words that have the same or almost the same meaning.

The brown pony is **little.**
The gray pony is **small,** too.

Antonyms are words that have opposite meanings.

Jim rode the **young** pony.
Wendy rode the **old** horse.

little  small

Guided Practice

Tell which pairs of words are synonyms and which pairs of words are antonyms.

Example: high, low   *antonyms*

1. fast, slow
2. soft, hard
3. glad, happy
4. breezy, windy

5. sleepy, tired
6. dry, wet
7. big, huge
8. opened, closed

 **THINK**

■ How can I decide which words are synonyms and which words are antonyms?

REMEMBER

- **Synonyms** are words that have the same or almost the same meaning.
- **Antonyms** are words that have opposite meanings.

More Practice

Write each sentence. Replace each underlined word with a synonym or antonym from the word box.

Example: The wind was <u>cool</u>. *The wind was cold.*

skinny	large	stable	cold	awake
crispy	frightened	speedily	tall	last
pretty	warm	quickly		

  9. I walked into the <u>barn</u>.
10. My pony was <u>asleep</u>.
11. My pony stood up on his <u>thin</u> legs.
12. A <u>big</u> dog barked at my pony.
13. "Do not be <u>afraid</u>," I whispered.
14. I fed my pony a <u>crunchy</u> carrot.
15. He ate the carrot <u>quickly</u>.
16. I patted his <u>ugly</u> brown coat.
17. We rode to the <u>first</u> willow tree.
18. The <u>cold</u> wind blew my hair.
19. We stood in the <u>short</u> grass.
20. Then, we rode home <u>slowly</u>.

Extra Practice, page 287

WRITING APPLICATION A Travelogue

Imagine a place where there are more animals than people. Write a travelogue for this place. Be sure to use synonyms and antonyms in your travelogue.

GRAMMAR —AND— WRITING CONNECTION

Combining Sentences

You use adjectives to describe nouns. When you write two sentences that tell about the same person, place, or thing, you can often combine the sentences by adding an adjective.

Separate: Felix has a rabbit.
The rabbit is white.
Combined: Felix has a white rabbit.

Working Together

COOPERATIVE LEARNING

With your classmates talk about how you would combine sentences with adjectives. Then, tell how you would combine each pair of sentences.

Example: The park was full of pets.
It was a public park.
The public park was full of pets.

1. Corrine brought her dog.
   The dog was huge.
2. Donna held her dog on a leash.
   The dog was brown and golden.
3. David fed the dog.
   He gave the dog a biscuit.

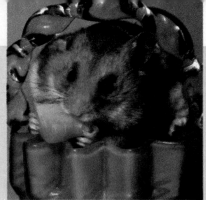

Revising Sentences

Cathy is writing a story about a pet show. Help Cathy combine each pair of sentences by adding an adjective to the first sentence.

4. Sylvie showed her bird.
   The bird was colorful.
5. The bird had long feathers.
   The feathers were red.
6. A rabbit hopped away.
   The rabbit was tiny.
7. A ferret bared its teeth.
   The ferret was hungry.
8. A goat won first prize.
   The goat was white.
9. It wore a ribbon.
   The ribbon was blue.
10. A snake won second prize.
    The snake was striped.

Imagine that you are writing about a pet show for your school newspaper. Write a news article about the show. Reread your article. Combine any sentences that you can.

UNIT CHECKUP

LESSON
1

What Is an Adjective? (page 262) Write each sentence. Draw one line under each adjective. Draw two lines under the noun it describes.

1. I taught my puppy a new trick.
2. I held up a long stick.
3. My frisky dog jumped over it.
4. I threw it into the thick bushes.
5. He scooted away on his strong legs.
6. My happy dog came back with the stick.

LESSON
2

More About Adjectives (page 264) Write each sentence. Draw one line under each adjective. Draw two lines under the noun it describes.

7. I have one guinea pig named Henrietta.
8. There are many stories about her.
9. I have written several stories.
10. One story is about her babies.
11. Henrietta had four babies.
12. I took ten pictures of the babies.

LESSON
3

Adjectives That Compare (page 266) Write the sentences. Complete each sentence with the correct adjective in ( ).

13. Polly is (younger, youngest) than Jolly.
14. She is (calmer, calmest) than Molly.
15. She is the (smaller, smallest) bird of all.
16. Jolly is (smarter, smartest) than Polly.
17. His feathers are (darker, darkest) than hers.
18. He is the (older, oldest) of all the birds.

LESSON 4

Using *a*, *an*, and *the* (page 268) Write the sentences. Complete each sentence with the correct article in ( ).

19. I have _____ amusing turtle. (a, an)

20. Once, he ran in _____ turtle race. (a, an)

21. I waited by _____ starting line. (the, an)

22. He decided to take _____ nap. (a, an)

LESSON 5

Mechanics: Commas in a Series (page 270) Write the sentences. Use commas where they belong.

23. Rex came home muddy grimy and smelly.

24. I got out the soap towel and brush.

25. Ben Carl and I caught Rex.

26. Rex barked whined and growled.

LESSON 6

Vocabulary Building: Synonyms and Antonyms (page 272) Write each pair of words. Write **synonym** if they are synonyms. Write **antonym** if they are antonyms.

27. happy, merry

28. angry, mad

29. frozen, melted

30. fat, thin

31.–40.

Writing Application: Adjective Usage (pages 262–270) The following paragraph contains 10 errors with adjectives. Rewrite the paragraph correctly.

Our neighborhood had an dog show last week. My dog was an cuter dog in the show. She wore a orange collar and a orange bow in her hair. Barry's dog was the larger dog in the show. He won an ribbon. My dog was the smartest of the two dogs. Barney Fluffy and Lady won ribbons.

POST -A- WORD

Cut ten words from magazines. Paste these words onto a large piece of paper. Write a synonym and an antonym next to each word. Then, cut out pictures from magazines to show the words' meanings.

ANIMAL CLUES

Without naming it, describe a favorite animal. Have a friend guess the animal that you are describing. Use adjectives to describe the animal. You might describe an elephant using the words *large, gray, wrinkled.* Take turns giving clues and guessing animals.

Animal Actors

Play this game with two friends. Write adjectives such as *big, fast,* and *slow* on cards. Then, act like an animal, such as a dog. The person who guesses the animal must pick a card. If the card says *big,* he or she must act like a bigger animal. If the card says *fast,* then a faster animal should be acted out. Take turns guessing and acting out animals.

*Waterfall, only
a foot high, makes a large cool
music at evening...*

—ISSA

*Who can stay indoors
on such a day in the sun
dazzling on new snow!*

—KIKAKU

Try It Out! Haiku is a form of Japanese poetry that has only three lines in each poem. The first and third lines each have five syllables. The second line has seven syllables. Write a haiku of your own. Describe an animal. Keep in mind the number of syllables.

EXTRA PRACTICE

Three levels of practice

What Is an Adjective? (page 262)

LEVEL A. Write each sentence. Draw two lines under the adjective that describes each underlined noun.

1. Scamp and Fagan live in the big house.
2. Fagan is a gentle dog.
3. Fagan has a short tail.
4. He has brown fur.
5. Scamp is a puppy with soft fur.
6. Scamp can give a loud bark.
7. Scamp and Fagan can do funny tricks.

LEVEL B. Write each sentence. Draw one line under each adjective. Draw two lines under the noun that each adjective describes.

8. Fluffy clouds fill the sky.
9. The hot sun warms my face.
10. It is a good day for a parade.
11. Cathy puts her cat in a little wagon.
12. Ray has a blue hat for his dog, Buster.
13. The happy children begin the march.
14. The noisy parade winds down the street.

LEVEL C. Write each sentence. Complete each sentence with an adjective.

15. The parade passes a _____ house.
16. A woman holds a _____ cat.
17. She waves a _____ flag.
18. Can my cat join your _____ parade?
19. The children march to the _____ oak tree.
20. They rest under a _____ oak tree.

EXTRA PRACTICE

Three levels of practice
More About Adjectives (page 264)

LEVEL A. Write each sentence. Draw a line under the adjective that tells how many.

1. Rick works several days a week.
2. He works three hours on Saturday.
3. Rick works with many animals.
4. He feeds five hamsters.
5. He gives a few carrots to the rabbits.
6. Three birds eat their dinner.
7. Rick feeds two turtles.

LEVEL B. Complete each sentence with the adjective that tells how many.

8. There are (green, two) parrots in the cage.
9. One parrot talks for (three, long) hours.
10. The other parrot says (many, funny) words.
11. Rick teaches the parrots (sad, several) songs.
12. The parrots sing the songs (happy, five) times.
13. Rick claps his hands for the (two, smart) parrots.

LEVEL C. Write the sentences. Complete each sentence with an adjective that tells how many.

14. The pet shop has _____ customers.
15. The owner helps _____ of them.
16. Some people already have _____ pets.
17. Charlie watches the _____ kittens.
18. He buys a kitten for _____ dollars.
19. He will feed it _____ times a day.
20. Charlie now has _____ pets.

EXTRA PRACTICE

Three levels of practice
Adjectives That Compare (page 266)

LEVEL A. Write each sentence. Draw a line under the adjective that compares.

1. Kate has a smaller horse than Jan.
2. Jan has a smarter horse than Kate.
3. Bob has a faster horse than Kate.
4. Amber is the fastest horse of all.
5. He has the smallest hooves I have ever seen.
6. Amber is also the strongest horse of all.
7. Amber has the softest coat of all.

LEVEL B. Write the sentences. Complete each sentence with the correct form of the adjective in ( ).

8. Lucy is the (smart) of my two parakeets.
9. Lucy is a (small) parakeet than Ricky.
10. Ricky does (hard) tricks than Lucy.
11. Fred does the (hard) tricks of all.
12. Lucy has the (long) cage of all.
13. Ricky has the (loud) chirp of all.

LEVEL C. Write the sentences. Complete each sentence with an adjective that compares.

14. Christine has a _____ dog than Lee.
15. My dog is the _____ dog in town.
16. Goldy has _____ fur than Blacky.
17. Goldy has a _____ appetite than Silky.
18. Goldy takes the _____ naps of all.
19. She also has the _____ bark of any dog.
20. Silky has the _____ eyes of all.

EXTRA PRACTICE: Lesson 3

GRAMMAR

PRACTICE + PLUS

Three levels of additional practice for a difficult skill
Adjectives That Compare (page 266)

LEVEL A. Write each sentence. Draw a line under the adjective that compares.

1. My fish are the slowest I know.
2. Minnie is the fastest one.
3. She is a smarter fish than Dot.
4. Minnie does harder things.
5. Dot is a faster swimmer than Minnie.
6. Minnie is the youngest fish I have.
7. She is also the quickest fish.
8. She is the lightest color.
9. Dot has a longer tail than Minnie.
10. Dot has brighter eyes, too.
11. Dot is my oldest fish.
12. Mickie is my newest fish.
13. Mickie is the greatest eater of all.
14. I bought them a deeper fishbowl.
15. It is a clearer bowl than the old one.
16. It has greener plants.
17. It is the deepest bowl on my block.
18. Dot is the proudest fish in the neighborhood.

LEVEL B. Complete each sentence with the correct form of the adjective in ( ).

19. It was the _____ pet concert! (great)
20. We saw the _____ sights ever. (wild)
21. Sandy wore _____ clothes than Miep. (bright)
22. Scamp wore the _____ scarf in the group. (long)
23. Scamp sang _____ notes than Miep. (high)
24. Mac was _____ than Skippy. (loud)

PRACTICE + PLUS

Complete each sentence with an adjective that compares.

25. Spanky is _____ than Mr. Tom.

26. Mousey is the _____ of all the pets.

27. He is _____ than the cat.

28. Of the two cats, Berta is _____ .

29. Of course, my pet is _____ of all!

30. Beth thinks her dog is _____ than mine.

31. Amy thinks hers is the _____ of all.

32. My pet is _____ than the others.

33. He has the _____ paws.

34. He also has the _____ fur.

35. His tail is much _____ , too.

36. Beth's dog has _____ eyes than my dog.

37. His eyes are the _____ of all the pets.

38. My pet's eyes have a _____ color.

39. My dog is the _____ pet on the block.

40. Beth's dog has a _____ doghouse than my dog.

EXTRA PRACTICE

Three levels of practice
Using a, an, and the (page 268)

A. Write the sentences. Underline the articles in each sentence.

1. Would you want an elephant?
2. A baby elephant is very big.
3. It might trample the grass in your yard.
4. It will find the peanuts and eat them.
5. It will squirt you with a water spray.
6. It might not be the best pet.
7. A dog would be better.

B. Write the sentences. Complete each sentence with the correct article in ( ).

8. Sparky and I play on (the, a) grass.
9. I throw (a, an) ball, and he chases it.
10. Sparky carries (a, an) apple back to me.
11. I laugh at (the, an) silly way he trots.
12. Sparky eats (an, a) apple.
13. He brings me (a, the) apple core.

C. Write the sentences. Complete each sentence with **a** or **an**.

14. I know _____ pet store with unusual pets.
15. Eric bought _____ aardvark that eats ants.
16. Ralph bought _____ snake.
17. Doreen bought _____ monkey.
18. Carla bought _____ pet rock!
19. I bought _____ iguana.
20. My sister bought _____ eel.

GRAMMAR

Three levels of practice

Mechanics: Commas in a Series (page 270)

LEVEL A. Write the sentences that use commas correctly.

1. Sandy feeds the colt, the lamb, and the pig.
2. Their names are, Iris Daisy and Fern.
3. The lamb is woolly white and, little.
4. Sandy has milk, apples, and bananas.
5. She goes to the stable, the barn, and the yard.
6. Iris, walks trots, and gallops.

LEVEL B. Write the sentences. Add the missing comma to each sentence.

7. My dog is large, shaggy and brown.
8. His tongue is long pink, and wet.
9. My dog eats, sleeps and chases cars.
10. He eats my socks my shoes, and my homework.
11. He cries, barks and howls at the moon.
12. We hike, play and watch TV together.
13. Mom Dad, and I love our dog.

LEVEL C. Write each sentence. Add commas where needed.

14. Ralph has a tail paws and a button nose.
15. He is a gentle kind and courageous dog.
16. He guards the children the house and the yard.
17. Ralph runs jumps and catches a ball.
18. He eats tomatoes steak and muffins.
19. Ralph licks my nose my cheek and my hand.
20. I pet his nose his head and his back.

Three levels of practice

Vocabulary Building: Synonyms and Antonyms (page 272)

LEVEL A. Write the sentences. Draw a line under the word in each sentence that is an antonym of the underlined word.

1. Buster is a <u>little</u> dog with a big bark.
2. He has white fur with <u>black</u> spots.
3. His fur is <u>smooth</u>, but his tongue is bumpy.
4. Buster is <u>gentle</u>, but he can be rough.
5. He sleeps near me and <u>wakes</u> when I do.
6. Buster acts <u>brave</u> when I feel afraid.

LEVEL B. Choose the synonym in ( ) for each underlined word. Rewrite each sentence, using the synonym.

7. Brian has a <u>smart</u> parrot. (clever, famous)
8. It is <u>little</u> and colorful. (small, cute)
9. The parrot plays <u>mean</u> tricks on the dog. (nasty, unhappy)
10. The parrot's chatter is <u>noisy</u>. (nosy, loud)
11. The parrot is <u>quiet</u> when it sleeps. (tired, silent)
12. The parrot <u>sleeps</u> on one foot. (naps, sits)

LEVEL C. Complete each sentence with an antonym for the underlined word.

13. Kevin is <u>clean</u>, but his dog is _____ .
14. Kevin runs <u>slowly</u>, but the dog runs _____ .
15. The bath is <u>empty</u>, but it will be _____ .
16. Kevin <u>holds</u> the dog and _____ the soap.
17. The dog <u>hates</u> baths but _____ being clean.
18. Kevin <u>washes</u> the dog, then _____ his fur.
19. The dog <u>runs</u> from the house, and Kevin _____ after him.
20. The dog <u>sits</u> under a tree while Kevin _____ nearby.

Writing Descriptions

Read the quotation and look at the picture on the opposite page. The writer has chosen his words carefully.

When you write a description, take time to choose the right words for the word picture you create.

Focus A description uses details to tell about the way something looks, feels, smells, tastes, or sounds. Adjectives add information about the details.

What would you like to describe? On the following pages you will find a story filled with description. You will find some photographs, too. You can use them to find ideas for writing.

Fern looked at her father. Then she lifted the lid of the carton. There, inside, looking up at her, was the newborn pig. It was a white one. The morning light shone through its ears, turning them pink.

—E.B. White
from *Charlotte's Web*

What do you know about spiders? One summer day, a lady found a spider in a head of lettuce. How do you think she felt when she spotted the spider?

The Lady and the Spider

by Faith McNulty

On a summer day in a lady's garden, a spider stood on a lettuce leaf. She looked about and saw hills of green and valleys of green. Between two leaves she saw a green cave. Walking daintily on her eight legs, she went inside. With the tips of her long front legs, she felt the sides and the ceiling and the floor. The cave suited her. It was a leafy den just the right size to be her home.

When night came, dew formed on the leaves. Drops of water trickled into a hollow beside the spider's den. They made a tiny pool. The moon rose. Moths wakened and flew dizzily about the garden in search of other moths. One saw moonlight shine in the pool. It flew into the water. Its wings became wet. Unable to fly, it drowned.

In the morning when the sun rose, the spider looked into the pool and saw the moth. She walked to the water's edge and had breakfast.

Each day the lady came to tend her garden. She planted seeds, and pulled up weeds, and sprinkled water. She looked among the leaves for bugs. She did not want bugs to eat her garden. Once she saw the spider walking on a leaf but paid no heed. She knew spiders do not eat lettuce.

Detail sentences provide more information about the main idea.

When the lady's footsteps shook the ground, the spider ran and hid. One day the lady's dress brushed the leaves around the spider's home. The spider felt an earthquake, but the lady did not know what she had done.

For many days the garden grew. The lettuce leaves grew bigger. Each day the spider walked on the leaves searching for food. At noonday, when the sun was high, small flies—the kind with golden eyes—sat quietly on the leaves to warm their wings and rub their hands together. They were the spider's lunch. Birds also dined in the lady's garden. They perched on the fence and looked about sharply, peering here and there, searching for bugs.

One day the spider was having lunch. She was eating a large blue fly. A bird swooped down. Just in time, the spider saw its swift, dark shadow. She leaped into her den. The bird flew off with the fly.

As the days grew hot, the lady knew it was time to pick the lettuce. Each day she came to the garden with a basket and a knife and cut off a head of lettuce for her lunch. Each day the lettuce that she picked was closer to the head of lettuce in which the spider lived.

One day, when the sun came up and warmed the walls of her den, the spider went out and walked down a green hill to her sparkling pond to see what might be there for breakfast. Just at that moment the lady came into the garden. She bent down, grasped the head of lettuce in which the spider lived, and cut it off at the roots. She shook off the dew drops. She put the lettuce with the spider hidden among its leaves into her basket. Of course the lady had no idea the spider was there. As the leaf beneath her feet shook, the spider dashed toward her den. Her den was gone. The lady's thumb had crushed it. The spider clung to the leaf while the whole green world trembled and shook around her. The lady carried the head of lettuce to her kitchen and laid it on the counter beside the sink. When her world became still, the spider stood up and walked about among the leaves. She tried to see with her eight eyes. She tried to feel with the tips of her legs. She tried to think with her tiny brain. It was no use. The spider could not know that she had made her home in a head of lettuce in a lady's garden, and that the lady intended to eat that lettuce for lunch.

Details are placed in an order that makes sense.

The lady bent over the sink. She picked up the lettuce. She parted the leaves and looked for bugs. She did not see the spider, crouched deep in a dark cranny between two leaves. The lady put the lettuce into the sink. She put in the stopper and turned on the water. It poured clean and cold over the leaves. Huge drops of water splashed around the spider. She was caught in an icy river. She lost her grip. She spun in the stream, and was carried down, and then pushed up, and down again, by the surging water.

The lady turned off the faucet. The water in the sink became calm. The head of lettuce floated, rocking on tiny waves. Part of it was under water and part above. The spider struggled upward to the surface. Her front legs found the edge of a leaf. She was heavy with water. With all her strength she pulled herself up onto a leafy island. The leaf was cold. It was wet. The spider walked about, waving her long front legs, searching for a dark, dry, safe place to hide.

The lady looked down, and a tiny motion caught her eye. She saw a small spider, adrift on a raft of lettuce, trying to escape. The lady picked up the leaf with the spider clinging to it and opened the lid of the garbage pail. Just before the leaf dropped from her fingers, a thought crossed her mind. She looked again at the spider. The spider, searching for a place to hide, waved her legs.

She waved and waved. Looking closely, the lady saw things she had never noticed before. She saw how the spider's color matched the leaves. She saw the tiny dots that were her eyes. She saw how delicately she moved on her slender legs and how she waved and waved and waved.

The lady thought: Isn't it wonderful that a creature so small can live and love life, find food, and make a home just like me! The lady closed the lid of the garbage pail. Holding the leaf carefully, with the spider on board, she went to the garden. She bent over a head of lettuce and gently dropped the spider into its leaves. "Good luck in your new home," said the lady, and walked back to the kitchen for lunch.

The spider landed lightly in a sun-warmed, sweet-smelling valley. She sat still until she was warm and dry. Then she walked up a green hill and down a green hill, searching with the tips of her long front legs. Soon she found a nook just the right size. There she waited safe and snug. Waited for lunch... for the sun to set...and the moon to rise...and for her tiny, very important life to go on.

Thinking Like a Reader

1. How would you feel if you were the spider in the story?
2. What things would you enjoy?
3. What things would you find difficult or scary?

Write your responses in your journal.

Thinking Like a Writer

4. Which details does the author use to let you know that the spider is small and helpless?
5. Which details do you like best?

Write your responses in your journal.

LITERATURE

Brainstorm *Vocabulary*

In "The Lady and the Spider," there are many words with the suffix *ly*. For example, *daintily* and *dizzily*. Find as many of these words as you can and write them in a personal vocabulary list. Use these words in your writing.

Talk It Over
Changing Places

Imagine that the lady and the spider could change places. With your classmates, act out a scene between the lady and the spider. They might discuss what new or strange things they noticed when they changed places. Have one classmate play the role of the lady and another play the role of the spider. Other classmates could play the roles of neighbors.

Quick Write *Write a Note*

Imagine that you are a spider living in a head of lettuce. Write a note to a friend inviting her or him to visit you in your home. Be sure to describe clearly what your home looks like and where it is. Keep your note in your writing folder.

Idea Corner
A Sense of Nature

While living in the head of lettuce, the spider was aware of many things going on in nature. Make a list of some of the things going on around you. Write about how things look, feel, taste, sound, and smell. Your list might look like this.

- smell of flowers and trees
- taste of fresh honey
- vivid colors of flowers
- touch of breezes on my face
- loud roar of the ocean

PICTURES

Finding Ideas for Writing

Look at the pictures. Think about what you see.
What ideas for descriptive writing
do the pictures give you?
Write your ideas in your journal.

PICTURES: Ideas for Descriptive Writing

COOPERATIVE
LEARNING

WRITING

TOGETHER

GROUP WRITING: A Descriptive Paragraph

A descriptive paragraph can be about a person, a place, or a thing. The **purpose** of a descriptive paragraph is to paint a clear and colorful picture for an **audience.** What will make a descriptive paragraph clear?

- Main-Idea Sentence
- Sensory Details
- Order of Details

Main-Idea Sentence

Read the paragraph that Andrew wrote.

> <u>Daisy is the most unusual dog I have ever seen.</u> Her floppy ears are different shades of brown. She has flecks of white below her eyes. Daisy's furry body is very small, while her paws are very large. Her bark is louder than that of any dog in my neighborhood.

The underlined sentence gives the main idea of the paragraph. It tells what the paragraph is about. The other sentences in the paragraph, called detail sentences, tell you more about the main idea.

Guided Practice: Writing a Main-Idea Sentence

With your classmates, choose a pet that you would like to describe. Write a main-idea sentence about the pet.

Sensory Details

When you write descriptive paragraphs, you provide details that describe how things **look**, **sound**, **smell**, **taste**, and **feel**. These details are called **sensory details.** They provide vivid pictures for the audience. Read Andrew's paragraph again.

- Which words describe Daisy's ears?

Guided Practice: Using Sensory Details

Look back at the pet you chose with your class. Think of sensory details to describe it. Draw a picture of the animal's face. Next to the eyes, write words that tell how the animal looks. Next to the nose, list words describing smell. Next to the ears and the cheeks, write words describing sound and touch.

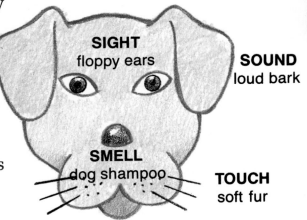

SIGHT floppy ears

SOUND loud bark

SMELL dog shampoo

TOUCH soft fur

Order of Details

Descriptive paragraphs should put details in an order that makes sense. One kind of order is **top-to-bottom.** This means that a place or thing is described from its top to its bottom. Words like *top, above, over, middle, halfway, between, bottom, below,* and *under* help the reader see the description.

Read the paragraph about Daisy again. Which word lets you know where the flecks of white appear?

Putting a Description Together

With your class, you have written a main-idea sentence. You created a face chart that added details to your main-idea sentence. Are there any more details that you can add to your face chart?

Andrew decided to add the following details about Daisy to his face chart.

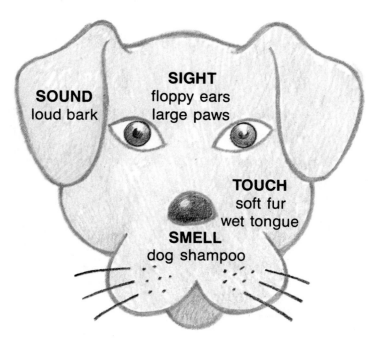

SOUND
loud bark

SIGHT
floppy ears
large paws

TOUCH
soft fur
wet tongue

SMELL
dog shampoo

Guided Practice: Writing a Descriptive Paragraph

Write three or four detail sentences to add to the main-idea sentence that you wrote with your class. Be sure to use your face chart to help you add sensory details to your paragraph. Arrange your detail sentences in order from top to bottom.

Can a friend draw a picture based on your descriptive paragraph?

Checklist: Descriptive Writing

A checklist will help you remember what to include when you write descriptive paragraphs. Make a copy of the checklist below and complete it. Keep it in your writing folder.

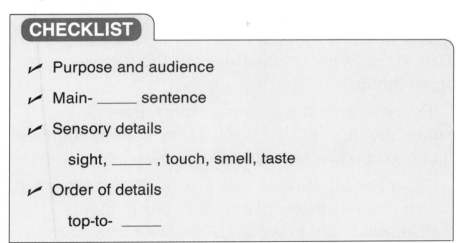

CHECKLIST

✔ Purpose and audience

✔ Main- _____ sentence

✔ Sensory details

   sight, _____ , touch, smell, taste

✔ Order of details

   top-to- _____

2 THINKING AND WRITING: Classifying

When you write, you can group together, or **classify,** items that have something in common. What they have in common is the name of the group. You can group things according to size, shape, weight, or even color. What do the things in the pictures have in common?

Everything in the pictures can be classified as something heavy. That is what they have in common. Their group can be called *heavy things.*

Classifying things can make your writing more vivid. It can paint a clearer picture for your audience. Before you begin to write, think about how things can be classified. Look at these sentences from a student's notebook.

1. The old sofa was heavy and hard to move.
2. The old sofa was heavier than an elephant and just as hard to move.

Thinking Like a Writer

- Which sentence is more interesting?
- What picture does the sentence paint in your mind?

THINKING APPLICATION Classifying

Four third-grade students are writing paragraphs about the animals that they like. They decided to show what the animals have in common. Help the students with their paragraphs. Discuss with your classmates how you would classify each group of animals.

1. Wendy wants to write a paragraph about dolphins and porpoises. What would she call this group?

2. Terrance wants to write about dogs, cats, and horses. What do these three animals have in common?

3. Shawn plans on writing about goldfish and guppies. What other fish could be classified with goldfish and guppies?

4. Debra wants to write about guinea pigs and mice. What do they have in common?

3 INDEPENDENT WRITING: A Description

Prewrite: Step 1

You know a lot about writing a descriptive paragraph. Now you are ready to choose something to describe. Jane, a student your age, wanted to describe an animal. She thought her cousin would be a good **audience.** Here's how Jane chose an animal to describe.

Choosing a Topic

1. First, Jane made a list of animals.
2. Next, she thought about each animal.
3. Last, she chose the animal that she most wanted to write about.

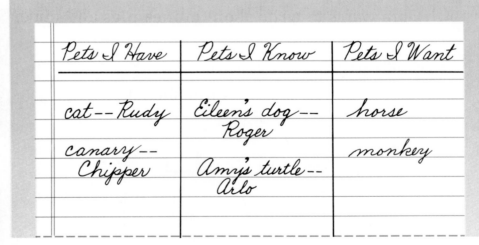

Pets I Have	Pets I Know	Pets I Want
cat -- Rudy	Eileen's dog -- Roger	horse
canary -- Chipper	Amy's turtle -- Arlo	monkey

Jane decided to write about a pet monkey she would like to have. She explored her idea by making a chart.

Exploring Ideas: Charting Strategy

SIGHT	SOUND	SMELL	TOUCH	TASTE
pale face big eyes brown fur	squealing chattering	fruit milk	soft furry	

Before beginning to write, Jane tried to form a clear picture of the monkey. She made some changes in her details chart.

SIGHT	SOUND	SMELL	TOUCH
pale face big eyes brown fur curly tail	squealing chattering	fruit milk	soft furry

Thinking Like a Writer

- What did she add? What did she take out?
- Why do you think she crossed out that part?

YOUR TURN

Think of an animal you would like to describe. Use **Pictures** or your journal for ideas. Follow these steps.

- Make a list of animals. Choose the one you like.
- Remember purpose and audience.

Make a chart. Do not forget that you can add to or take away from your chart at any time.

Write a First Draft: Step 2

Jane made a checklist so that she would remember what to include in her paragraph. Jane is now ready to write her first draft.

Jane's First Draft

My pet monkey, Waldo, has pink ears and a pail face. His big browne eyes look at me playfully. Waldo has the louder squeal I've ever heard. When i feel sad, he puts his arms around my neck. He hugs me. Waldo likes to swing by his curly tail. He smells like bananas, mangos and milk.

Jane put her ideas down on paper. She did not worry about making mistakes. She would revise her paragraph and correct errors later.

Planning Checklist
- Purpose and audience
- Main-idea sentence
- Sensory details sight, sound, touch, smell, taste
- Order of details top-to-bottom

YOUR TURN

Write your first draft. As you begin to write, ask yourself these questions:

- What is my purpose and who is my audience?
- What will my audience want to know?

TIME-OUT You might want to take some time out before you revise. That way you will be able to revise your writing with a fresh eye.

Revise: Step 3

After Jane finished her first draft, she read it to herself. Then, she shared her writing with a classmate. She wanted some suggestions for improving her paragraph.

I wish I had a pet monkey. I wonder what their fur feels like.

That's a good detail to add. Thanks for the idea.

Jane looked back at her planning checklist. She put a check next to *touch* so that she would remember to add this detail when she revised. Jane now has a checklist to use as she revises.

Jane revised her paragraph. Notice that she did not correct any of the small errors yet. She could do this later. Turn the page to see Jane's revised draft.

Revising Checklist
- Purpose and audience
- Main-idea sentence
- Sensory details sight, sound, touch, ✔ smell, taste
- Order of details top-to-bottom

WRITING PROCESS

My pet monkey, Waldo, has pink ears and a pail
face. His big browne eyes look at me playfully.
Waldo has the louder squeal I've ever heard.
When i feel sad, he puts his arms around my
neck. He hugs me. Waldo likes to swing by his
curly tail. He smells like bananas, mangos and milk.

, and   *His brown fur is very soft.*

Thinking Like a Writer

- Which sentence did she add?
- Which sentences did she combine?

YOUR TURN

Read your first draft. Make a checklist. Ask yourself
these questions.

WISE
WORD
CHOICE

- How can I make my description clearer?
- Which sensory details could I add to make my
  paragraph more vivid?

You might want to ask a friend to read your paragraph
and make suggestions before you revise it.

Proofread: Step 4

Jane knew that her work was not complete until she proofread her paragraph. She made a proofreading checklist to use.

Part of Jane's Proofread Draft

My pet monkey, Waldo, has pink ears and a ~~pail~~ *pale* face. His big ~~browne~~ *brown* eyes look at me playfully. Waldo has the ~~louder~~ *loudest* squeal I've ever heard.

When ~~i~~ feel sad, he puts his arms around my neck. ~~He hugs me.~~ *, and He hugs me.* *His brown fur is very soft.* Waldo likes to swing by his curly tail. He smells like bananas, mangos, and milk.

YOUR TURN

Proofreading Practice

Use this paragraph to practice your proofreading skills. Write the corrected paragraph on a separate piece of paper.

> A spotted face look over the treetops. The giraffe eats the green leaves that the antelope, monkey and zebra can not reach. The giraffe is tall than the elephant It is the taller of all the animal.

Proofreading Checklist
- Did I indent my paragraphs?
- Did I spell all words correctly?
- Which punctuation errors do I need to correct?
- Which words do I need to capitalize?

Applying Your Proofreading Skills

Now proofread your descriptive paragraph. Read your checklist again. Review **The Grammar Connection** and **The Mechanics Connection,** too.

Proofreading Marks

⁋ Indent
∧ Add
⅄ Take out
≡ Make a capital letter
/ Make a small letter

THE GRAMMAR CONNECTION

Remember these rules about adjectives.

- To compare two nouns, add *er* to the adjective.
- To compare more than two nouns, add *est* to the adjective.

The elephant is larg**er** than the giraffe.
The giraffe is the tall**est** of all the animals.

Check your descriptive paragraph. Have you used adjectives that compare correctly?

THE MECHANICS CONNECTION

Remember this rule about using commas.

- Use a comma to separate words in a series of three or more words.

The zoo has giraffes, elephants, and crocodiles.

Check your descriptive paragraph. Have you used commas in a series correctly?

Publish: Step 5

Jane copied her paragraph about Waldo neatly. She drew a picture of the monkey and attached it to her paragraph. Jane gave the paragraph and the picture to her cousin when she came over for a visit.

YOUR TURN

Write your final copy in your best handwriting. Think of a way to share your work. You may want to use one of the **Sharing Suggestions** in the box below.

SHARING SUGGESTIONS

Make a greeting card in the shape of your animal. Give the card to a relative.	Add your paragraph with a picture of your animal to a class book of animals.	Write a story for your friends by leaving blank spaces where the name of the animal should go. Have your friends guess the animal.

SPEAKING AND LISTENING:
Listening for Descriptive Details

Poetry is another kind of descriptive writing. Poems describe people, places, or things. Poets use sensory details to help the audience create a vivid picture in their minds.

With a friend, take turns reading and listening to this poem by Karla Kuskin. Pay special attention to the sensory words. Can you picture the dragon in your mind?

The Gold-Tinted Dragon

What's the good of a wagon
Without any dragon
To pull you for mile after mile?
An elegant lean one
A gold-tinted green one
Wearing a dragonly smile.
You'll sweep down the valleys
You'll sail up the hills
Your dragon will shine in the sun
And as you rush by
The people will cry
"I wish that my wagon had one!"

—Karla Kuskin

When you read poetry aloud, keep the following speaking guidelines in mind.

SPEAKING GUIDELINES: Reading Poetry

1. Speak slowly and loudly.
2. Say each word clearly.
3. Practice reading the poem aloud until you can read it without stopping.

- Why is it important to say each word clearly?
- Why should I practice reading the poem aloud?

SPEAKING APPLICATION Reading a Poem

Choose a favorite poem that describes an animal or use "The Gold-Tinted Dragon." Make a list of the sensory words that helped create a picture in your mind. Then, replace each word on the list with another sensory word. How does the picture of the animal change? Read the poem to your classmates with and without your changes. Your classmates will use the following listening guidelines as they listen to your poem.

LISTENING GUIDELINES: Listening to Poetry

1. Listen carefully to what is being read.
2. Listen for sensory details.
3. Use the sensory details to create a picture in your mind.

5 WRITER'S RESOURCES: The Thesaurus

Remember that synonyms are words that have the same or almost the same meaning, and antonyms are words that have opposite meanings. Synonyms and antonyms can be found in a book called a **thesaurus.** A thesaurus can help you find the exact words you want to use to make your writing clearer and more colorful.

In a thesaurus, words are listed in alphabetical order. Under each entry word is a list of synonyms, their definitions, and an example sentence.

big *adj.* of great size. Danny made a **big** pile of leaves.

huge extremely big. That elephant is **huge.**

enormous much greater than the usual size. An **enormous** truck drove up to the house.

large of great size; big. This coat is too **large** for me.

antonyms: *See* **little.**

What are the synonyms for the word **big?** Which synonym would you use if you were describing a dinosaur?

Practice

1. Replace the word **big** in each sentence with a synonym from the thesaurus. Write each sentence.
   a. The *big* elephants pulled up trees with their trunks.
   b. The dinosaurs were *big* animals.
2. Use the thesaurus on page 447. Write two sentences using synonyms for the word *laugh*.
3. Write an antonym for each word.
   a. like
   b. old
   c. hard
   d. quiet

WRITING APPLICATION A Short Story

Pick two words that describe a pet you have or one you know. Use the thesaurus to find words that have similar meanings. Use all the words to write a short story about the pet. You will use it in the **Curriculum Connection** on page 318.

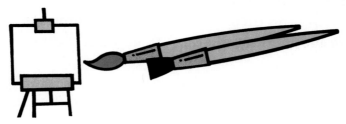

Writing About Art

Writers, painters, and photographers all create pictures. Writers use words. Painters use colors and lines. Photographers use cameras and lights.

Writers often describe paintings and photographs. Their words help an audience to see the work of art. A good writer makes the images clear and vivid to the audience. The audience can then imagine the painting or photograph.

ACTIVITIES

Oral Descriptions   Describe to your class the animal that you wrote about in your story. Include sensory details in your description. Have your classmates guess what animal you are describing.

Describe a Photograph   Make a list of sensory details that would describe the photograph on the next page. Try to include at least one word for each of the senses.

Respond to Literature   The following is from "The Story of Doctor Dolittle" by Hugh Lofting. Dr. Dolittle was a doctor who kept many pets. One day

his parrot, Polynesia, convinced him that he should become an animal doctor. Polynesia taught Doctor Dolittle how to talk to the animals.

The Story of Doctor Dolittle

"But animals don't always speak with their mouths," said the parrot in a high voice, raising her eyebrows. "They talk with their ears, with their feet, with their tails—with everything. Sometimes they don't *want* to make a noise. Do you see now the way he's twitching up one side of his nose?"

"What's that mean?" asked the Doctor.

"That means, 'Can't you see that it has stopped raining?'" Polynesia answered. "He is asking you a question. Dogs nearly always use their noses for asking questions."

Imagine that you could talk to Polynesia. Make a list of four questions that you would ask her.

UNIT CHECKUP

LESSON

Group Writing: A Descriptive Paragraph (page 300)
Read the paragraph. Write the main-idea sentence.

The three-story house made a perfect pet hotel. The attic space was just right for the tropical birds and reptiles. The second story had several rooms for cats and dogs.

LESSON

Thinking: Classifying (page 304)

Write these two groups on a piece of paper: **CITY PETS** and **FARM ANIMALS.** List three animals that could go in each group.

LESSON

Write a Description (page 306)

Imagine that you are a pet dog, cat, or turtle. Write a letter to your master explaining what you want in your living space.

LESSON

Speaking and Listening: Listening for Descriptive Details (page 314)
Why should you practice reading a poem aloud?

LESSON

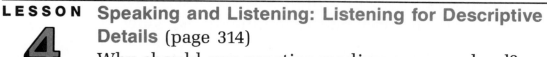

Writer's Resources: The Thesaurus (page 316)
Use the thesaurus on pages 447-454 to find two synonyms for each of these words:

brave   dry   fast   hard

THEME PROJECT

PET TALK

Little Orphan Annie is a character in a comic strip that appears in many newspapers. Annie and her dog, Sandy, are very close to one another. They are almost always together. Look at the comic strip below. What do you think Sandy is saying?

If your pet could talk, what would he or she say?

- Write a conversation between you and your pet.
- Act out the conversation with a friend.
- Have your friend play the part of you. You can play the part of your pet.
- Perform your scene for the class.

UNIT

11

Pronouns

In this unit you will learn about pronouns.
Pronouns are words that take the place of nouns.

Discuss Read the poem on the opposite page. How
do the books you choose tell something about you?

Creative Expression The unit theme is
Favorites. Everyone has something that is a
favorite—a song, a sweater, a fruit, or even a pillow.
Make a poster of some of your favorite things. Ask
your friends to add their favorite things to the poster.
Keep a list of your favorite things in your journal.

THEME: *FAVORITES*

*Reach for a book
on a library shelf
and lose and find
your very own self.*

—Eve Merriam
from "Reach for a Book"

1 WHAT IS A PRONOUN?

A pronoun is a word that takes the place of one or more nouns.

> **Singular Pronouns:** I, you, he, she, it, me, him, her
> **Plural Pronouns:**   we, you, they, us, them

Use a pronoun with the correct form of the verb.

Ned goes to the pond.   The **children** go to the pond.
He goes ice-skating.   **They** go ice-skating, too.

When a verb follows the pronoun *I*, do not add *s* or *es* to the verb.

I go to the pond with Ned.

Guided Practice

Tell which word in each pair is a pronoun.

Example: we, child   *we*

1. him, dance
2. talk, us
3. her, smile
4. they, boy
5. you, kite
6. bird, it
7. me, log
8. see, we

?! THINK

■ How can I decide if a pronoun is singular or plural?

REMEMBER

- A **pronoun** is a word that takes the place of one or more nouns.

More Practice

A. Write the sentences. Draw a line under the pronoun in each sentence.

Example: I like to skate.

9. I shout, "Hooray, hooray."
10. They clap loudly.
11. He makes a figure on the ice.
12. It is an eight.
13. She skates for the medal.
14. You cheer loudly.
15. She gets the medal.

B. Write the sentences. Complete each sentence with the correct verb in ( ).

Example: I (live, lives) in Oregon.   *I live in Oregon.*

16. She (live, lives) in Colorado.
17. He (practice, practices) for the Olympics.
18. They (watch, watches) him practice.
19. I (take, takes) Peter to the tryouts.
20. We (arrive, arrives) early.

Extra Practice, page 342

WRITING APPLICATION A Letter

Write a letter to your favorite sports star. Explain to that star why you are a fan. Exchange letters with a classmate. Circle the pronouns in each other's work.

Debi Thomas,
Olympic athlete

2 SUBJECT PRONOUNS

When you write, you may want to use a pronoun as the subject of the sentence. Use a **subject pronoun** as the subject of a sentence.

Singular Subject Pronouns: I, you, he, she, it
Plural Subject Pronouns: we, you, they

Bob and **Sue** show Lois the animals.
They show Lois the animals.

Lois pets the horse.
She pets the horse.

she

Guided Practice

Tell which word in each sentence is the subject pronoun.

Example: She left the city last summer.   *She*

1. We invite Lois to the farm.
2. She is excited about the visit.
3. They teach Lois about horses.
4. I show Lois the stable.
5. You would like the farm.
6. He rides the pony.

?! THINK

■ How can I decide when to use a subject pronoun?

it

REMEMBER

■ A **subject pronoun** is used as the subject of a sentence.

More Practice

A. Write the sentences. Underline the subject pronoun in each sentence.

Example: <u>He</u> invites Judy to the ranch.

  7. I visit a horse ranch.
  8. They saddle the horses.
  9. He wears a very large hat.
10. We watch a rodeo.
11. We sit on the fence.
12. I call the horse Thunder.
13. It is a beautiful stallion.
14. He holds the reins tightly.
15. They cheer for the horse.

B. Write the sentences. Replace each underlined noun with a subject pronoun.

Example: <u>Farmers</u> work hard. *They work hard.*

16. <u>The farm</u> is a busy place.
17. <u>Ann and Tim</u> work on a farm this summer.
18. <u>The farmer</u> has pigs, cows, and chickens.
19. <u>Ann</u> feeds the pigs and cows.
20. <u>The chickens</u> lay many eggs.

Extra Practice, page 343

WRITING APPLICATION A Journal Entry

Write a journal entry about your favorite summer activity. Describe the activity and why you enjoy it.

3 OBJECT PRONOUNS

You know that you can use a subject pronoun as the subject of a sentence. Use an **object pronoun** after an action verb or words such as *for, at, of, with,* and *to.*

> **Singular Object Pronouns:** me, you, him, her, it
> **Plural Object Pronouns:**   us, you, them

Sandy plays the **violin** well.
Sandy plays **it** well.

Sandy played for **Dan** and **Sue.**
Sandy played for **them.**

The pronouns *you* and *it* can be used as both subject pronouns and object pronouns.

violin

it

Guided Practice

Tell which word in each sentence is an object pronoun.

Example: Sandy showed her the beautiful violin.   *her*

1. Sandy has played it for three years.
2. Donna watches her practice every day.
3. The teacher encourages her.
4. Mrs. Jones invites you to the concert.
5. Please play for us.
6. The teacher listens to them.

?! THINK

■ How can I decide when to use an object pronoun?

REMEMBER

■ An **object pronoun** is used after an action verb or words such as *for, at, of, with,* and *to.*

More Practice

A. Write the sentences. Underline the object pronouns.

Example: The music makes <u>her</u> smile.

  7. Carl and Ann tune the violins for us.
  8. Carl plays the horn for her.
  9. Carl blows it loudly.
 10. Carl calls to us.
 11. Luis stands behind him.
 12. Luis plays with me.
 13. Jack plays two instruments for you.
 14. Jack plays them at the concert.

B. Write the sentences. Replace the underlined word or words with the correct object pronoun in ( ).

Example: Joe likes <u>music</u>. (it, her)   *Joe likes it.*

 15. My sister plays <u>the violin</u>. (it, us)
 16. She plays the violin with <u>Tom</u>. (him, it)
 17. He sings with <u>Ann and Gail</u>. (them, you)
 18. I sing a song with <u>Tony</u>. (them, him)
 19. My father listens to <u>my sister and me</u>. (us, her)
 20. My sister enjoys <u>the recital</u>. (me, it)

Extra Practice, page 344

WRITING APPLICATION A Review

Write a review of a concert. Describe the instruments and how they sounded. Underline the object pronouns.

4 POSSESSIVE PRONOUNS

A **possessive pronoun** takes the place of a possessive noun. A possessive pronoun shows who or what owns something.

⇨ Use the pronouns *her, his, your, my,* and *its* to take the place of singular possessive nouns.

⇨ Use the pronouns *their, your,* and *our* to take the place of plural possessive nouns.

> **His** favorite book is about King Arthur.
> That is **our** favorite book, too.

Guided Practice

Tell the possessive pronoun in each sentence.

Example: Your book is on the shelf.   *Your*

1. Which is your favorite King Arthur tale?
2. Her favorite is about the Round Table.
3. Arthur had a Round Table for his knights.
4. It was in his castle.
5. Arthur solved their problems at the table.
6. Our book has many tales.

?! THINK

■ How can I decide when to use a possessive pronoun?

REMEMBER

■ A **possessive pronoun** shows who or what owns something.

More Practice

A. Write the sentences. Draw a line under each possessive pronoun.

Example: <u>His</u> life was exciting.

  7. My favorite tale is about Merlin.
  8. I like the story about his bird.
  9. Our class read it last week.
10. His bird fascinates me.
11. My bird speaks one language.
12. Your bird does, too.
13. His bird speaks many languages.
14. Its vocabulary is amazing.

B. Write the sentences. Change the underlined possessive noun to a possessive pronoun.

Example: <u>Al's</u> book is here.   *His book is here.*

15. <u>Dawn's</u> class read about Sir Lancelot.
16. <u>Lancelot's</u> strength was remarkable.
17. He is <u>the children's</u> favorite knight.
18. They liked <u>Lancelot's</u> good deeds.
19. <u>The boys'</u> class wanted him to save Guinevere.
20. <u>Darren's</u> book had colorful drawings.

Extra Practice, Practice Plus, pages 345–347

WRITING APPLICATION A Note

With your class, write a note to your favorite author. Circle the possessive pronouns.

COOPERATIVE
LEARNING

5 MECHANICS: Contractions

A **contraction** is a shortened form of two words. One or more letters are left out and an apostrophe (') takes their place.

I + am = **I'm**	they + are = **they're**	I + will = **I'll**
he + is = **he's**	we + are = **we're**	it + will = **it'll**
it + is = **it's**	she + will = **she'll**	you + have = **you've**
she + is = **she's**	you + will = **you'll**	we + have = **we've**
she + has = **she's**	he + will = **he'll**	they + have = **they've**
he + has = **he's**	we + will = **we'll**	I + have = **I've**
you + are = **you're**	they + will = **they'll**	

Guided Practice

Tell which contraction would replace the underlined words in each sentence.

Example: <u>She will</u> pack for the trip. *She'll*

1. <u>They will</u> visit the Grand Canyon.
2. <u>It is</u> located in Colorado.
3. <u>We will</u> take many pictures.
4. <u>You have</u> never seen such a sight!

 THINK

- How can I decide where to place the apostrophe (') in a contraction?

REMEMBER

■ A **contraction** is a shortened form of two words.
■ One or more letters are left out and an apostrophe (') takes their place.

More Practice

Write the sentences. Write the two words that make up each contraction.

Example: I've had a great time.   *I have*

5. She's gone on vacation.
6. We've been to a special place.
7. It's called Muir Woods.
8. You'll see redwood trees.
9. They're very tall trees.
10. We'll meet with Ms. Monroe.
11. She's a park ranger in Muir Woods.
12. She'll show us around.
13. I'll visit one of the nature classes.
14. I'm writing a report for school.
15. You've never seen such trees anywhere.
16. I've noticed the wildflowers.
17. We're surprised at the colors.
18. He's watching a deer.
19. You're lucky to see the park.
20. I'm glad I saw a deer.

Extra Practice, page 348

WRITING APPLICATION A Poster

Create a poster for a wildlife park. Explain why people should go there on vacation. Describe how the park looks. Underline the contractions in your work.

6 VOCABULARY BUILDING: Homophones

Words that sound alike but have different spellings and different meanings are called **homophones**. The other words in a sentence can help you determine the meaning of each homophone.

The **pear** was delicious.
That is a pretty **pair** of shoes.

Is there something in your **eye**?
I will help you.

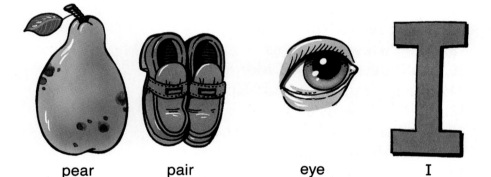

pear   pair   eye   I

Guided Practice

Tell which pairs of words are homophones.

Example: pair, pear   *homophones*

1. eye, I
2. up, under
3. be, bee
4. blue, blew
5. rode, road

6. hole, whole
7. afraid, scared
8. hard, soft
9. break, brake
10. look, see

?! THINK

■ How can I decide which words are homophones?

REMEMBER

■ **Homophones** are words that sound alike but have different spellings and different meanings.

More Practice

A. Write the sentences. Underline the homophone in each sentence that matches a homophone in the box.

Example: Have you <u>seen</u> the desert?

> nose   hole   sea   buy   flour   scene

11. I can hardly wait to see Arizona.
12. Alan knows all about the desert.
13. The whole place looks so flat.
14. A lizard runs by us.
15. This cactus has a flower.

B. Write the sentences. Complete each sentence with the correct homophone in ( ).

Example: Chop _____ for the fire. (would, wood)
Chop wood for the fire.

16. We travel up a winding _____ . (road, rode)
17. The color of the sunset is _____ . (read, red)
18. The desert sun _____ unreal to me. (seems, seams)
19. A desert gets very little _____ . (rain, rein)
20. Plants carry water in _____ stems. (there, their)

Extra Practice, page 349

 WRITING APPLICATION A Story

Write a story about the desert. Describe some of the things you would find there. Have a friend name any homophones in your story.

COOPERATIVE LEARNING

VOCABULARY: Homophones

Using *I* and *me*

When you talk about yourself, you use the pronouns *I* and *me*.

I collect stamps.
People ask **me** questions about stamps.
Dennis and **I** share stamps.

I is always written with a capital letter. When you talk about yourself and someone else, always name yourself last.

To help you decide whether to use *I* or *me* in a sentence, try the sentence without the other noun.

Bob asked **Denise and me** for stamps.
Bob asked **me** for stamps.

Working Together

COOPERATIVE
LEARNING

With your classmates, talk about when to use *I* and *me*. Then, use **I** or **me** to complete each sentence.

Example: José and _____ collect stamps.
José and I collect stamps.

1. Mr. Dent showed José and _____ a rare stamp.
2. Mr. Dent told _____ the price of the stamp.
3. _____ bought it for my collection.

Revising Sentences

Gina is writing about her grandmother's roller skates. Help Gina complete her story by adding **I** or **me** to each sentence.

4. Mandy and _____ collect old toys.
5. _____ searched two weeks for a toy.
6. Grandma gave _____ her roller skates.
7. She told Mandy and _____ about the skates.
8. Mandy and _____ laughed at the wooden wheels.
9. Mandy followed _____ on her skateboard.
10. _____ skated down the block.

Write a letter to a friend telling him or her about something you collect. Circle the pronouns *I* and *me* in your letter.

UNIT CHECKUP

LESSON **What Is a Pronoun?** (page 324) Write the sentences.

1
Underline the pronouns.

1. He plays on a basketball team.
2. They play for two hours.
3. We think Earl is the best player.
4. Mr. Charles gave him a basketball.
5. Carla asked him for an autograph.
6. She is a big fan.
7. Look for me at the game tonight.

LESSON **Subject Pronouns** (page 326) Write each sentence

2
with the correct verb in ( ).

8. She (wear, wears) a swimsuit.
9. I (follow, follows) Mike to the beach.
10. We (run, runs) into the ocean.
11. He (swim, swims) to a boat.
12. It (float, floats) near the shore.
13. You (play, plays) in the waves.
14. They (splash, splashes) in the cold water.

LESSON **Object Pronouns** (page 328) Write each sentence

3
with the correct object pronoun in ( ).

15. Jane gave _____ a nickname. (her, she)
16. The nature walks fascinated _____ . (we, me)
17. We collected rocks and labeled _____ . (them, us)
18. We lit a fire and sang around _____ . (them, it)
19. We invited _____ to sing. (him, it)

Possessive Pronouns (page 330) Write the sentences. Underline the possessive pronouns.

20. My family owns a horse.
21. Its name is Misty.
22. Our friend teaches Misty tricks.
23. His goal is to win a race.
24. My sister brushes Misty.
25. Her hands work quickly.

Mechanics: Contractions (page 332) Write the words that form each contraction.

26. we're	30. I'm	34. they'll
27. you'll	31. you're	35. I've
28. they're	32. she's	36. we'll
29. he's	33. we've	37. I'll

Vocabulary Building: Homophones (page 334) Write the sentences. Complete each sentence with the correct homophone in ( ).

38. _____ is your life jacket. (Here, Hear)
39. Pull up the _____ . (sale, sail)
40. _____ is the anchor? (Where, Wear)

Writing Application: Pronoun Usage (pages 324–332) The following paragraph contains 10 errors with pronouns. Rewrite the paragraph correctly.

41.–50.   They goes skating around the pond. He bring extra socks and two pairs of gloves. She take a warm jacket with she. We practices skating backwards. I invites Carl to skate with we. Hes eager to skate with we. Donna ties her skates for him.

OLD FRIENDS

Think of a favorite storybook character. Imagine that you meet this character. Tell a friend about your meeting. Describe what you and your character did. Tell where you went and what you saw. Use the pronouns *I, he, she, you, we,* and *they* when you tell your story.

Hear, Here!

Play this game with a friend. Tell your friend the first sentence of a story. Include homophones in your sentence. For example, you might say *I see the sea from my window.* Have your friend continue the story. Make sure the new sentence has homophones. Take turns adding sentences with homophones to the story.

COMIC FUN

Choose a favorite cartoon character. Make up a cartoon strip about the character. Draw your cartoon character. Write what your character is saying. Use some of the pronouns below.

He, she, they, us, we, them, it, our

You Name It!

Choose three contestants for your game show. You will be the host. First, write some questions about your school on index cards. Use pronouns instead of common and proper nouns. One question might be: *They* score lots of runs. (Answer: the baseball team.) Number each question and have the contestants take turns choosing and answering questions.

Handy Homophones

Trace and cut out six outlines of your hand. Have a friend do the same thing. Then think of three homophone pairs and write one word on each hand. Put all the hands together face down. Take turns picking two hands. When you pick a homophone pair, clap the hands together.

G R A M M A R

Three levels of practice

What Is a Pronoun? (page 324)

LEVEL
A. Write each sentence. Draw a line under the pronoun in each sentence.

1. I like blueberries.
2. They are Sue's favorite fruit.
3. Do you like blueberries?
4. We could make a pie.
5. She made a dessert called Blueberry Buckle.
6. It was delicious.
7. He finished the dessert quickly.

LEVEL
B. Write the sentences. Complete each sentence with the correct verb in ( ).

8. She (eat, eats) the last peach.
9. It (taste, tastes) sweet.
10. He (like, likes) blueberries in his cereal.
11. They (finish, finishes) the strawberries.
12. I (buy, buys) more strawberries.
13. You (bake, bakes) delicious pies.
14. She (give, gives) Joe a piece of pie.

LEVEL
C. Write the sentences. Complete each sentence with the correct pronoun in ( ).

15. _____ am very happy. (We, I)
16. _____ are on the way home. (We, He)
17. _____ look for blackberries. (She, They)
18. _____ gathers many blackberries. (We, He)
19. _____ help pick the berries. (She, They)
20. Let _____ carry the blackberries. (they, me)

EXTRA PRACTICE

Three levels of practice
Subject Pronouns (page 326)

LEVEL A. Write the sentences. Underline the subject pronoun in each sentence.

1. We like the beach.
2. I always bring a big umbrella.
3. You get sunburned at the beach.
4. We found many starfish at the beach.
5. They are very beautiful.
6. She collects shells.
7. He helps carry the shells.

LEVEL B. Write the sentences. Complete each sentence with the correct subject pronoun in ( ).

8. _____ jumps the waves. (I, He)
9. _____ are very high. (They, It)
10. _____ jump the waves with Donald. (It, I)
11. _____ splash water at each other. (He, We)
12. _____ is so much fun! (You, It)
13. _____ join the fun. (You, It)
14. _____ goes into the water. (She, They)

LEVEL C. Replace each underlined noun with a subject pronoun.

15. Anne plays in the water.
16. Shells wash up onto the beach.
17. Jason finds a beautiful shell.
18. Donald and I are hungry.
19. The sun sinks in the sky.
20. Donald builds a sand castle.

EXTRA PRACTICE

Three levels of practice

Object Pronouns (page 328)

LEVEL A. Write the sentences. Underline the object pronouns.

1. Carl explained the hobby to you.
2. He showed them the ring.
3. The new hobby interests him.
4. Dana showed the necklace to me.
5. Dana showed the beads to her.
6. Carl helped him make jewelry.
7. Carl will explain it.
8. Carl will teach us.

LEVEL B. Replace each underlined noun with the correct object pronoun in ( ).

9. I will draw cartoons. (it, them)
10. The art teacher helps Jane and me. (him, us)
11. I draw a cartoon. (it, them)
12. My work pleases the teacher. (they, her)
13. The teacher smiles at Paul. (us, him)
14. I show the cartoon to Dad. (you, him)
15. He proudly shows it to Amy and Jan. (them, me)

LEVEL C. Complete each pair of sentences with an object pronoun.

16. I want to make a puppet.
    I will make _____ out of papier-mâché.
17. First, I'll cut newspapers into strips.
    Then, I'll soak _____ in water.
18. My mother gave Carol and me glue.
    She also gave colored paper to _____ .
19. I tell Al about my project. I ask _____ for advice.
20. Al helps me. He shows _____ what to do.

EXTRA PRACTICE

Three levels of practice

Possessive Pronouns (page 330)

LEVEL A. Write the sentences. Draw a line under the possessive pronoun in each sentence.

1. What is your favorite game?
2. Mary and I work on our computer.
3. Mary writes her story.
4. My story is ready.
5. Rick needs the computer for his homework.
6. Their computer is very busy.
7. Its memory has a lot of information.
8. My homework is finished.

LEVEL B. Write the sentences. Change each underlined possessive noun to a possessive pronoun.

9. Rick's computer game is fun.
10. Mary's moves are excellent.
11. The children's smiles are bright.
12. The computer's lights flash.
13. Mary's sister joins the game.
14. Rick's fingers hurry over the keys.
15. Our parents' stories make us laugh.
16. The girls' laughter is loud.

LEVEL C. Write the sentences. Complete each pair of sentences with a possessive pronoun.

17. I tell Dad about the game. He says _____ game is fun.

18. Mary and I are on one team. _____ team will win.

19. Mom turns on the computer. _____ lights flash.

20. You can make up a game, too. _____ game can be as much fun as ours!

PRACTICE + PLUS

Three levels of additional practice for a difficult skill

Possessive Pronouns (page 330)

LEVEL
A. Write the sentences. Draw a line under the possessive pronoun in each sentence.

1. Where are my suitcases?
2. Did you pack your bags?
3. Dad wants to visit his hometown.
4. The town will celebrate its history.
5. Our family will spend the weekend.
6. Do not forget your camera!
7. I can see the parade from my seat.
8. Mom waves her flag.
9. Two boys bang their drums.
10. Another boy plays his flute.
11. The mayor gives her speech.
12. Her words thrill the crowd.
13. Dad claps his hands.
14. Mom takes our picture.
15. My father's hometown is a great place!
16. Do you like your hometown?
17. Her hometown has many tall buildings.
18. Their house is in the country.
19. Our backyard has a huge rose garden.
20. Many birds play in my birdhouse.
21. Our friends watch the birds.
22. Birds splash in their birdbath.
23. A robin feeds her babies.
24. Her feathers are red.
25. The backyard is my favorite place.

PRACTICE + PLUS

LEVEL
B. Write the sentences. Change the underlined possessive noun to a possessive pronoun.

26. <u>Tim's</u> science project is fascinating.
27. It is more interesting than <u>Pete's</u>.
28. The <u>children's</u> help is necessary.
29. <u>Lucy's</u> toolbox has the correct tools.
30. <u>Bill's</u> beakers are the right size.
31. <u>Mr. Berg's</u> ideas are valuable.
32. Tim needs <u>Brad's</u> book.
33. <u>My friends'</u> eyes are on Tim.
34. Tim shakes <u>the principal's</u> hand.
35. Tim makes <u>the newspaper's</u> front page.

LEVEL
C. Write the sentences. Complete each pair of sentences with a possessive pronoun.

36. My family enjoys gardening.
What does _____ family enjoy doing?
37. We have a big vegetable garden.
_____ vegetables are delicious.
38. Mom eats a tomato.
She enjoys _____ taste.
39. I often help with the garden.
_____ job is easy.
40. Friends help pick the vegetables.
They don't mind using _____ hands.

GRAMMAR

Three levels of practice
Mechanics: Contractions (page 332)

LEVEL A. Write the sentences. Draw one line under the contraction in each sentence.

1. He's lost his way.
2. It's hard to read the compass.
3. We've got to find the right trail.
4. She's got a good sense of direction.
5. Soon, we'll be back at the camp.
6. They'll be happy when we return.

LEVEL B. Write the sentences with a contraction in place of the underlined words.

7. They have been waiting for us.
8. They are happy to see us.
9. We have been gone a while.
10. I am so hungry.
11. She will get your dinner.
12. We have had a big adventure.
13. You have been so brave!

LEVEL C. Complete each sentence with a contraction.

14. _____ finished dinner.
15. _____ watched the sun go down.
16. _____ sit around the campfire.
17. _____ dark outside.
18. _____ sing songs.
19. _____ a good singer.
20. _____ sing another song.

EXTRA PRACTICE

Three levels of practice
Vocabulary Building: Homophones (pages 334)

LEVEL A. Write each sentence. Underline the homophones in each sentence.

1. Lee's favorite aunt sent her an ant farm.
2. Lee will write to her aunt right away.
3. Eight ants escaped and ate Mom's plant.
4. The whole group escaped through a hole.
5. Would they hide in the woodpile?
6. Two children tried to find them.

LEVEL B. Write the sentences. Complete each sentence with the correct homophone in ( ).

7. Aunt Tess, I think (you're, your) the best.
8. You are a (deer, dear) person to send me the ant farm.
9. Some ants got out through a (whole, hole).
10. Should I (by, buy) an anteater?
11. What (would, wood) you do?
12. It is hard (to, two) find them.
13. I know they are (here, hear).

LEVEL C. Write the sentences. Write the correct homophone for each underlined word.

14. Hear is how you catch the ants.
15. You need an aunt trap.
16. By one at the local store.
17. Put it in the flour bed.
18. You're problem will be solved.
19. Keep the ants in a pale.
20. Right and tell me what happens.

UNIT
12

Writing Book Reports

Read the quotation and look at the picture on the opposite page. Julius Lester's favorite stories were the folk tales his father used to tell. Now he is sharing his favorite things by writing them in books.

A book report is a way of sharing a book with others.

Focus A book report tells more than just the title and author of the book. It also tells something about the story and your opinion of the book.

Which of your favorite books would you like to tell a friend about? The story and the photographs in this unit may give you some ideas for writing.

THEME: *FAVORITES*

*The readers of my books receive the
best of me. I hope that they bring
the best of themselves to my books.*

—Julius Lester

LITERATURE

Reading Like a Writer

AWARD WINNING SELECTION

What would you like to change about yourself? The knee-high man wants to be bigger than he is. How do you think he feels as he looks for ways to become bigger?

from The Knee-High Man

by Julius Lester

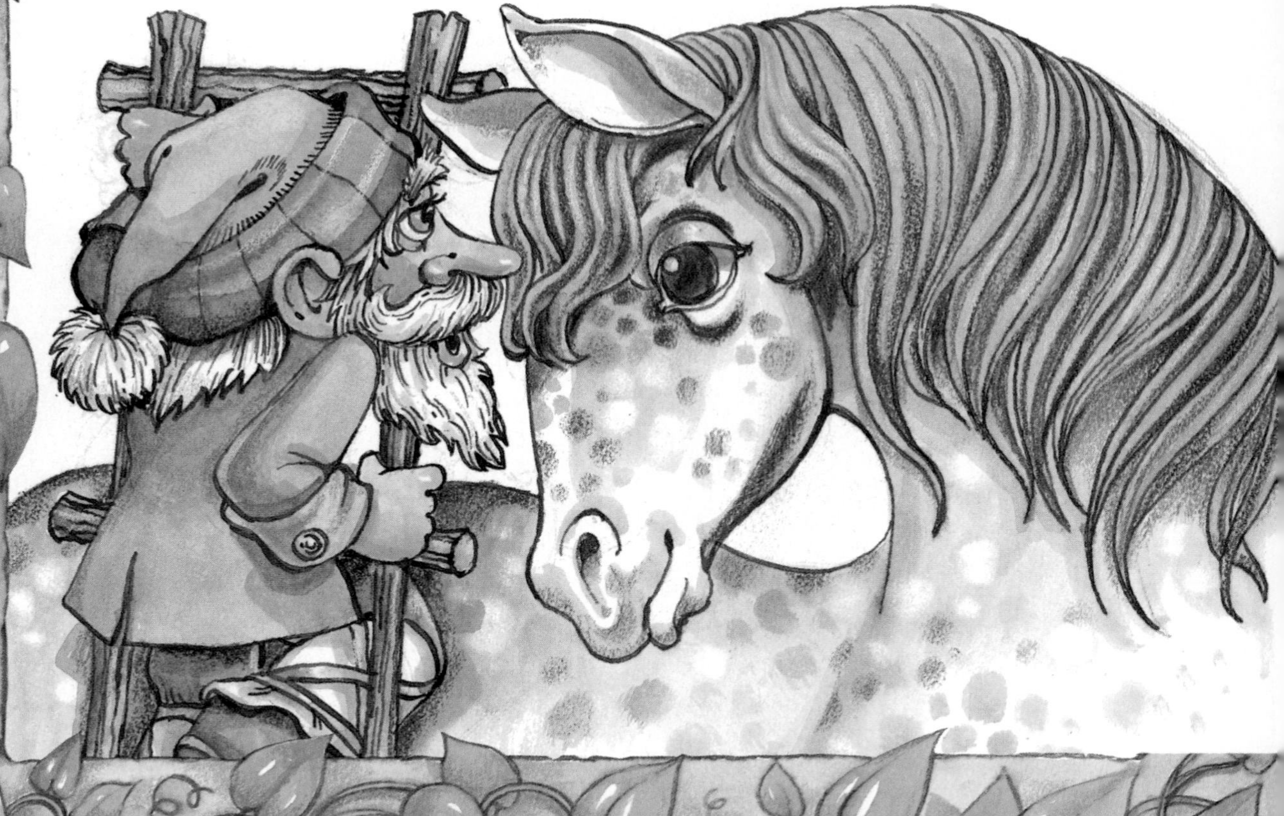

These details could be used in a book report.

Once upon a time there was a knee-high man. He was no taller than a person's knees. Because he was so short, he was very unhappy. He wanted to be big like everyone else.

One day he decided to ask the biggest animal he could find how he could get big. So he went to see Mr. Horse. "Mr. Horse, how can I get big like you?"

Mr. Horse said, "Well, eat a whole lot of corn. Then run around a lot. After a while you'll be as big as me."

The knee-high man did just that. He ate so much corn that his stomach hurt. Then he ran and ran and ran until his legs hurt. But he didn't get any bigger. So he decided that Mr. Horse had told him something wrong. He decided to go ask Mr. Bull.

"Mr. Bull? How can I get big like you?"

Mr. Bull said, "Eat a whole lot of grass. Then bellow and bellow as loud as you can can. The first thing you know, you'll be as big as me."

So the knee-high man ate a whole field of grass. That made his stomach hurt. He bellowed and bellowed and bellowed all day and night. That made his throat hurt. But he didn't get any bigger. So he decided that Mr. Bull was all wrong too.

Now he didn't know anyone else to ask. One night he heard Mr. Hoot Owl hooting, and he remembered that Mr. Owl knew everything. "Mr. Owl? How can I get big like Mr. Horse and Mr. Bull?"

"What do you want to be big for?" Mr. Hoot Owl asked.

"I want to be big so that when I get into a fight, I can whip everybody," the knee-high man said.

Mr. Hoot Owl hooted. "Anybody ever try to pick a fight with you?"

The knee-high man thought a minute. "Well, now that you mention it, nobody ever did try to start a fight with me."

Mr. Owl said, "Well, you don't have any reason to fight. Therefore, you don't have any reason to be bigger than you are."

"But, Mr. Owl," the knee-high man said, "I want to be big so I can see far into the distance."

Mr. Hoot Owl hooted. "If you climb a tall tree, you can see into the distance from the top."

The knee-high man was quiet for a minute. "Well, I hadn't thought of that."

Mr. Hoot Owl hooted again. "And that's what is

In a book report, remember not to give away the ending.

wrong, Mr. Knee-High Man. You hadn't done any thinking at all. I'm smaller than you, and you don't see me worrying about being big. Mr. Knee-High Man, you wanted something that you didn't need."

Thinking Like a Reader

1. Do you think Mr. Hoot Owl gave the knee-high man good advice? Why or why not?

2. Has anyone ever given you advice about a similar problem? Did you think it was good advice? Why or why not?

Write your responses in your journal.

Thinking Like a Writer

3. Why does the writer have the knee-high man do funny things?

4. What is the writer saying about the importance of the knee-high man's wish to become big?

Write your responses in your journal.

Brainstorm *Vocabulary*

The knee-high man wanted to get big. Think of as many synonyms as you can for the word *big*. Then, think of as many antonyms as you can. Write these words in a personal vocabulary list. Choose another word from the story. Think of as many synonyms and antonyms as you can for that word. You can use these words in your writing.

Talk It Over *Read Aloud*

Work with your classmates to read aloud "The Knee-High Man." Choose students to read the parts of each animal and the knee-high man. Have another student read the rest of the story. Try to speak as you think the characters in the story would speak.

Quick Write
For and Against

Write three reasons why you think it might be fun to be bigger than you are. Then, write three reasons why you think it might be fun to be smaller than you are. Read each reason to a friend. Have your friend decide which reasons make the most sense.

Idea Corner
Becoming Different

The knee-high man wanted to be something that he was not. Think of other stories or books that you have read in which someone wanted to change. Did you agree with the change that they wanted to make? Why are people often better off staying the way they are? Keep the titles of these stories and books in your writing folder.

PICTURES

SEEING LIKE A WRITER

Finding Ideas for Writing

Look at the pictures. Think about what you see.
What ideas for writing a book report
do the pictures give you?
Write your ideas in your journal.

PICTURES: Ideas for Writing Book Reports

1 GROUP WRITING: A Book Report

The **purpose** of a book report is to tell other people about a book that you have read. You want to convince your **audience** to read the book. Book reports tell the title, author, and something about the story. They also tell why you liked the book. What should you include when you want to recommend a book to others?

COOPERATIVE LEARNING

- Clear Summary
- Convincing Opinion

Clear Summary

Look at the book report Ron wrote.

> **Title: The Good-Luck Pencil**
> **Author: Diane Stanley**
>
> This book is about a girl who finds a magic pencil. Mary Ann thinks her life is dull and wishes for things that would make it exciting. She wishes that her mother was a famous ballerina, her father was an astronaut, and she was a champion piano player. At the end of the book, Mary Ann realizes that her dull life isn't so bad.
>
> I really liked this book. It was funny and exciting. The pictures were colorful. My favorite part was when Mary Ann's life went back to the way it was before. I think everyone should read The Good-Luck Pencil.

Ron began his book report with the title of the book and the author. In the first paragraph he gave a **summary**, or told what the book was about. He included all of the events that he thought someone who wanted to read the book should know.

Guided Practice: Writing a Summary

With your classmates, talk about books that you have read and liked. Choose one book. Write a three-sentence summary of the book. Be sure to include the most important details.

Convincing Opinion

When you want someone to agree with you, you use **persuasive language** to convince the person of your opinion. You use specific words to tell the person why you feel the way you do.

Look back at Ron's book report. The second paragraph tells why he thinks other people should read the book.

- Which words tell you how Ron felt about *The Good-Luck Pencil*?
- Did Ron persuade you to read the book?
- Which part of Ron's book report persuaded you to read the book?

Guided Practice: Writing a Convincing Opinion

Look back at the book you chose with your classmates. Write an opinion about the book that would persuade someone to read it. Remember to use persuasive language as you give your opinion.

Putting a Book Report Together

You and your classmates have written a summary of a book. You have given your opinion about the book. You have also tried to persuade someone to read the book. Are there any details that you would like to add to your summary? Is there anything else you would like to add in order to persuade someone to read the book?

Ron made the following cover for his book report.

Guided Practice: Writing a Book Report

Use your summary and convincing opinion to write a book report for the book you chose with your class. Be sure to include the title and author. Make a cover for your report.

Have a friend read your book report. Did your convincing opinion persuade him or her to read the book?

CHECKLIST: A Book Report

When you write a book report, there are some points you will want to remember. To help you remember what to include in a book report, you can make a checklist.

Look at this checklist. Finish it and keep it in your writing folder. You now have a checklist to use when you write a book report.

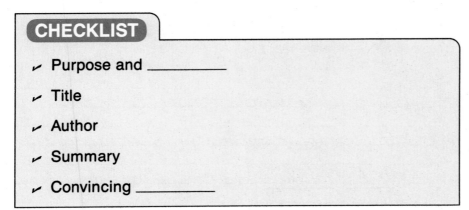

CHECKLIST

- ✓ Purpose and _____
- ✓ Title
- ✓ Author
- ✓ Summary
- ✓ Convincing _____

2 THINKING AND WRITING: Telling Fact from Opinion

Facts are statements that can be proved true. **Opinions** tell what people think or believe. Opinions cannot be proved.

The following page from a writer's journal has notes for a book report.

> 1. Biographies are the best books to read.
>
> 2. A biography is the story of someone's life.
>
> 3. *Arthur Mitchell* was written by Tobi Tobias.
>
> 4. Tobi Tobias is a good writer.
>
> 5. *Arthur Mitchell* is my favorite book.

Sentences 2 and 3 are facts. You can look up the meaning of the word *biography* in the dictionary. You can look in the card catalog to prove that Tobi Tobias wrote that book.

Sentences 1, 4, and 5 are the opinions of the writer. You may agree or disagree with opinions.

Thinking Like a Writer

- Which part of a book report gives facts?
- Which part of a book report gives opinions?

THINKING APPLICATION Telling Fact from Opinion

Four students are writing book reports. Help each student decide which sentences are facts and which are opinions. Discuss your thoughts with your classmates. Write your ideas on a separate piece of paper.

1. David is writing a book report about Arthur Mitchell. Which sentences in David's report are facts?
   a. Arthur Mitchell danced with the New York City Ballet Company.
   b. He started the Dance Theater of Harlem.
   c. The Dance Theater of Harlem is the best dance company in New York.

2. June is writing about the photographer, Gordon Parks. Which sentence in June's book report is an opinion?
   a. Gordon Parks is the best photographer in the country.
   b. Gordon Parks won many awards.
   c. He told the story of black people.

3. Alan is writing a book report about Helen Keller. Alan wants his report to contain only facts. Which sentences should he include?
   a. Anne Sullivan taught Helen Keller how to read Braille.
   b. Anne was the best friend Helen ever had.
   c. Anne taught Helen Keller sign language.

4. Holly's book report is about plants. She needs one more opinion. Which sentence is an opinion?
   a. Plants give us most of our food.
   b. Plants give us wood.
   c. Plants are pretty to look at.

3 INDEPENDENT WRITING: A Book Report

Prewrite: Step 1

You have learned some important points about writing a book report. Now think about your favorite book. This is how Ken chose a favorite book to share with his friends.

Choosing a Book

1. First, Ken thought of his favorite books.
2. Next, he listed the detail he liked best from each book.
3. Then, he chose a book to write about.

Ken chose a book called *The Dream Eater* by Christian Garrison. He thought about which details he wanted to include in his book report.

Exploring Ideas: Listing Strategy

> The Dream Eater
>
> 1. A boy named Yukio has bad dreams.
> 2. Everyone in his village also has nightmares.
> 3. Yukio meets a baku that eats dreams.
> 4. The baku eats all the bad dreams.

Ken thought that he had included many important details in his list. Before beginning to write, he thought more about the story. He decided to add another detail.

The Dream Eater

1. A boy named Yukio has bad dreams about two monsters.

2. Everyone in his village also has nightmares.

3. Yukio meets a baku that eats dreams.

4. The baku eats all the bad dreams.

Thinking Like a Writer

- What did he add?
- Why did he add that part?

YOUR TURN

Choose a book you would like to read. Use **Pictures** or your journal for ideas. Follow these steps.

- Think of your favorite books.
- List one detail from each book.
- Choose the book you want to share with your friends.
- Think about your purpose and audience.

Read the book. Make a list of the details in the book. Remember you can add to or take away from your list at any time.

Write a First Draft: Step 2

Ken used a planning checklist so he would remember to include everything in his book report. Ken is now ready to write his first draft.

Ken's First Draft

Title: The Dream Eater
Author: Christian Garrison

This book is about a village where all the people have Nightmares. A boy named Yukio has a dream. He dreams about two monsters. Yukio meets a baku that Eats dreems.

me enjoyed reading this book. The pictures was very exciting.

Ken did not worry about errors as he wrote. He knew he could revise and correct errors later.

Planning Checklist
■ Purpose and audience
■ Title
■ Author
■ Summary
■ Convincing opinion

YOUR TURN

Write your first draft. As you write, ask yourself:

■ What will my audience want to know?
■ What is the best way to give my opinion?

TIME-OUT You might want to take some time out before you revise. That way you will be able to revise your writing with a fresh eye.

Revise: Step 3

After Ken finished his first draft, he read it over to himself. Then, he shared his writing with a classmate. He wanted some suggestions for improving his book report.

Ken looked at his planning checklist once more. He checked off **Convincing opinion** so he would remember that when he revises. Ken now has a checklist to use as he revises.

Ken made some changes in his report. He did not correct the small errors. He would do this later. Turn the page. Look at Ken's revised draft.

Revising Checklist
- ■ Purpose and audience
- ■ Title
- ■ Author
- ■ Summary
- ✓ ■ Convincing opinion

Ken's Revised Draft

Title: The Dream Eater
Author: Christian Garrison

This book is about a village where all the people have Nightmares. A boy named Yukio has a dream. He dreams about two monsters. Yukio meets a baku that Eats dreems.

me enjoyed reading this book. The pictures was very exciting. My favorite part was when the baku ate the dreams.

Thinking Like a Writer

WISE
WORD
CHOICE

- Which sentence did Ken add?
- Which sentences did he combine? How does this improve the paragraph?

YOUR TURN

Read your first draft. Make a checklist. Ask yourself:

- How can I make my summary clearer?
- Will my audience want to read the book?

You might want to ask a friend to read your report and make suggestions before you revise it.

Proofread: Step 4

Ken knew that he needed to proofread his book report. He used a proofreading checklist while he proofread.

Part of Ken's Proofread Draft

people have Nightmares. A boy named Yukio has a dream. He dreams about two monsters. Yukio meets a baku that Eats dreems *(dreams)*.

I me enjoyed reading this book. The pictures *were* was very exciting. My favorite part was when the baku ate the dreams.

YOUR TURN

Proofreading Practice

Use this paragraph to practice your proofreading skills. Write the corrected paragraph on another piece of paper.

> I wrote a letter to Grandma betty, Aunt sarah, and Uncle Sid. I told them me was reading *Charlotte's Web* by e.b. White. Me birthday was too weeks later. They sent I other books by E.B. white.

Proofreading Checklist
- Did I indent my paragraphs?
- Which words do I need to capitalize?
- What punctuation errors do I need to correct?
- Did I spell all words correctly?

Applying Your Proofreading Skills

Now proofread your book report. Read your checklist again. Review **The Grammar Connection** and **The Mechanics Connection,** too. Use the proofreading marks to show changes.

THE GRAMMAR CONNECTION

Remember these rules about using *I* and *me.*

- Use **I** in the subject of the sentence.
- Use **me** in the predicate of the sentence.

   I read a good book.
   Nathan gave the book to **me.**

Check your book report. Have you used *I* and *me* correctly?

THE MECHANICS CONNECTION

Remember these rules about writing titles.

- Use a capital letter to begin the first word and each important word in a title.
- Underline the title of a book.

   <u>The Dream Eater</u>   <u>The Good-Luck Pencil</u>

Check your book report. Have you used capital letters in your book title correctly?

Proofreading Marks

- ¶ Indent
- ∧ Add
- ℐ Take out
- ≡ Make a capital letter
- / Make a small letter

Publish: Step 5

Ken made a poster for *The Dream Eater*. He drew scenes from the book on the poster. Then, he attached the book report to the center of the poster. Ken's friends thought his poster was colorful. They were eager to read the book.

YOUR TURN

Use your best handwriting to make a final copy of your book report. How will you share your work? Look at the ideas in the **Sharing Suggestions** box below.

SHARING SUGGESTIONS		
Start or add to a file called "Best Books."	Write a scene based on the book. Create parts for your classmates.	Write a letter to the author telling why you enjoyed the book.

4 SPEAKING AND LISTENING: Giving a Persuasive Talk

When you want to persuade someone to agree with you, you use **persuasive language**. If you give good reasons, your listeners may agree with your ideas. The best reasons are always backed up by facts.

Ken thinks gymnastics is fun. His school will hire a coach if ten students sign up for a gymnastics club. Ken tries to persuade his friends on the baseball team to sign up for the gymnastics club.

Ken used the following reasons when he tried to persuade his friends.

1. Gymnastics is fun.
2. You can learn to do handstands and flips.
3. Gymnastics will make your arms stronger for playing baseball.
4. Gymnastics will make your legs stronger for running.

When you give a persuasive talk, keep these speaking guidelines in mind.

SPEAKING GUIDELINES: A Persuasive Talk

1. Keep your **purpose** and **audience** in mind.
2. Give reasons that make sense.
3. Provide facts to back up your reasons.

■ Why should facts back up reasons?

SPEAKING APPLICATION A Persuasive Talk

Choose a hobby club you might want to start at school. Make a list of reasons why you think the club should be started. Think of friends who might like the idea. Keep them in mind as you write your reasons. Then, try to persuade those friends to join the club. Your friends should keep these listening guidelines in mind as you tell them your idea.

LISTENING GUIDELINES: A Persuasive Talk

1. Listen for persuasive language.
2. Listen for facts and opinions.
3. Decide if the reasons make sense.

5 WRITER'S RESOURCES: Parts of a Book

Knowing the parts of a book will help you decide if you want to read the book.

The first page of every book is the **title page.** It tells the name of the book and the author.

The **table of contents** follows the title page. It lists the name and the page number of each chapter in the book. Here is part of the table of contents of a book called *America's Olympic Superstar Mary Lou Retton* by George Sullivan.

Contents

An **index** is found at the back of most nonfiction books. It helps you to find information quickly. The index lists in alphabetical order all the topics in the book and their page numbers.

Practice

Use the title page, table of contents, and index of this textbook to answer the following questions.

1. The title is _____ .
2. The theme of Unit 12 is _____ .
3. There are _____ units in the book.
4. The title of Unit 1 is _____ .
5. Information about subject pronouns can be found on pages _____ .
6. Information about common nouns can be found on pages _____ .
7. Unit 13 has _____ pages.
8. The index begins on page _____ .
9. The index has _____ pages.
10. The book has _____ pages.
11. *Fish Fry* begins on page _____ .
12. Classifying is taught on pages _____ .
13. The special verb *be* is taught in Unit _____ .
14. Irregular verbs are taught in Unit _____ .
15. The theme of Unit 6 is _____ .
16. *Dear Aunt Helen* was written by _____ .
17. Unit _____ is the longest unit.
18. How many extra practice pages are in Unit 3? _____
19. Making Introductions begins on page _____ .
20. The book has _____ Unit Checkups.

WRITING APPLICATION A Table of Contents

Create a table of contents for a book that you would like to write. Include chapter titles and page numbers. Keep your table of contents in your writing folder.

Writing About Health

Remaining in good health is an important concern. Eating foods that are good for you will keep you healthy and strong. A balanced diet will give you the energy you need to be at your best every day. A balanced diet includes plenty of fruits and vegetables, meats, dairy products, and grains.

Exercise is also very important if you want to stay healthy and in good shape. Exercise makes you look good. It also keeps your heart and lungs functioning at their best.

ACTIVITIES

Create a Health Plan   Find out more about which foods are the most healthful. You can find this information in an encyclopedia or in another resource in the library. Create a poster of these foods. Draw a picture of each food and describe why it is healthful. Share your poster with classmates.

Describe a Photograph   Look at the photograph on the following page. Which foods have you tasted? Which would you like to try?

Respond to Literature What do you like to eat for breakfast? Do you like eggs? Cereal? Do you drink milk or juice? People in other countries have their favorite breakfasts just as you have yours. Read the following from a book called *Foodworks*, to find out what people eat in Israel, Japan, and England.

A Matter of Taste

Kids in Israel wake up to a meal of cottage cheese, yogurt, hardboiled eggs, olives, tomatoes, cucumbers, bread or pita (circles of flat bread that open into a pocket) and fruit—usually oranges. Sometimes they have sardines or smoked fish.

The English, on the other hand, like a really big breakfast, starting with cold cereal. Then, bring on the fried eggs, bacon and sausages, fried tomatoes, fried mushrooms, toast and marmalade!

Ever tried soup for breakfast? The Japanese love clear soup flavoured with a soybean paste called *miso.*

Describe what you eat for breakfast to someone in another country.

UNIT CHECKUP

LESSON 1

Group Writing: A Book Report (page 360) Read this paragraph from a book report. Write three words that helped persuade you to read the book.

Everybody should read *James and the Giant Peach.* It is an exciting adventure story. The talking insects are funny. James's aunts are also funny. The story has a happy ending.

LESSON 2

Thinking: Telling Fact from Opinion (page 364) Write the sentences. Next to each sentence write **F** if it is a fact. Write **O** if it is an opinion.

1. There are many books in the library.
2. The children's library is the best.
3. Biographies are the most interesting books to read.
4. A biography is the story of someone's life.

LESSON 3

Writing a Book Report (page 366) Write a summary of a book that you liked. Be sure to include the main details of the book.

LESSON 4

Speaking and Listening: Giving a Persuasive Talk (page 374) Give three reasons why your friends should go to a party you are giving.

LESSON 5

Writer's Resources: Parts of a Book (page 376) Use the title page, table of contents, and index of this book to answer the following questions.

1. On what page does Unit 5 begin?
2. What is the theme of Unit 14?
3. Which unit is about writing letters?

THEME PROJECT

A SURVEY

Everyone has a favorite color, game, and food. Everyone's favorites are different.

The following graph shows the favorite colors of 65 students in Ken's school. Which color is the most popular? Which colors are the least popular?

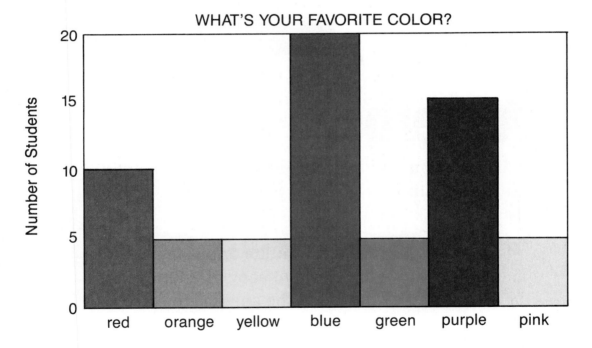

WHAT'S YOUR FAVORITE COLOR?

Create your own survey about any topic you want. You might ask about a favorite pet, subject, or sport.

- First, select a topic
- Then, make a list of all the people you will ask.
- Next, ask each person on your list the same question.
- Last, make a graph like the one above to show the answers.

Adverbs

In Unit 13 you will learn about adverbs. When you use adverbs in your writing, you can use them to tell *how, where,* and *when.*

Discuss Read the poem on the opposite page. The writer is wondering about some mysteries in nature. How might she find the answers to these questions?

Creative Expression The unit theme is *Mysteries.* Have you ever read a mystery story? Were you able to understand the clues? Write a list of clues for a mystery you would like a friend to solve. Write your list in your journal.

THEME: *MYSTERIES*

I don't know why
*   the sky is blue*
*   or why the raindrops*
*   splatter through*
*   or why the grass*
*   is wet with dew . . . do you?*

— Myra Cohn Livingston
from "I Don't Know Why"

1 WHAT IS AN ADVERB?

An adverb is a word that tells more about a verb.

When you write, you use a verb to show an action. An adverb is a word that describes a verb. It tells **how, where,** or **when** an action takes place.

Emilia reads the recipe **carefully.**
Emilia looks **downstairs** for another recipe.
She bakes muffins **today.**

Guided Practice

Tell which word in each sentence is an adverb.

Example: Father beats the eggs lightly.   *lightly*

1. Father walks downstairs.
2. He cooks breakfast quickly.
3. Father cracks two eggs easily.
4. He mixes the batter carefully.
5. Then, he pours the mix into a pan.

 THINK

■ How can I decide if a word is an adverb?

REMEMBER

- An **adverb** is a word that tells more about a verb.
- An **adverb** tells how, where, or when.

More Practice

A. Write the sentences. Underline each adverb. Draw two lines under the verb it describes.

Example: <u>Today</u> we <u><u>eat</u></u> pancakes.

6. Father gladly cooks the pancakes.
7. He neatly arranges them on a plate.
8. Next, he sets the table.
9. He calls us upstairs.
10. He quickly leaves the room.
11. Our puppy Gus sits nearby.
12. We enter the kitchen eagerly.
13. We search everywhere for the pancakes.
14. We see pancake crumbs there.

B. Write the sentences. Write if the underlined adverb tells **how, where,** or **when**.

Example: We walk <u>quickly</u>.   *how*

15. We <u>slowly</u> follow the trail of crumbs.
16. The trail leads us <u>outside</u>.
17. <u>Finally</u>, we see our puppy.
18. Gus <u>joyfully</u> finishes the pancakes.
19. Father sends him <u>indoors</u>.
20. <u>Immediately</u> we make more pancakes.

Extra Practice, page 400

WRITING APPLICATION A Mystery Story

Write a story about a mystery. Describe what the mystery was. Identify the adverbs in each sentence.

ADVERBS THAT TELL HOW

You know that an adverb tells more about a verb. Some **adverbs** tell **how** an action takes place. Adverbs that tell how usually end in *ly.*

Don enters the room **quietly.**

He turns **slowly** toward the window.

A shadow moves **quickly.**

Don **bravely** walks to the window.

Guided Practice

Tell which word in each sentence is an adverb that tells how. Then, tell the verb it tells more about.

Example: I sit wearily on my bed.   *wearily, sit*

1. Shadows dance playfully on my wall.
2. I study them quietly.
3. The moonlight shines brightly.
4. The trees sway wildly.
5. I look out the window excitedly.

?! THINK

■ How can I decide if an adverb tells how?

REMEMBER

■ **Adverbs** that tell *how* usually end in *ly.*

More Practice

Write the sentences. Draw a line under each adverb that tells how. Draw two lines under the verb it describes.

Example: We talk softly.

> We <u>talk</u> <u>softly</u>.

6. Anna plays roughly with the kitten.
7. Bill busily studies for a test.
8. Footsteps approach rapidly.
9. They tap loudly across the roof.
10. Bill and Anna call their Dad nervously.
11. Mr. Bond swiftly calls the police.
12. Mr. Ryan answers briskly.
13. Mr. Ryan talks calmly to Mr. Bond.
14. He walks briskly to his car.
15. The family waits anxiously.
16. Mr. Ryan arrives quickly.
17. He shines a light directly on the roof.
18. A raccoon jumps fearfully to the ground.
19. It quickly disappears into the woods.
20. We will rest safely tonight.

Extra Practice, page 401

WRITING APPLICATION A Review

Write a review of a mystery movie you have seen. Tell what happened. Use an adverb that tells *how* in each sentence.

COOPERATIVE
LEARNING

3 ADVERBS THAT TELL WHERE AND WHEN

You know that **adverbs** can tell **how** an action takes place. Adverbs can also tell **where** and **when** an action takes place.

The boat carries them **far.**
The scuba divers arrive **early.**

Here are some adverbs that tell **where** and **when.**

Where		When	
there	ahead	first	soon
outside	around	always	early
up	far	next	today
here	away	later	then
nearby	everywhere	tomorrow	yesterday

Guided Practice

Tell which word in each sentence is an adverb that tells *where or when.* Then, tell the verb it tells more about.

Example: I sail tomorrow.   *tomorrow, sail*

1. The divers arrive early.
2. The boatful of divers pulls away.
3. Finally, the boat stops.
4. The captain drops the anchor here.
5. Now they look for a rare fish.

early

far

near

?! THINK

■ How can I decide if a word is an adverb?

REMEMBER

■ Some **adverbs** tell *where* and *when* an action takes place.

More Practice

Write each sentence. Draw a line under each adverb. Write **where** if the adverb tells where. Write **when** if the adverb tells when.

Example: Other fish swim <u>nearby</u>.   *where*

6. First, the divers put on wet suits.
7. Next, they wear safety vests.
8. Then, they lift their air tanks.
9. The boat drifts nearby.
10. The leader of the group goes ahead.
11. The divers swim away.
12. Many plants grow there.
13. The divers look around.
14. Angelfish swim in the sea today.
15. Soon, the divers see a rare fish.
16. They saw it yesterday.
17. Red and yellow fish swim overhead.
18. Later, the divers take photos.
19. Sometimes the fish look in the camera.
20. The tired divers swim up.

Extra Practice, Practice Plus, pages 402–403

COOPERATIVE
LEARNING

WRITING APPLICATION A Journal Entry

Imagine that you went scuba diving with a famous underwater explorer. Write a journal entry about the dive. Exchange papers with a classmate. Identify the adverbs in each other's work.

GRAMMAR

4 MECHANICS: Using Commas

When you write, you use a **comma** to show a pause. Use a comma in the following ways:

➡ Use commas to separate three or more words in a series.

➡ Use a comma after a person being spoken to.

➡ Use a comma after the words *yes* and *no* when they begin a sentence.

Spring comes slowly, gently, and sweetly.
Susan, look at the colorful new flowers.
Yes, they are colorful.

slowly   gently   sweetly

Guided Practice

Tell where commas belong in each sentence.

Example: No I did not plant the seeds.
No, I did not plant the seeds.

1. Susan where are the seeds?
2. Jack do you have them?
3. Yes they are in my pocket.
4. They cheer loudly happily and gladly.
5. Jack digs deeply carefully and quickly.
6. Yes they have enough water.

?! THINK

■ How can I decide when to use commas?

REMEMBER

■ Use a **comma** to separate three or more words in a series, after the name of a person being spoken to, and after the words *yes* and *no*.

More Practice

A. Write the sentences. Draw one line under each sentence that uses commas correctly.

Example: <u>No, the grass was not cut.</u>

7. Donald, will you cut the grass?
8. It grew quickly steadily and speedily.
9. Staci will you help Donald?
10. Yes, I like mowing the lawn.

B. Write each sentence. Use commas correctly.

Example: Joe did the farmer plant the crops?
Joe, did the farmer plant the crops?

11. The rain falls gently lightly and evenly.
12. The farmer works hard steadily and fast.
13. We happily swiftly and carefully plant seeds.
14. Yes this is hard work.
15. Carol please take a break.
16. The birds sing sweetly clearly and joyfully.
17. Jodi do you hear the birds?
18. No I wasn't listening.
19. Jim I can hear it now!
20. Yes it sounds sweet.

Extra Practice, page 404

WRITING APPLICATION A Post Card

Write a post card to a friend describing how you might spend a spring day. Underline the commas.

5 VOCABULARY BUILDING:
Borrowed Words

Words that come from other languages are called **borrowed words.** Here are some of the words that we have borrowed:

Spanish	French	Native American
alligator	ballet	moccasin
fiesta	prince	moose
ranch	pumpkin	skunk
rodeo	button	canoe
Italian	**Dutch**	**German**
pizza	cookie	pretzel
violin	stoop	dachshund
spaghetti	easel	kindergarten
umbrella		

Guided Practice

Look at each underlined word. Find it on the chart. Tell from which language the word is borrowed.

Example: I wear an <u>alligator</u> costume.   *Spanish*

1. Someone comes dressed as a <u>prince</u>.
2. Another dresses as a <u>ballet</u> dancer.
3. A musician plays the <u>violin</u>.
4. The host serves delicious <u>cookies</u>.

?! THINK

■ How do I know if a word is a borrowed word?

REMEMBER

- A **borrowed word** is a word from another language. The dictionary tells you from which language a word is borrowed.

More Practice

Write the sentences. Answer each question with a borrowed word from the box.

Example: What animal has a white stripe? *skunk*

spaghetti	dachshund	easel	pretzel
alligator	moccasins	umbrella	pizza
skunk	ranch	canoe	violin

5. Where are horses raised?
6. What animal lives in a swamp?
7. What do you wear on your feet?
8. What is a food with cheese on top?
9. What can you paddle down the river?
10. What do you carry when it rains?
11. Where do you put your painting?
12. What is made of twisted pieces of dough?
13. What kind of dog is short and long?
14. What instrument do you play with a bow?
15. What food is long and stringy?

Extra Practice, page 405

WRITING APPLICATION An Advertisement

COOPERATIVE
LEARNING

With your classmates, write an advertisement for a fiesta or a costume party. Be sure to include as many borrowed words as you can. Underline the borrowed words in your advertisement.

GRAMMAR —AND WRITING CONNECTION

Combining Sentences

If you write two sentences that tell about the same action, you can sometimes combine them by adding words that tell **where** or **how.**

Where:

SEPARATE: Bob dropped the bag. It fell over there.

COMBINED: Bob dropped the bag over there.

How:

SEPARATE: A voice shouted. It shouted loudly.

COMBINED: A voice shouted loudly.

Working Together

COOPERATIVE LEARNING

With your classmates, combine these pairs of sentences by adding words that tell *where* or *how.*

Example: Tony waited. He waited calmly.
Tony waited calmly.

1. Tony stared.
   He looked out the window.
2. He saw Tom standing.
   He saw Tom there.
3. Tom carried a bag.
   He carried it carefully.

Revising Sentences

Combine each pair of sentences by adding words that tell *where* or *how*.

4. Tony called to Tom.
   He shouted loudly.
5. Tom walked down the road.
   He walked briskly.
6. Tony followed Tom.
   He followed slowly.
7. A deer approached.
   It walked quietly.
8. Tom held the milk.
   He held it eagerly.
9. The deer drank the milk.
   It drank hungrily.
10. Tony solved the mystery.
    He solved it easily.

Tony discovered that Tom was feeding a deer. Think of another ending to the story. Where else could Tom have gone? Write a new ending to the mystery.

Reread your ending. Combine any sentences you can by adding words that tell *where* or *how*.

UNIT CHECKUP

LESSON

1

What Is an Adverb? (page 384) Write each sentence. Draw one line under each adverb. Draw two lines under the verb it describes.

1. Today, the people explore the cave.
2. First, they fasten their hats.
3. They enter the cave slowly.
4. They crawl bravely along the ground.
5. Their lights shine ahead.
6. They see a stream there.

LESSON

2

Adverbs That Tell How (page 386) Write each sentence. Complete each sentence by making the word in ( ) tell *how*.

7. _____ Alan ran into the house. (Quick)
8. "I'm home!" he called _____ . (cheerful)
9. _____ he heard strange voices. (Sudden)
10. _____ he climbed the stairs. (Nervous)
11. He peeked _____ into his bedroom. (brave)
12. A tape played _____ on his recorder. (loud)
13. Alan sighed _____ with relief. (deep)

LESSON

3

Adverbs That Tell Where and When (page 388) Write each sentence. Draw a line under the adverb. Write **where** if the adverb tells *where*. Write **when** if the adverb tells *when*.

14. Today, Amy goes to the library.
15. She goes upstairs to the children's room.
16. First, Amy heads for the card catalog.
17. She looks for a mystery book there.
18. Soon, she finds an interesting title.

Mechanics: Using Commas (page 390) Write each sentence. Use commas where needed.

19. I sleep soundly comfortably and well.
20. Yes the thunder is loud.
21. Martha do you see the flashing lights?
22. Max barks sharply angrily and noisily.
23. I gently patiently and calmly pet him.
24. Yes I'll stay with him.
25. Martha please stay with us.

Vocabulary Building: Borrowed Words (page 392) In a dictionary check each word below. Write each word with its correct definition.

| piano | pretzel | umbrella | moccasin | pumpkin |

26. leather shoe with beads
27. a round, orange fruit
28. protection from the rain
29. baked dough often shaped in a loose knot
30. a musical instrument with a keyboard

Writing Application: Adverb Usage
(pages 384–390) The following paragraph contains 10 sentence errors. Rewrite the paragraph correctly.

31.–40.   The class travels quick to the museum. We sing happily, loud and eager. Our teacher quiet leads the way. Final, we arrive. We look around excited. I walk slow through the huge rooms. Sudden, I spot my favorite room. The dinosaurs stand fierce.

ENRICHMENT

MYSTERY MEAL

Complete the story with borrowed words from the list below.

> moccasin skunk gate taco

A _____ is missing from my plate. Put on your other _____. Please come and help me. I will open the _____. Look, a _____ is eating it!

ADVERB SNAKES

Cut three pieces of paper in the shape of a snake. Write the word *how, when,* or *where* on each snake. Then, think of adverbs that tell how, when, and where. Write the adverbs on the correct snake. Every time you learn a new adverb, add it to the correct snake.

PICTURE THE ADVERB

Think of adverbs that tell how. For example, you might choose *quickly, slowly,* or *eagerly.* Write these adverbs on a large piece of paper. Then, cut out pictures from newspapers or magazines for each adverb. Your pictures can be of anything you want. Paste the pictures next to the adverbs.

WORLDLY WORDS

When you speak, you may be using words from many different languages. Look at this list of words:

| bouquet | chocolate | moose | sofa |

Use a dictionary to find out what languages they are from. Think of other words that you use every day. Find out about these words. Then, you and a friend can make a poster of the words and the countries that they come from.

SHOW ME

Do you like to paint or cook? Do you like to build models? Write an instruction booklet that tells how to make something. Be sure to use adverbs to make the instructions clear. You should also draw pictures to show some of the steps.

EXTRA PRACTICE

Three levels of practice
What Is an Adverb? (page 384)

LEVEL A. Write the sentences. Underline the adverbs.

1. Today, my family leaves for vacation.
2. We look everywhere for our dog.
3. He is not there.
4. Happily, we find him in our car.
5. On the way to the lake, we sing gaily.
6. A deer runs gracefully across the road.
7. Suddenly, it stops.
8. We quickly take a picture.
9. The deer disappears quietly.
10. We drive away.

LEVEL B. Write the sentence in each pair that has an adverb. Underline the adverb.

11. Lou visits the old cabin.
    He stays there for a week.
12. The door creaks loudly.
    Lou enters the cabin.
13. It is dark and dusty inside.
    Lou finds a candle.

LEVEL C. Write each sentence with an adverb.

14. Lou hears a voice _____ .
15. He _____ runs from the room.
16. _____ the candle blows out.
17. Lou _____ runs to the door.
18. He opens it _____ .
19. Four eyes _____ stare at him.
20. _____ Lou solves the mystery.

EXTRA PRACTICE

Three levels of practice
Adverbs That Tell How (page 386)

LEVEL A. Write the sentences. Underline the adverbs.

1. Lee quickly looks for his homework.
2. Lee carefully searches his room.
3. He stares sadly at his sister.
4. June watches him curiously.
5. Lee speaks softly to June.
6. She helps him happily.
7. Lee hugs June warmly.
8. They open the closet eagerly.
9. June studies the room thoughtfully.
10. June suddenly sees the records.
11. Records are placed neatly on a table.

LEVEL B. Write the sentences with the adverb that tells *how.*

12. June looks through the records _____ .
    a. yesterday   b. quickly
13. _____ she hands Lee his homework.
    a. Finally   b. Cheerfully
14. Lee thanks June _____ .
    a. sincerely   b. now
15. He _____ finishes his homework.
    a. usually   b. patiently

LEVEL C. Write each sentence with an adverb that tells *how.*

16. The dog is hiding _____ under the bed.
17. He looks _____ at me.
18. Did he _____ eat my homework?
19. I talk to him _____ .
20. He wags his tail _____ .

EXTRA PRACTICE

Three levels of practice
Adverbs That Tell Where and When (page 388)

Write the sentences. Underline the adverb that tells *where* or *when* in each sentence.

1. Dana lost her bike today.
2. She left it nearby.
3. It is not here.
4. Are you sure you left your bike there?
5. She looks everywhere.
6. Dana calls me later.
7. She finally found her bike in the garage.
8. Now we can go for a ride.
9. Dana meets me outside.
10. Soon we ride to a park.

Write the sentences. Complete each sentence with the adverb in ( ) that tells *where* or *when.*

11. I (happily, often) solve mysteries.
12. (First, Carefully) I look for clues.
13. (Quietly, Next) I organize them.
14. (Proudly, Soon) I have the answers.

Write each sentence with an adverb that tells *where* or *when.*

15. Jason hears a noise _____ .
16. _____ Jason finds footprints in the snow.
17. He sees many footprints _____ .
18. _____ Jason follows the footprints.
19. Jason sees something _____ .
20. He finds a lost puppy _____ .

PRACTICE + PLUS

Three levels of additional practice for a difficult skill
Adverbs That Tell Where and When (page 388)

LEVEL A. Read each pair of adverbs. Write the adverb that tells where or when.

1. now, carefully
2. upstairs, really
3. only, yesterday
4. there, absolutely
5. lively, soon

6. up, gladly
7. loudly, later
8. slowly, first
9. today, nicely
10. last, sweetly

LEVEL B. Write each sentence. Draw a line under the adverb that tells *where* or *when.* Write **where** or **when** next to each adverb.

11. Yesterday, I read a mystery.
12. Then, I lost the book.
13. I left it here.
14. Soon, I found it.
15. It was upstairs.

LEVEL C. Write the sentences. Complete each sentence with an adverb.

finally	soon	today	there	down

16. _____ we follow the treasure map.
17. We see the spot with the *x* _____ .
18. We dig _____ .
19. Will we find the treasure _____ ?
20. _____ we find the treasure.

EXTRA PRACTICE

Three levels of practice
Mechanics: Using Commas (page 390)

LEVEL
A. Write the sentence in each pair that uses commas correctly.

1. Ann smiles slowly brightly and widely.
   Ann smiles slowly, brightly, and widely.
2. Jack, are you ready for an adventure?
   Jack are you ready for an adventure?
3. Yes I can't wait.
   Yes, I can't wait.

LEVEL
B. Write the sentences that use commas correctly.

4. Donna, will you come with us?
5. They smile cheerily, sweetly, and easily.
6. Nell moves quickly, quietly, and nervously.
7. Donna help Nell.
8. Yes, I will help her.
9. Nell where is the map?
10. Nell, folds the map easily and neatly.

LEVEL
C. Write the sentences. Add commas where needed.

11. Nell digs slowly carefully and neatly.
12. Jack help Nell dig a hole.
13. Yes I will help her.
14. Nell give me a shovel.
15. Jack digs quickly easily and excitedly.
16. Donna do you want to dig with us?
17. Nell do you see the treasure?
18. Yes I can see something.
19. Nell screams suddenly happily and loudly.
20. Jack look at the buried treasure!

EXTRA PRACTICE

Three levels of practice
Vocabulary Building: Borrowed Words (page 392)

LEVEL A. Write the sentences. Answer each question with a borrowed word from the box.

> tacos   skunk   pajamas   ranch   wigwam

1. Where will Tess and Liz sleep?
2. What will Tess and Liz wear?
3. What will Tess and Liz eat?
4. What do Tess and Liz smell?
5. Where do Tess and Liz live?

LEVEL B. Complete each riddle with a word from the box.

> kindergarten   chili   snoop   button   chipmunk

6. I close your jacket. I am a _____ .
7. I am very tasty. I am _____ .
8. I am a kind of detective. I am a _____ .
9. I am a cute animal. I am a _____ .
10. Children visit my class. I am a _____ .

LEVEL C. Look up each borrowed word in a dictionary. Write the correct definition next to each word.

11. dachshund
12. guitar
13. shawl
14. ballet
15. prairie

a. a flat land covered with grass
b. a kind of dance
c. a small dog
d. clothing worn over the shoulder
e. an instrument with six or more strings

MAINTENANCE

Unit 1   Understanding Sentences

Statements and Questions (page 4), **Commands and Exclamations** (page 6). Write each sentence correctly.

1. laura will play baseball
2. do you have a bat
3. look over there

Subjects in Sentences (page 8), **Predicates in Sentences** (page 10). Write each sentence. Draw a line between the subject and the predicate.

4. Lorna closes her eyes.
5. She counts to ten.
6. Casey and Holly hide behind a tree.

Unit 3   Understanding Nouns

Singular Nouns and Plural Nouns (page 68). Write the plural form of each noun.

7. puppy
8. man
9. strawberry
10. fox
11. bush
12. child
13. mouse
14. dress

Singular Possessive Nouns (page 74), **Plural Possessive Nouns** (page 76). Write the possessive form of each noun.

15. Wally
16. teacher
17. father
18. neighbors
19. student
20. women
21. friends
22. sisters

Unit 5   Understanding Action Verbs

Verbs in the Present (page 138), **Verbs in the Past** (page 140), **Verbs in the Future** (page 142). Write the verbs. Write **past, present,** or **future** next to each verb.

23. Alexander Bell invented the telephone.
24. Dial the number correctly.
25. Someday, I will invent something.
26. My invention will surprise everyone.

Irregular Verbs (page 146). Write each sentence. Choose the correct verb in ( ).

27. He had (came, come) to my house.
28. He had (run, ran) all the way.
29. David (begin, began) to sing.
30. Then, he (eat, ate) his lunch.

Unit 7 The Special Verb *be*

Verbs in the Present (page 204), **Verbs in the Past** (page 206). Underline the *be* verb in each sentence.

31. Manny was sad.
32. Carol was far away.
33. She is a good letter writer.
34. They were pen pals.
35. The letters are funny.

Suffixes (page 210). Write each word. Underline the suffix in each word.

36. dependable
37. careful
38. friendly
39. quickly
40. careless

41. closely
42. helpless
43. senseless
44. hopeful
45. wishful

Unit 9   Understanding Adjectives

More About Adjectives (page 264). Write each sentence. Underline each adjective.

46. Bonzo is a hungry dog.
47. Sonia has several treats.
48. She gives many treats to Bonzo.

Adjectives That Compare (page 266). Complete each sentence with the correct form of the adjective in ( ).

49. Helen has a (big) cat than Mirna.
50. Mirna's cat is (fat) than Helen's.
51. Max's cat is the (strong) of all.

Using *a, an,* and *the* (page 268). Complete each sentence by writing *a* or *an.*

52. Lori finds _____ black cat.
53. It has _____ orange face.
54. It has _____ long tail.

Synonyms and Antonyms (page 272). Write each sentence. Draw one line under the synonyms and two lines under the antonyms.

55. Tom is a little mouse with big ideas.
56. The tiny mouse lives in a small cage.
57. He has black fur and a white tail.

Unit 11   Understanding Pronouns

Subject Pronouns (page 326), **Object Pronouns** (page 328). Write each sentence. Draw one line under each subject pronoun. Draw two lines under each object pronoun.

58. Do you have a favorite game?
59. Donny will teach the game to her.
60. It is an exciting game.

Possessive Pronouns (page 330) Write each sentence. Underline each possessive pronoun.

61. Where are my shoes?
62. The children look for their things.
63. Anton has lost his backpack.
64. Where are my books?

Contractions (page 332) Write the contraction for each word.

65. it is
66. I have
67. you are
68. he is

69. I will
70. they are
71. they have
72. we will

73. he will
74. she is
75. we are
76. I am

Homophones (page 334) Write the sentences with the correct homophone in ( ).

77. Billy read his poem (allowed, aloud).
78. (Would, Wood) you open the door?
79. Isn't the (sea, see) beautiful?

Unit 13 Understanding Adverbs

What Is an Adverb? (page 384) Write the word in each pair that is an adverb.

80. house, happily
81. quietly, his
82. mother, swiftly

83. often, table
84. chair, then
85. runs, now

86. never, cry
87. go, upstairs
88. quickly, jump

Adverbs That Tell How (page 386). Write the adverb that tells *how.*

89. carefully, here
90. there, quickly

91. nervously, first
92. next, loudly

93. finally, eagerly
94. then, slowly

Adverbs That Tell Where and When (page 388). Write the adverbs that tell *where* or *when.*

95. soon, friendly
96. there, happily
97. quickly, tomorrow

98. here, slowly
99. speedily, yesterday
100. first, sadly

UNIT

14

Writing Research Reports

Read the quotation and look at the picture on the opposite page. Think about a book you have read this year. Tell about what was new to you.

When you write a research report you try to find the most important and interesting facts about your subject.

Focus A research report gives detailed information about a topic.

What would you like to learn more about? On the following pages, you will find an interesting article and some photographs. You can use them to find ideas for writing.

THEME: *MYSTERIES*

Each book should be important, interesting, and contain an element of surprise for every reader. . . .

— Franklyn Branley

Why do you think birds fly south as soon as the weather gets colder? Where do you think they go? The following article explains about bird migration and tells why it is still a great mystery.

The Great Mystery–
Following the Seasons

Hundreds of barn swallows sit in rows on telephone wires. Suddenly, with a great twittering, they all rush into the air. Staying close together in a big flock, they fly away. It is late summer and the barn swallows have begun to migrate.

Every autumn millions of geese, ducks, storks,

cuckoos, bobolinks, and other birds migrate. They leave the north, where they spent the summer, and fly south. Sometimes many birds fly together. Some birds fly alone.

When birds migrate they often fly great distances. Sometimes they cross oceans and continents. But the birds always go to the same warm parts of the world where their ancestors have gone for thousands of years. The birds stay all winter in these warm places.

This information could be included in a research report.

In the spring they migrate back to the north. Sometimes they go back to the same nests they used the summer before.

Birds aren't the only animals that migrate. Monarch butterflies, ladybugs, and many other insects migrate, too. So do some fish and mammals.

It is usually still warm when birds and insects begin to migrate. How do they know winter is coming? How do they know where to go? What makes them always go to the same place?

Scientists know that something in a bird's or insect's body makes it leave at the right time and steers it the way it should go. But no one is sure of all the causes. Migration is a great mystery!

Thinking Like a Reader

1. List one fact that you learned by reading this article.
2. Where would you guess insects go when they migrate?

Write your responses in your journal.

Thinking Like a Writer

3. Which details does the writer use to let the reader know that migration is a mystery?

Write your response in your journal.

LITERATURE

Brainstorm
Vocabulary

The article begins, "Hundreds of barn swallows sit in *rows* on the telephone wires." Can you think of a name of a flower that is a homophone for the word *rows*? Choose three words from the article. Write a homophone for each one. Write these words in a personal vocabulary list. You can use these words in your writing.

Talk It Over
Bird Talk

Create a scene in which birds migrate for the winter. Have your classmates play the parts of the birds. Explain why the birds are migrating. Tell where they are going and when they will be coming back.

Quick Write *Write an Ad*

You have read that some birds fly south in the winter. Write an ad telling birds about a good place to spend the winter. Your ad might look something like this:

> Spend the winter at cozy "Feathered Nest Hotel." Everything a bird could want at your wingtips. Birdbaths in every nest. Gourmet birdseed served three times daily.

Idea Corner
More Information

In this article you learned a little about bird migration. Where could you go to learn more about this yearly event? Write your response in your journal.

PICTURES

SEEING LIKE A WRITER

Finding Ideas for Writing

Look at the pictures. Think about what you see.
What ideas for writing a report do the pictures give you?
Write your ideas in your journal.

PICTURES: Ideas for Writing Research Reports

1 GROUP WRITING: A Research Report

COOPERATIVE
LEARNING

The **purpose** of a research report is to provide an **audience** with information about one subject. What do you need to do before you write a research report?

- Choose a Topic
- Narrow Your Topic
- Find Information/Take Notes

Choose a Topic

In order to **choose a topic,** think about subjects that you want to learn more about. Would you like to learn about flowers? Are you curious about a certain animal? Michael wanted to find out about deserts.

Narrow Your Topic

Michael decided to write a report about deserts. He knew that he could not write about every desert. Michael **narrowed** his topic and wrote only about the Sahara Desert. Here is part of Michael's report.

The Sahara is the largest and hottest desert in the world. Its annual rainfall is less than 8 inches. Parts of the desert get less than 1 inch of rain each year. The average temperature in the summer is over 100 degrees. In the winter the temperature only reaches about 60 degrees. The Sahara has patches of green, which are oases. These oases get their water from springs.

Guided Practice: Brainstorming Topics

With your classmates, brainstorm topics for a research report. Decide on a topic and narrow it if it is too broad. For example, if you want to research whales, you might narrow your topic and research white whales.

Find Information/Take Notes

Where do you find the information for your research report? Michael went to the library and looked up deserts in the encyclopedia. He also looked in the card catalog to find nonfiction books about the Sahara Desert. Here is part of an encyclopedia article Michael read about deserts. Notice how the deserts are alike and how they are different.

> Some deserts are rolling, sandy places where hardly any kinds of plants can grow. Some are flat plains that are covered with many kinds of plants. Even the world's biggest, hottest desert, the Sahara, has small patches of trees and grass in some places. Such a patch of greenery is called an oasis.

Michael took **notes** on the articles as he read them. He wrote down the most important facts. He did not use complete sentences.

Guided Practice: Finding Information

With your class, go to the library and research the topic that you chose. Look in the encyclopedia or in nonfiction books. Find at least two articles about the topic. Take notes on the articles.

Putting a Research Report Together

With your classmates, you have chosen a research topic and narrowed the topic. You went to the library and found articles about the topic. Then, you took notes on the articles. Now think about which information you want to include in your research report.

Guided Practice: Writing a Research Report

Write the first paragraph of the report you researched with your class. Use your notes to make sure the information is correct.

Share your paragraph with a friend. Did your friend learn something that he or she didn't already know?

Checklist: A Research Report

Use this checklist when you want to write a research report. Finish the checklist. Keep it in your writing folder.

CHECKLIST

- ✓ Purpose and _____
- ✓ Choose a topic
- ✓ Narrow your _____
- ✓ Find information

  encyclopedia

  nonfiction books
- ✓ Take notes

2 THINKING AND WRITING: Summarizing

A **summary** is like a main-idea sentence. It tells in a few sentences the main idea and the important details. Look at the details from a writer's journal.

> • don't know why dinosaurs died out
> • some thought weather
> • others thought no food

Now look at this summary.

> Scientists do not know why dinosaurs died out. It might have been the weather. It might have been the lack of food. It still remains a mystery.

This summary has a main-idea sentence and a few important details. The last sentence ties together the ideas in the paragraph.

Thinking Like a Writer
- Which sentence tells the main idea?
- Which details support the main idea?

The main idea of this summary is in the first sentence. It says that scientists do not know why dinosaurs died out. The other sentences tell possible reasons why they died out.

THINKING APPLICATION Summarizing

Each student below wants to write a summary. Help the students with their summaries. Discuss your ideas with your classmates.

1. Juan's paragraph will be about a cactus. Write a summary using Juan's details.
   - can survive without much water
   - can live in bright sunlight
   - can take the heat of the desert

2. Diane wants to write about Siamese cats. Write a summary using the following details.
   - originally came from Thailand
   - have curved tails
   - always have blue eyes

3. Toby is writing about oceans. Write a main-idea sentence for her summary.

   Some think that water formed billions of years ago when the earth cooled. Others think that steam turned to clouds, which then cooled. The oceans were what remained.

4. Dale is writing about icebergs. Add a main-idea sentence to Dale's summary.

   Icebergs can be as tall as mountains and many miles wide. They float near the North and South poles. These chunks of ice broke off from large sheets of ice.

5. Sherri is writing about shooting stars. Write a summary of Sherri's details.
   - dots of dust on fire
   - most are small
   - burn up when they enter atmosphere

3 INDEPENDENT WRITING: A Research Report

Prewrite: Step 1

You have learned some important points about research reports. Now it's time to pick your own topic to write about. Daryl, a third-grade student, picked a topic for his research report in this way.

Choosing a Research Topic

1. First, Daryl looked through nonfiction books and the encyclopedia.

2. Then, he listed possible topics.

3. Last, Daryl decided on the best topic for his report.

bears

meteors

rain

Daryl liked the last idea on his list. He decided to narrow his topic and write about rainbows. He thought that his classmates would be interested in learning about rainbows.

Daryl went to the library and found two books and an encyclopedia article about rainbows. He took notes as he read.

Exploring Ideas: Note-taking Strategy

- long ago people thought they were magic
- pot of gold at end
- sunlight shines on raindrops
- sunlight divides colors
- heavier rain makes longer rainbow

Before beginning to write, Daryl looked through the articles again. He changed his notes.

- sunlight shines on raindrops
- sun must be behind you; rain, in front of you
- sunlight divides colors
- heavier rain makes longer rainbow

Thinking Like a Writer

- What did Daryl add? What did he take out?
- Why do you think he took out those parts?

YOUR TURN

Pick a topic to research. Use **Pictures** or your journal for ideas. Follow these steps.

- Select a topic and narrow it.
- Research the topic in the library.
- Think about your purpose and audience.

Take notes on the articles. Remember, you can add to or take away from the notes at any time.

Write a First Draft: Step 2

Daryl knows what his research report should include. He used his planning checklist so he would remember to include everything. Daryl is now ready to write his first draft.

Daryl's First Draft

A rainbow is caused by the sun shining bright on raindrops. Sunlight shines through a raindrop. it breaks down into diferent colors. a rainbow forms when many rays of sunlight break up in the rain.

Daryl did not worry about errors. He knew he could correct them later.

YOUR TURN

Write your first draft. As you prepare to write, ask yourself these questions.

- What will my audience want to know?
- What do I need to explain so that they will understand my report?

⏱ **TIME-OUT** You might want to take some time out before you revise. That way you will be able to revise your writing with a fresh eye.

Planning Checklist
- Purpose and audience
- Choose a topic
- Narrow your topic
- Find information
  - encyclopedia
  - nonfiction books
- Take notes

Revise: Step 3

After Daryl finished his first draft, he read it over to himself. Then, he asked a classmate to read it. He wanted to know how he could improve his report.

Daryl looked back at his planning checklist. He checked *Take notes* so he would remember to add the information from his notes when he revised. He now has a checklist to use as he revises.

Daryl revised his writing. He still did not correct any small errors. Turn the page. Look at Daryl's revised research report.

Revising Checklist
- Purpose and audience
- Choose a topic
- Narrow your topic
- Find information
  - encyclopedia
  - nonfiction books
- ✓ Take notes

WRITING PROCESS

Daryl's Revised Draft

A rainbow is caused by the sun shining ~~bright on raindrops.~~ Sunlight shines through a raindrop. *and* ~~it~~ breaks down into diferrent colors. a rainbow forms when many rays of sunlight break up in the rain.

The sun must shine behind you while it rains in front of you.

Thinking Like a Writer

WISE
WORD
CHOICE

- Which sentence did Daryl add?
- How does this improve the report?
- Which sentences did he combine?

YOUR TURN

Read your first draft. Make a checklist. Ask yourself the following questions.

- Which facts can I add to make my report more interesting?
- Which information should I leave out of my report?

If you wish, ask a friend to read your report and make suggestions. Then, revise your report.

Proofread: Step 4

Daryl knew that he still had to proofread his report. He used a proofreading checklist while he proofread.

Part of Daryl's Proofread Draft

brightly
~~bright~~ on raindrops. Sunlight shines through
and *different*
a raindrop. it breaks down into (diferrent)
colors. a rainbow forms when many rays
of sunlight break up in the rain.
The sun must shine behind you while it
rains in front of you.

YOUR TURN

Proofreading Practice

Below is a paragraph that will help you practice your proofreading skills. Correctly write the paragraph on another piece of paper.

Waves in the ocean are Caused by the wind. The wind blloows the water and makes. the waves go up and down. The Tide are what pulls the waves crashing into shore. Then, the tide takes them quick back out again.

Proofreading Checklist
- Did I indent my paragraphs?
- Which words do I need to capitalize?
- Which punctuation errors do I need to correct?
- Did I spell any words incorrectly?

Applying Your Proofreading Skills

Now proofread your report. Read your checklist again. Review **The Grammar Connection** and **The Mechanics Connection**, too. Use the proofreading marks to show changes.

THE GRAMMAR CONNECTION

Remember this rule about placing adverbs correctly.

■ Adverbs are usually found at the beginning or the end of a sentence.

> **Happily** she walks to school.
> She walks to school **happily.**

Check your report. Have you placed adverbs correctly?

Proofreading Marks

¶	Indent
∧	Add
୫	Take out
≡	Make a capital letter
/	Make a small letter

THE MECHANICS CONNECTION

Remember this rule about using commas with adverbs.

■ When you use three or more adverbs together, use a comma to separate them.

> She walks quickly, happily, and proudly.
> He smiles fondly, cheerfully, and gaily.

Check your report. Have you used commas and adverbs correctly?

Publish: Step 5

Daryl enjoyed writing his research report. He decided to make a copy for each student in his class. He also drew a colorful poster of a rainbow and hung it on the chalkboard in the front of the room.

YOUR TURN

Make a final copy of your research report. Think of a way to share your report. You might want to use one of the **Sharing Suggestions** in the box below.

SHARING SUGGESTIONS

Make a class newspaper with short articles based on everyone's reports.	Write questions and answers on separate pieces of colored paper. Use the same color paper for the question and its answer.	Make a poster with three facts from your report. Title the poster "DID YOU KNOW?" Illustrate it.

W R I T I N G

EXTENSION

SPEAKING AND LISTENING: Giving an Oral Report

4

An **oral report** is a good way to share information with many people at once.

When you give an oral report, you put the important information from your report in outline form. The outline will help you remember those points as you give your oral report.

Fern made the following outline for her report about why trees lose their leaves in autumn.

Report title: The Life of a Leaf

I. Summer
    a. trees get water from ground
    b. water flows from roots to trunk to leaves
    c. leaves are green and healthy
II. Autumn
    a. thin layer of cork grows at stem of leaves
    b. leaves can no longer get water
    c. leaves change color and die
III. Winter
    a. dead leaves are blown from trees
    b. trunk of tree gets water from frozen ice in ground
IV. Spring
    a. ice in ground melts
    b. tree's roots take in water
    c. new leaves grow

In order for your oral report to go smoothly, you must practice giving it. If you appear to know your subject well, your **audience** will be interested in what you have to say.

When you give an oral report, keep these speaking guidelines in mind.

SPEAKING GUIDELINES: An Oral Report

1. Place your report in outline form.
2. Practice reading your report from your outline.
3. Look at your listeners.
4. Speak slowly and in a clear voice.
5. Speak with enthusiasm.

■ Why is it important to practice giving an oral report?

 ## SPEAKING APPLICATION An Oral Report

Use your research report to prepare an outline for an oral report. Practice your oral report with a friend or family member. Give your oral report to the class.

Your class will keep these listening guidelines in mind when they listen to your oral report.

LISTENING GUIDELINES: An Oral Report

1. Look at the speaker.
2. Do not talk to others.
3. Take notes on things you want to know more about.
3. Ask questions at the end.

5 WRITER'S RESOURCES: The Atlas and the Almanac

Where would you look if you wanted to see which state was closest to your own? You might look in an atlas. An **atlas** is a book of maps. It includes maps of each state, the entire country, and also other countries. An atlas gives you information about distances from one place to another. It shows you where bodies of water are located.

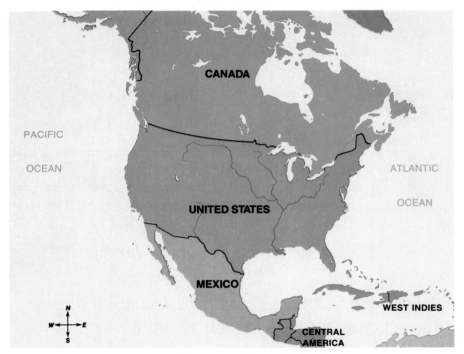

Where could you find information about your state? You can look in the encyclopedia, in nonfiction books, and in an almanac. An **almanac** is a book of facts. It is published every year. It gives facts about many subjects. It tells about current events as well as things that happened in the past.

Practice

Write whether you could use an atlas or an almanac to answer the following questions.

1. Which countries surround Switzerland?
2. Where was the lowest temperature in the United States last year?
3. Who was the president of France last year?
4. Which states does the Mississippi River run through?
5. Which states surround Texas?
6. How many people live in Italy?
7. How much rain fell in Bermuda over the last five years?
8. Where is Peru?
9. How many people in Canada could read and write last year?
10. How many people in Oklahoma got married last year?
11. How many people live in England?
12. How far is New Mexico from Texas?
13. How many people own cars in France?
14. How far is New York from Connecticut?
15. How many people in New Jersey graduated college?

 WRITING APPLICATION A Personal Atlas and an Almanac

Create a personal atlas and an almanac for your neighborhood. Draw maps of houses, apartment buildings, and stores. Write down a list of different facts. You might want to tell some information about the neighbors you know, what certain stores sell, and how many children your age live in the neighborhood.

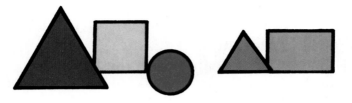

Writing About Mathematics

Numbers are an important part of your life. They are everywhere. You find them on street signs, menus, and in telephone books. When you buy something, the cost of the item is expressed in a number. The date, the time, your age, and even a simple recipe all use numbers.

ACTIVITIES

Create a Code   Make up a code where numbers stand for letters of the alphabet. For example, a=1, b=2, and so on. Or you can have z=1 and y=2. Use your code to write notes to friends.

Describe a Photograph   Look at the photo on the following page. How is the boy in the picture using numbers?

Respond to Literature   Working with numbers can be fun. You can play games or do tricks that have numbers in them. The following trick was taken from a book called *Entertaining with Number Tricks* by George Barr. See if your friends can figure out what you are doing. Can you think of another trick involving numbers?

Eleven Fingers

This fast stunt dealing with numbers seems to catch some people off balance. It consists of slowly counting your fingers and finding that you have 11 of them. Proceed as follows.

Use your right pointing finger to touch each finger on your outstretched left hand as you count "1, 2, 3, 4, 5." Then use your left pointing finger to count each finger on your right hand: "6, 7, 8, 9, 10."

Say this is strange, because this morning when you got up you counted your fingers and you had 11. Announce that you are going to count them once more. Again point to each finger on your right hand, but this time count backward: "10, 9, 8, 7, 6." Now stop, open your left hand and say, "And 5 are 11!"

Practice this until your timing is perfect.

UNIT CHECKUP

LESSON 1

Group Writing: A Research Report (page 418) Narrow the following topics by thinking of some topics that would be easier to write a research report about.

transportation   jewelry   flowers   animals

LESSON 2

Thinking: Summarizing (page 422) Write the main-idea sentence of the following paragraph

    Scientists sent *Voyager 2* into space to help them learn about other planets. *Voyager 2* sent back pictures of the planets and their moons. These pictures help scientists answer questions about our solar system.

LESSON 3

Writing a Research Report (page 424) Think of a topic you would like to write a research report about. Research the topic in an encyclopedia. Write notes for your report.

LESSON 4

Speaking and Listening: Giving an Oral Report (page 432) In the library, find an article about how bees make honey. Use the article to write a summary and give an oral report.

LESSON 5

Writer's Resources: The Atlas and the Almanac (page 434) Write whether you would use an **atlas** or **almanac** to answer these questions.

1. How far is New York from California?
2. What kinds of animals are found in Australia?
3. Who was George Washington's vice president?
4. What state is south of Kansas?

THEME PROJECT  PUZZLE

All of the things around you are made up of shapes. You can see circles, squares, rectangles, and triangles wherever you look. Study the picture below. How many shapes can you find?

You can draw a picture that has many different shapes hidden in it. Have your friends count the number of shapes in your drawing.

■ Draw a simple picture. You can draw a scene, an animal, or even a boat. If you want, all of the things in your picture can have the same shape. You can draw all circles or all squares.

■ Count the number of shapes in your picture.

■ See if your friends can guess the number of shapes in your picture.

Writer's Reference

C O N T E N T S

GRAMMAR

Sentences

A **sentence** expresses a complete thought. A sentence contains a subject and a predicate.

    The happy child / sings loudly.
        subject   **predicate**

There are **four** sentence types. Notice the end punctuation of each sentence type.

My homework is easy.	(statement—ends with a period)
Is your homework easy?	(question—ends with a question mark)
Do your homework.	(command—ends with a period)
Science is terrific!	(exclamation—ends with an exclamation mark)

A **subject** tells what or whom the sentence is about.

    Jack sang at the top of his voice.

A **predicate** tells what the subject does or is.

    Jack and Susan **danced.**

Nouns

A **noun** is a word that names a person, place, or thing.

    family   city   sidewalk

A **singular noun** names one person, place, or thing.

    girl   tree   dog

A **plural noun** names more than one person, place, or thing.

girls   trees   dogs

A **common noun** names any person, place, or thing. A **proper noun** names a special person, place, or thing.

common—dog, plant, child
proper—Atlantic Ocean, Flag Day, Grandpa Joe

A **possessive noun** is a noun that shows ownership.

A **singular possessive** noun shows what one person owns. Add an **apostrophe (')** and **s** to a singular noun to make it a singular possessive noun.

Sam**'s** pail   Joan**'s** house

A **plural possessive noun** shows what more than one person owns. Add an **apostrophe** to a plural noun that ends in **s** to form the plural possessive.

teams' uniforms   monkeys' hats

If a plural noun does not end in **s**, add **'s** to show possession.

children's toys   geese's beaks

Verbs

A **verb** shows action or tells what something is or is like.

dance   danced   is   was

The **tense** of a verb tells when the action takes place.

Present-tense verbs tell that something is happening now.

I dance today.

Past-tense verbs tell that something has already happened.

I danced at the party yesterday.

Future-tense verbs tell that something will happen later.

I will dance tomorrow.

Helping verbs help other verbs show an action in the past.

have cooked   **had** talked   **has** smiled

Most verbs add **ed** to form their past tense.

ask—ask**ed**   walk—walk**ed**

Some verbs form the past tense in a special way. An **irregular verb** does not add **ed** to form its past tense.

Present	Past	Past with *has, have, had*
begin	began	begun
do	did	done
eat	ate	eaten
give	gave	given
go	went	gone
grow	grew	grown
see	saw	seen
sing	sang	sung

Adjectives

An **adjective** is a word that describes a noun. An adjective tells **what kind** or **how many**.   **red** car   **wise** king   **four** ideas

A, an, and **the** are special adjectives called **articles.** Use **a** before a singular noun beginning with a consonant. Use **an** before a singular noun beginning with a vowel. Use **the** before singular nouns and plural nouns.   **A** girl   **The** girls   **An** owl

Pronouns

A **pronoun** takes the place of a noun.

Subject pronouns are used as the subject of a sentence.

Subject Pronouns are *I, you, he, she, it, we,* and *they.*

Object pronouns are used after action verbs or words such as *for, at, of, with,* and *to.*

> **Object pronouns** are *me, you, him, her it, us, and them.*

Possessive pronouns are pronouns that show ownership.

> **Possessive pronouns** are *my, your, his, her, its, our, and their.*

Adverbs

An **adverb** is a word that tells more about a verb. An adverb tells **how, where,** or **when.**

He walks **slowly.**   She lives **here.**   I will see you **soon.**

MECHANICS

PUNCTUATION

End Punctuation

Use end punctuation to end a sentence.

A **period** (.) ends a statement or a command.
A **question mark** (?) ends a **question.**
An **exclamation mark** (!) ends an exclamation.

Periods

Use a period to show the end of an abbreviation and with initials.

Mr.   Mrs.   Dr.   Susan L. Smith

Commas

Use a comma between the names of cities and states.

Fort Worth, Texas   San Diego, California

Use a comma between the day and the year in dates.

January 9, 1990   November 11, 1996

Use a comma to separate words in a series.

Jenny, Dale, and Phillip are my best friends.

Use a comma after the greeting and closing in a letter.

Dear Staci,   Sincerely,

Use a comma after the words *yes* or *no* when they begin a sentence.

Yes, I will go to your party. No, my sister will go instead of me.

Use a comma after the name of a person being spoken to.

Tony, did you have fun in the park?
Donna, let's go swimming.

Apostrophes

Use apostrophes (') with nouns to show possession.

Add **'s** to singular nouns or plural nouns that do not end in **s.**

Janet's book   Valerie's pen   children's stories

Add an (') to plural nouns ending in **s.**

kites' tails   giraffes' necks

Use apostrophes (') in contractions to show where letters are missing.

don't   we'll   I'm

Quotation Marks

Put quotation marks at the beginning and at the end of what a person says.

"Do you want to play tennis with me?" asked Susan.

Story and poem titles use quotation marks.

"The Last Leaf"   "The Swing"

Capitalization

Capitalize the first word in a sentence.

My class visited the zoo yesterday.

Capitalize the names of specific persons, places, or things.

George Washington   Canada   Lake Michigan

Capitalize the first and all important words in a book title.

The Good-luck Pencil   Very Last First Time

Capitalize the days of the week and the months of the year.

Monday   Thursday   August   April   September

Capitalize all words in the greeting of a letter. Capitalize only the first word in a letter's closing.

Dear Friend,   Very truly yours,

Abbreviations

Capitalize and put a period after abbreviations.

Dr.   Ms.   Mon.   Nov.

Use a colon (:) with time.   3:30 P.M.   8:42 A.M.

USAGE

Verbs

A **singular subject** must be used with a **singular verb**. A **plural subject** must be used with a **plural verb.**

The **girl eats** an apple.   The **boys eat** the apples.

Pronouns

When you use **I** or **me** with a noun, name yourself last.

Daniel and **I** sang.   They talked to Daniel and **me.**

THESAURUS FOR WRITING

What Is a Thesaurus?

A **thesaurus** is a reference book that can be very useful in your writing. It provides synonyms for many common words. **Synonyms** are words that have almost the same meaning. By choosing exact and colorful words, you can make your writing more interesting. For example, you may write this sentence: Joey **walked** across the street.

Walked is not a very interesting word. If you look up *walk* in the thesaurus, you will find: *march, stride, stroll.* Each of these words means *to walk,* but each one suggests a different way of walking.

Using the Thesaurus

The words in a thesaurus are listed in alphabetical order. You look up words in a thesaurus as you would in a dictionary. If you looked up the word *beautiful,* you would find this entry:

Main Entry Word	**beautiful** *adj.* full of beauty;
Meaning	having qualities that are pleasing.
Example Sentence	What a *beautiful* sunset!
Synonym	**lovely** beautiful in a comforting way. This is a *lovely* room.
Synonym	**pretty** pleasing or attractive, especially said of something small or dainty. What a *pretty* doll!
Antonym	**antonyms:** ugly, unattractive

A **main entry** gives the part of speech, a definition of the word, and an example sentence. In some entries you will also find **antonyms,** or words that have opposite meanings.

Cross-references

In some cases you will find cross-references. For example, if you look up **allow,** you will find this cross-reference: *See* let. This means that when you look up *let,* the word *allow* will be listed.

A

allow *See* let.

angry *adj.* feeling or showing anger. Tina made me *angry*.
furious extremely angry. Janet was *furious* when she heard what I had done.

ask *v.* to put a question to. We will ask Mr. Lee to join us.
question to try to get information. The teacher began to *question* us about our homework.
inquire to seek information by asking questions. Please inquire at the front office.
antonym: answer.

awful *adj.* causing fear, dread, or awe. Jeremy watched an *awful* movie.
terrible causing terror or awe. That was a *terrible* storm.
dreadful causing great fear. She let out a *dreadful* scream.

B

beautiful *adj.* full of beauty; having qualities that are pleasing. What a *beautiful* sunset!
lovely beautiful in a comforting way. This is a *lovely* room.

pretty pleasing or attractive, often said of something small or dainty. What a *pretty* flower!
antonyms: ugly, unattractive

big *adj.* of great size. Danny made a *big* pile of leaves.
huge extremely big. That elephant is *huge!*
enormous much greater than the usual size. An *enormous* truck drove up to the house.
large of great size; big. This coat is too *large* for me.
antonyms: *See* little.

brave *adj.* willing to face danger; without fear. The *brave* man climbed the rocks.
bold showing courage; fearless. The *bold* man entered the dark woods.
courageous having courage. A *courageous* woman rescued the cat.
daring willing to take risks. The *daring* girl dove into the water.
antonyms: afraid, fearful

bright *adj.* filled with light; shining. The sun was so *bright* we sat in the shade.

brilliant shining or sparkling with light. The lake was *brilliant* in the sunlight.
shiny shining brightly. Jenny found a *shiny* new dime.
antonyms: dark, dull

C

cold *adj.* having a low temperature; lacking warmth. We felt *cold* in the tent.
chilly uncomfortably cool. The day was rainy and *chilly.*
icy very cold. An *icy* wind blew across the frozen lake.
antonyms: *See* hot.

cry *v.* to shed tears. The baby started to *cry.*
sob to cry with short gasps. Lenny began to *sob* when his dog ran away.
weep to show grief, joy, or other strong emotions by crying. Lisa began to *weep* when she got the good news.
antonyms: *See* laugh.

D

do *v.* to carry out. Ronny wants to *do* his homework.
execute to complete. Amy *executed* the plan.
perform to carry out to completion. Martin *performed* his part well.

F

far *adj.* a long way off; not near. The zoo is *far* from our house.
distant extremely far. We sailed to a *distant* island.
antonyms: near, close

fast *adj.* moving or done with speed. A *fast* car drove by the house.
quick done in a very short time. That was a *quick* lunch.
rapid with great speed, often in a continuing way. He ran at a *rapid* pace for two miles.
swift moving with great speed, often said of animals or people. A deer is a *swift* runner.
antonym: slow

funny *adj.* causing laughter. She told us a *funny* joke.
amusing causing smiles of enjoyment or laughter. Ted knows some *amusing* stories.
comical causing laughter through actions. The dogs looked *comical* in their hats.
humorous funny in a mild or regular way. Mack's friend is *humorous.*

G

good *adj.* above average in quality. That was a *good* movie.

THESAURUS

excellent extremely good. Susie wrote an *excellent* story about her trip.

fair somewhat good; slightly better than average. Terry did a *fair* job of painting the house.

fine of high quality; very good. We used a *fine* set of dishes.

antonyms: bad, poor

great *adj.* of unusual quality or ability. Jim is a *great* runner.

remarkable having unusual qualities. She has a *remarkable* voice.

superb of greater quality than most. Nell is a *superb* artist.

wonderful very good; excellent. It was a *wonderful* party.

H

happy *adj.* having, showing, or bringing pleasure. Dennis is such a *happy* child.

glad feeling or expressing joy or pleasure. Tony was *glad* to be home.

joyful very happy; filled with joy. Donna was *joyful* when she heard the good news.

antonyms: *See* sad.

hard *adj.* not easy to do or deal with. Cutting wood is *hard* work.

difficult hard to do; requiring effort. These math problems are *difficult.*

tough difficult to do, often in a physical sense. Construction work is a *tough* job.

antonym: easy

help *v.* to give support; be of service to. Leo will *help* you clean your room.

aid to give help to someone. Mr. Collins will *aid* us and change the flat tire.

hot *adj.* having a high temperature; having much heat. The sun is *hot.*

fiery as hot as fire; burning. The leaves burned in a *fiery* blaze.

antonyms: *See* cold.

hurt *v.* to cause pain or damage. Did you *hurt* your arm?

harm to damage. Mrs. Jones would never *harm* an animal.

injure to cause physical damage. John fell and *injured* his foot.

L

large *See* big.

laugh *v.* to show amusement. They always *laugh* at my stories.
chuckle to laugh softly, especially to oneself. Nan began to *chuckle* at the riddle.
giggle to laugh in a silly or nervous way. Jill likes to *giggle* at her younger brother.
antonyms: *See* cry.

let *v.* to give permission to. Mr. Gracey will *let* me go fishing.
allow to give permission to. The town does not *allow* swimming in the lake.
permit to allow someone to do something. John will *permit* you to use the pool.
antonyms: refuse, deny, forbid

like *v.* to enjoy something; to feel affection for someone or something. I *like* my friend Linda.
admire to have affection and respect for someone. Jeff *admires* his father.
enjoy to take pleasure in doing something. She *enjoys* walking on the beach.
love to like something a lot; to feel great affection for someone. Ray *loves* his dog.
antonyms: dislike, hate

little *adj.* small in size. Meg ate a *little* apple.
small not large. Sarah drew a *small* circle in the sand.
tiny very small. The baby has *tiny* feet.
antonyms: *See* big.

look *v.* to see with one's eyes. *Look* at the large stripes on the tiger.
glance to look quickly. I saw Ken *glance* at me and then turn away.
peer to look closely. Sam and Joe *peer* at the map.
stare to look at for a long time with eyes wide open. Sue and Tim *stare* at the moving car.

M

many *adj.* consisting of a large number. Dick has *many* books about animals.
numerous a great many. We have been to the park *numerous* times.
several more than a few but less than many. Carla played in *several* games this year.
antonym: few

mean *adj.* without kindness or understanding. Tom was *mean* to me when I dropped the ball.

nasty very mean. That was a *nasty* thing to say.

selfish concerned only about oneself. Kate is too *selfish* to care about me.

spiteful filled with bad feelings toward others. Pam sometimes behaves in a *spiteful* way.

antonyms: *See* nice.

nice *adj.* agreeable or pleasing. I had a *nice* time today.

gentle mild and kindly in manner. Ruth is *gentle* with her animals.

kind friendly; good-hearted. It was *kind* of you to send me a card.

pleasant agreeable; giving pleasure to. We had a *pleasant* time at Grandpa's house.

sweet being agreeable. Debbie is such a *sweet* girl.

O

old *adj.* having lived for a long time. The tree is *old.*

aged having grown old. I care for my *aged* aunt.

ancient very old; from times long past. We saw some *ancient* tools from China.

antonym: young

Q

quiet *adj.* with little or no noise. The town is *quiet* after a snowstorm.

calm free of excitement or strong feeling; quiet. The sea was *calm.*

peaceful calm; undisturbed. The woods are *peaceful* at the end of the day.

silent completely quiet; without noise. The children were *silent* in the library.

antonyms: loud, noisy

R

right *adj.* free from error; true. Theo's answer was *right.*

accurate without error or mistake. Connie's report was *accurate.*

correct agreeing with fact or truth. Let me show you the *correct* way to mow the lawn.

exact very accurate; completely correct. Larry knew the *exact* number of records in the pile.

antonyms: wrong, mistaken

S

sad *adj.* feeling or showing unhappiness or sorrow. She looked *sad* when I left.

depressed feeling low; sad. Donny was *depressed* when he could not find his dog.
miserable extremely unhappy. Hazel was *miserable* for the first week at camp.
antonyms: *See* happy.

say *v.* to make known or express in words. Mel will *say* hello to his friends.
declare to make known publicly or formally. We will *declare* Monday a holiday.
speak to express an idea, fact, or feeling. Dan will *speak* to us about the new rules.
state to express or explain fully in words. Joe will *state* his opinion at the meeting.

scared *adj.* afraid; alarmed. She gets *scared* by large dogs.
afraid feeling fear, often for a long time. Al is *afraid* of dogs.
fearful filled with fear. Dean felt *fearful* waiting in the dark.
frightened scared suddenly, or for a short time. Van was *frightened* when he heard the noise.
terrified extremely scared; filled with terror. Paul was *terrified* of the plane trip.

sick *adj.* having poor health. Do you feel *sick* today?
ill not healthy; sick. Mark stayed in bed because he was *ill.*
antonyms: well, healthy

small *See* little.

smart *adj.* intelligent; bright; having learned a lot. Toni is a *smart* girl.
clever mentally sharp. Ben is a *clever* boy.
intelligent able to learn, understand, and reason. Nancy is *intelligent* enough to figure out the answer.
wise able to know or judge what is right, good, or true. My grandfather is a *wise* man.
antonym: stupid

smile *v.* to turn up the corners of your mouth in a happy or friendly way. Linda had to *smile* at the puppy.
grin to smile broadly, with great happiness or amusement. Keith started to *grin* when I came in.
antonyms: frown, scowl

strange *adj.* unusual; out of the ordinary. I saw a *strange* bird.
odd different; not ordinary. He was wearing a very *odd* hat.

weird strange or odd, in a frightening or mysterious way. The movie told a *weird* story.

sure *adj.* firmly believing in something. I am *sure* that I am right.

certain free from doubt; very sure. Russ is *certain* that the date was April 28.

definite positive or certain, often in a factual way. She was *definite* in her views.

antonyms: doubtful, unsure

surprised *adj.* feeling sudden wonder. Neil was *surprised* when I suddenly walked in the door.

amazed overwhelmed with wonder or surprise. Everyone was *amazed* by her magic tricks.

astonished greatly surprised; shocked. Greg was *astonished* when he saw the zebra.

T

tell *v.* to express in written or spoken words. Mandy will *tell* us about her trip.

announce to state or make known publicly. Mrs. Grimes had to *announce* that the school would be closed on Friday.

thin *adj.* not fat. Jim lost ten pounds and looks *thin*.

lean with little or no fat. Jim was tall and *lean* by the end of the summer.

slim thin, in a good or healthy way. Exercising has kept Janice *slim*!

antonyms: fat, plump, chubby

W

walk *v.* to move or travel on foot. Val will *walk* to school.

march to walk with regular steps. The band will *march* in the parade.

stroll to walk in a relaxed or leisurely manner. Amy and Sally plan to *stroll* by the lake.

want *v.* to have a desire or wish for. Lou and Dana *want* to fly the kite.

wish to have a longing or strong need for. Ellen and Gary *wish* they could go to the city.

wet *adj.* covered or soaked with water or other liquid. He was very *wet* when he got home.

damp slightly wet. The grass is still *damp* from the rain.

moist slightly wet; damp. The rain made the grass *moist*.

antonym: dry

LETTER MODELS

You can use these models to help you when you write.

THANK-YOU NOTE

147 Columbus Street
Alexandria, Virginia 22307
June 9, 19--

HEADING

Dear Cousin Sally,

GREETING

   Thank you for the great train set you sent me for my birthday. My sister and I had hours of fun playing with the trains. The sounds they make are so real. I can't wait for you to come over and play with us.

BODY

Your cousin,

CLOSING

Gail

SIGNATURE

INVITATION

21 Cedar Lane
Rutland, Vermont 05701
June 30, 19--

HEADING

Dear Donald,

GREETING

   Please come to my sister's graduation party on Sunday, July 11, at 1:30. The party will be at my Cousin Dana's house. Directions are attached to this invitation. The party is a surprise, so don't mention it to my sister. I hope you can come.

BODY

Your friend,

CLOSING

Sam

SIGNATURE

SPELLING STRATEGIES

When you write, it is important to spell all words correctly. This will help to make your meaning clear. Use the following strategies to help you to improve your spelling.

1. Study the basic spelling rules.
2. Learn to recognize commonly misspelled words.
3. Check your work carefully after you have finished writing.
4. Use a dictionary to check the spelling of any words you are unsure of.

Spelling Rules

Here are some rules to help you spell certain kinds of words correctly.

Words with *ie* and *ei*	Spell the word with *i* before *e* when the sound is *e,* except after *c*
	i before *e*: chief, believe, field, piece except after *c:* receive, ceiling, deceive
	Spell the word with *ei* when the sound is not *e,* especially if the sound is *a.*
	Sound is *a:* neighbor, weigh, eight

There are some exceptions to the rules above. It is best to memorize the spelling of the following words.

Exceptions: either, seize, weird, friend

Adding *s* and *es*	In most cases, add *s* to a noun to make it plural.
	Examples: tree+s=trees shirt+s=shirts
	Add *s* to most verbs when they are used with singular subjects.
	Example: The boy walks slowly.

If a noun ends in *s, ch, sh,* or *x,* add *es* to spell the plural.

Example: bush+es=bushes

If a verb ends in *sh, ch, ss, s, zz,* or *x,* add *es* when it is used with a singular subject.

Example: Sally watches the moon.

If a noun ends in a consonant and *y,* change the *y* to *i* before adding *es* to spell the plural.

Example: baby   babies

If a verb ends in a consonant and *y,* change the *y* to *i* before adding *es* when it is used with a singular subject.

Example: John hurries down the street.

Adding *ed, er, est*

If a word ends in a consonant and *y,* change the *y* to *i* before adding an ending that begins with any vowel except *i.*

Examples: sorry   sorrier
                 happy   happiest
                 worry   worried

In most cases, if a one-syllable word ends in a consonant following a vowel, double the final consonant when adding an ending that begins with a vowel.

Examples: drop   dropped
                 skip   skipping

If a word ends in a silent *e,* drop the *e* when adding an ending that begins with a vowel.

Examples: dive   diving
                 hike   hiked

OVERVIEW OF THE WRITING PROCESS

You have learned that writing is a process.

Prewrite

- Decide on a purpose and audience for your writing.
- Choose a topic that keeps your purpose and audience in mind.
- Explore ideas about your topic.
- Narrow your topic if it is too broad.

Write a First Draft

- Use your prewriting ideas to write your first draft.
- Get your ideas down on paper. Do not worry about errors.

Revise

- Read your draft. Share it with someone else to get ideas for improving your writing.
- Ask yourself these questions about your draft.

  What else will my audience want to know?
  How can I make my purpose clearer?
  How can I improve the organization of my writing?

Proofread

- Read your revised draft. Ask yourself these questions.

  Have I used complete sentences?
  Have I used capitalization and punctuation correctly?
  Have I spelled all words correctly?

Publish

- Make a neat copy of your proofread draft.
- Share your writing with the audience for whom you wrote it.

STUDY STRATEGIES

Studying is an important part of learning. You will often need to study written material, and sometimes you will have to take a test. These strategies will help you when you study.

General Study Guidelines

1. Plan your time carefully.
2. Keep a list of what you need to study.
3. Decide how much time to spend on each task.
4. Find a quiet, comfortable place to work.
5. Keep study materials handy.

Helpful Study Methods

There are a number of ways to study. One method, SQ3R, is described below.

SQ3R The name stands for the five steps you should follow when you read a unit or chapter.

1. **Study** the selection to find out what it is about.
2. Think of **questions** to help you understand the selection.
3. **Read** the material, answer the questions you made up, and look for important points in what you read.
4. **Record** answers to the questions and the important points by writing them down.
5. **Review** the selection and the notes you have written.

Special Study Tips

Follow Directions Carefully

1. Identify the steps you should follow.
2. Ask questions about steps you do not understand.
3. Follow directions step by step.

Set a Purpose for Studying

1. Before you begin studying, decide on the purpose of your work.
2. Sometimes you will want to find out why something happened, or to compare two similar events or people.
3. Use the directions to help you to identify your purpose.
4. Stick to your purpose as you work.

Outline Your Material

1. Make an outline of what you are studying.
2. Organize your outline according to the important points of what you are studying.

Map Your Material

1. Use a diagram or picture to outline what you are studying.
2. You might use a map, a time line, or a cluster to indicate what information is important and how it is organized.

Taking Tests

Taking tests is an important part of your schoolwork. You can use many of these study skills to make test-taking easier.

1. Preview the test. Look through the test quickly to see what it covers and how long it is.
2. Plan your time. Your teacher will tell you how much time you have to finish the test. Decide how much time to spend on each part of the test. Some parts may take longer than others. Writing a paragraph, for example, will usually take longer than punctuating sentences correctly. Keep track of the time as you work.
3. Follow directions. Listen to any directions your teacher gives you. Then, read the test directions carefully before you begin the test. As you work through the test, read any directions you see at the beginning of each new section.

G L O S S A R Y

OF WRITING, GRAMMAR, AND LITERARY TERMS

WRITING TERMS

audience	the reader or readers for whom a composition is written
detail sentences	sentences that tell more about the main idea
first draft	the first version of a composition, in which the writer gets his or her basic ideas down on paper
main-idea sentence	the sentence that tells the main idea of a paragraph
personal narrative	a piece of writing in which the writer tells about something that has happened in his or her life
prewriting	the stage in the writing process in which the writer chooses a topic, explores ideas, gathers information, and organizes his or her material before writing a first draft
prewriting strategies	particular ways of gathering, exploring, planning, and organizing ideas before writing the first draft of a composition

• **charting**   a way to gather ideas under different headings

Who	Beth
What	invitation to school play
Where	school auditorium
When	next Thursday
Why	Beth wants to be an actress

• **clustering**   a way to explore ideas by gathering details related to the writing topic

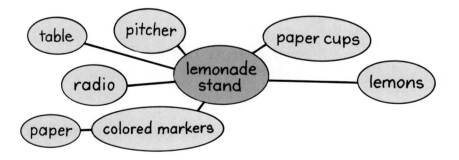

- **listing**   a way to gather reasons and details

> The Dream Eater
> 1. A boy named Yukio has bad dreams about two monsters.
> 2. Everyone in his village also has nightmares.
> 3. Yukio meets a baku that eats dreams.
> 4. The baku eats all the bad dreams.

- **note taking**   a way to gather information from different sources

> - sunlight shines on raindrops
> - sun must be behind you; rain, in front of you
> - sunlight divides colors
> - heavier rain makes longer rainbow

proofread   to correct errors in punctuation, capitalization, spelling, and grammar in a writing draft

publish   to share a composition with an audience

purpose   the writer's reason for writing a composition—for example, to explain, to entertain, or to persuade

revise   to improve the first draft of a composition by adding or taking out information, combining and reordering sentences, or changing word choice according to the purpose and audience

sensory details   in a description, the details that appeal to the reader's five senses—sight, hearing, touch, taste, and smell

supporting details   facts, examples, or sensory details that give more information about the main idea of a paragraph

time-order words   words that help make the sequence of events clear, such as *first, next, then,* and *finally*

topic sentence	the sentence that states the main idea of a paragraph
writing process	the steps for writing a composition, including prewriting, writing a first draft, revising, proofreading, and publishing

GRAMMAR TERMS

action verb	a word that expresses action Birds *fly* south in the winter.
adjective	a word that describes a noun The *happy* dog wagged his tail.
adverb	a word that tells more about a verb The baby crawled *quickly*.
article	the word *a, an,* or *the* John watched *the* birds.

be verb a verb that does not show action
    Tina *is* my pen pal.

common noun a noun that names any person, place, or thing
    Sam jumped into the cold *water.*

helping verb a verb that helps another verb to show an action in the past
    Dana *has* accepted the job.

irregular verb a verb that forms the past tense in a special way
    Donna *saw* the dog in the yard.

noun a word that names a person, place, or thing
    The *dinner* was delicious.

object pronoun a pronoun that is used after an action verb or words such as *for, at, of, with,* and *to*
    Mom made lunch for *them.*

plural noun a noun that names more than one person, place, or thing
    The *kites* sailed away.

possessive noun a noun that shows ownership
    The *boy's* shirt is new.

possessive pronoun a pronoun that shows who or what owns something
    Where is *your* sweater?

pronoun	a word that takes the place of one or more nouns *They* bought balloons at the circus.
proper noun	a noun that names a special person, place, thing *Leslie* is from *England.*
sentence	a group of words that expresses a complete thought *The seagull squawked as it flew through the air.*
singular noun	a noun that names one person, place, or thing The *flower* grew tall.
subject pronoun	a pronoun that is used as the subject of a sentence *He* cooked dinner for the whole family.

LITERARY TERMS

characters	the people in a story or play
dialogue	the conversations that people have in a story or a play

fiction	written works such as novels and short stories that tell about imaginary characters and events
haiku	a poem that has three lines and seventeen syllables and describes something in nature
nonfiction	written works that deal with real situations, people, or events, such as biographies
rhyme	writing with words that sound alike
rhythm	a set beat
setting	the time and place in which the events of a story happen
story poem	a poem that tells a story

INDEX

Bold-face numbers indicate the page on which the skill is taught.

A

a, **268**–269, 285. *See also*
  Articles.
Abbreviations, 78–79, 96
Action verbs
  and *be* verbs, 202
  definition of, **136**–137
  and object pronouns,
    328–329
Adjectives
  combining sentences
    with, 274–275
  definition of, **262**, 280
  in sentences, 262–263
  that compare, **266**–267,
    282–284
  that tell how many,
    264–265, 281
  Articles, **268**–269, 285
Adverbs
  combining sentences
    with, 394–395
  definition of, **384**
  in sentences, 384–385
  that tell how, 386–387,
    401
  that tell where and
    when, 388–389,
    402–403
Advertisements, writing,
  15, 67, 137, 393
Almanac, 194, 434–435
Alphabetical order
  in dictionary, **126**–127
  in encyclopedia, 195
  in index, 376
an, **268**–269, 285. *See also*
  Articles.
  268–269, 285
and, 16–17, 82–83
Antonyms, 272–273
Apostrophe
  in contractions, 208–209,
    222, 332

in possessive nouns, 74–77,
  92–95
Art connection, 318–319
Articles, 268–269, 285
Articles, writing, 11, 139
Atlas, 194, 434–435
Audience
  for book reports, 360, 366
  for descriptive
    paragraphs, 300, 306
  for instructions, 178, 184
  for letters, 239, 244
  for paragraphs, 42, 49
  for research reports, 418,
    424
  for stories, 110, 116

B

Base words
  and prefixes, 150–151, 167
  and suffixes, 210–211, 223
be **verbs,** 202–203, 218
Biographical sketches,
  writing, 141
Body, of letter, 238
Book reports
  audience for, 360
  checklist for, 363
  choosing book for,
    366–367
  draft of, 368
  opinion in, 361
  prewriting, 366–367
  proofreading, 371–372
  publishing, 373
  purpose of, 360
  putting together, 362
  revising, 369–370
  summary in, 360–361
Books. *See also* Reference
  sources
  for book report, 366–367
  fiction, 194
  in library, 194–195

nonfiction, 194
parts of, 376–377
Borrowed words, 392–393,
  405
Brainstorming, 42–44,
  110–112, 178–180,
  238–240, 300–302,
  360–362, 418–420

C

Capital letters
  abbreviations, 78–79, 96
  first word in sentence,
    2–3, 22
  in letters, 238
  pronouns, 336–337
  proper nouns, 72–73, 91
  titles and initials, 78–79,
    96
Card catalog, 194
Cartoons, writing, 69
Characters, in stories, 111
Charting strategy, 242–245,
  307
Classifying, 304–305
Closing, of letter, 238
Clustering strategy
  for instructions, 184–185
  for paragraphs, 48–49
Colon, 446
Combining sentences
  with adjectives, **274**–275
  with adverbs, **394**–395
  with *and,* **16**–17
  with nouns, **82**–83
  with predicates, **152**–153
Comma
  with adjectives, **270**–271,
    286, 312
  with adverbs, **390**–391,
    404, 430
  in addresses, 238–240
  in dates, 250
  in letters, 250